Commerce, Peace, and the Arts in Renaissance Venice

Drawing material from a wide range of original sources, this book identifies a network of early modern Venetian patrician merchant and banking families. The book explores their commercial activities and consequent preferences in international relations, as well as how both were served by cultural works, all within the monumental changes taking place in fifteenth- and sixteenth-century Venice.

In a study of patronage in the broadest sense, Linda L. Carroll reads vast quantities of unpublished primary sources, uncovering remarkable and unsuspected connections. She documents the well-known links between declining trade and the need for new investments in the mainland (re)gained by Venice, as well as links between problems of governance and political networks. She unveils the potential purposes of those at the highest levels who invited Ruzante to perform in what are interpreted as 'rudely' metaphorical truth-telling plays for their fellow Venetian patricians.

Focusing on patrons of art works in S. Maria Gloriosa dei Frari, the first chapter establishes interrelated commercial and political interests, connecting them to the works and the artists. The second chapter analyzes an important Venetian literary manuscript in the Bodleian Library of Oxford University and identifies its copyist, a central figure in the Venetian patrician turn from commercial to cultural pursuits and connected to the cultural worlds of Venice, Padua, and Rome. The third chapter demonstrates the economic and political tensions behind the presence of many high-ranking officials at a scandalous 1525 Ruzante performance, drawing on extensive documentation to provide a new picture of Beolco's relationships with his Venetian supporters, including Frari patrons. The fourth chapter explores Venice's first state lotteries and a connection between one of the managers and Machiavelli.

Linda L. Carroll is Professor of Italian at Tulane University, USA. She is the author of numerous books and articles explicating the exceptionally but opaquely candid plays of Angelo Beolco (Il Ruzante), whose *Prima oratione* she has edited and translated. She is co-editor of *Sexualities, Textualities, Art and Music in Early Modern Italy*.

Commerce, Peace, and the Arts in Renaissance Venice

Ruzante and the Empire at Center Stage

Linda L. Carroll

LONDON AND NEW YORK

First published 2016
by Routledge

2 Park Square, Milton Park, Abingdon, Oxfordshire OX14 4RN
52 Vanderbilt Avenue, New York, NY 10017

Routledge is an imprint of the Taylor & Francis Group, an informa business

First issued in paperback 2018

British Library Cataloguing in Publication Data
A catalogue record for this book is available from the British Library

Library of Congress Cataloging in Publication Data
Names: Carroll, Linda L.
Title: Commerce, peace and the arts in Renaissance
    Venice: Ruzante and the empire at center stage / by Linda L. Carroll.
Description: Farnham, Surrey ; Burlington, VT : Ashgate, 2016. |
    Includes bibliographical references and index.
Identifiers| LCCN 2015043206| ISBN 9781472478139 (hardcover : alk. paper)
    | ISBN 9781472478153 (epub)
Subjects: LCSH: Theater—Italy—Venice—History—16th century. | Art
    patronage—Italy—Venice—History—16th century. | Italian literature—
    16th century—History and criticism—Sources. | Ruzzante, 1502?-1542—
    Stage history—Italy. | Renaissance—Italy—Venice.
Classification: LCC PN2686.V42 C37 2016 | DDC 700.945/31109031—dc23
LC record available at http://lccn.loc.gov/2015043206

ISBN: 978-1-4724-7813-9 (hbk)
ISBN: 978-0-367-14048-9 (pbk)

Typeset in Times New Roman
by Swales & Willis Ltd, Exeter, Devon, UK

Contents

List of Figures   vi
Note on the Author   vii
Acknowledgments   viii
List of Abbreviations   xi

Introduction: Mercury, Venus, and the Muses: Commerce,
Peace, and the Arts in Renaissance Venice   1

1   Twelve Monuments, Five Altarpieces, Five Chapels, and
    a Fresco: Frari Patronage and Renaissance Venetian
    Political Economy   19

2   Bodleian Library Canonician Ital. 36: Stefano Magno
    and the Move from Commerce to Culture   64

3   *Concordiae dedicatum*: The Triumphanti, the Beolco,
    and the Politics of Prosperity in Renaissance Venice   107

4   1526: State Lotteries, the Final Ruzantine Performance,
    and a Machiavellian Coda   147

    Conclusion   154

Bibliography   156
Index   169

Figures

1.1	Plan of Santa Maria Gloriosa dei Frari	20
1.2	Funeral Monument of Jacopo Marcello	21
1.3	Lorenzo Bregno and Baccio da Montelupo, Funeral Monument of Benedetto Pesaro	22
1.4	Giovanni Bellini, *Frari Triptych: Madonna and Child with Saints Peter, Nicholas, Benedict and Mark*	23
1.5	Bartolomeo Vivarini, *Bernardo Triptych*	24
1.6	Funeral Monument of Doge Francesco Foscari	25
1.7	Antonio Rizzo, Funeral Monument of Doge Nicolò Tron	26
1.8	Alvise Vivarini and Marco Basaiti, *St. Ambrose and Saints*	27
1.9	Bartolomeo Vivarini, *Triptych of St. Mark with Sts. John the Baptist, Jerome, Nicholas and Paul*	28
1.10	Funeral Monument of Bishop Jacopo Pesaro	29
1.11	Titian (Tiziano Vecellio), *Ca' Pesaro Madonna*	30
1.12	Giammaria Mosca (Padovano), Funeral Monument of Alvise Pasqualigo	31
3.1	Archivio di Stato, Padova, *Notarile*, busta 2727, fol. 38^r	110

Note on the Author

Linda L. Carroll, who received her A.B. from Princeton University and M.A. and Ph.D. from Harvard University, is Professor of Italian at Tulane University. She is the author of numerous books and articles explicating the exceptionally but opaquely candid plays of Angelo Beolco (Il Ruzante), whose *Prima oratione* she has edited and translated. She also publishes on topics in art history and, together with Melanie L. Marshall and Katherine McIver, co-edited *Sexualities, Textualities, Art and Music in Early Modern Italy. Playing with Boundaries.* Her work as translator includes *Venice, Città Excelentissima: Selections from the Renaissance Diaries of Marin Sanudo*. Her edition of the first book of madrigals of Antonio Molino (co-edited with Anthony M. Cummings, Zachary W. Jones, and Philip Weller) was published in 2014 by the Istituto Italiano della Storia della Musica, Rome. Her work is planned to culminate in a volume on cultural evolution in Renaissance Italy and in an edition and translation of the complete plays of Ruzante.

Acknowledgments

The seeds of the present work were planted in 1968 during my participation in Gonzaga University's Florence Program. My interest in art history was developed by coursework with Carolyn Valone, whose combination of spirited insight and disciplinary rigor was inspiring, and by the viewing of as many works as time and funds allowed. My first viewing of Santa Maria Gloriosa dei Frari occurred that year under the expert guidance of (now Monsignor) Timothy Verdon, whose appreciation of the Giovanni Bellini *sacra conversazione* (*Frari Triptych: Madonna and Child with Saints Peter, Nicholas, Benedict and Mark*) of the Pesaro Chapel drew my attention to it. Venice's linguistic and theatrical traditions exerted a fascination from first contact that grew apace with knowledge of them that also revealed their cross-fertilization with Padua's, resulting in a dissertation offering the first history of the languages and literatures of Venice and Padua in English.

Subsequent research expanded to considerations of the social, political, and economic contexts of the arts in the Italian Renaissance, especially in Venice. Living and teaching in the port city of New Orleans with its Carnival and Carnival krewes provided stimulating points of comparison. The astonishingly modern figure and works of Angelo Beolco, better known by the name of the peasant character that he created and played, Ruzante, attracted my particular attention, especially his advancement in 1528 of the core concept of universal suffrage. Such a radically egalitarian proposal naturally raises the question of the circumstances prompting him to do so and the reasons why Venetian patricians, whose own social status was hardening into a caste in his time, invited him to entertain for them. The present work represents one phase of the research, planned to encompass the entire arc of Beolco's performing years and to include an edition and translation into English of his complete works.

Among the scholars whose works have inspired and guided me over the years are my graduate professor Paolo Valesio 'il miglior fabbro', the late Giovan Battista Pellegrini with his profound and extensive knowledge of the languages of Italy and their history, historian of Venice and beyond the late Kenneth M. Setton, scholar of Renaissance Italy's multivalent literary production Brian Richardson, scholar of theater in its many manifestations Richard Andrews, librarian and scholar *par excellence* Marino Zorzi, and congenial and thought-provoking discussant of the cultural history of Padua and Venice Margaret Bent. My thinking on freedom of expression has been constantly nourished and supported by the fellow members and staff of the American Association of University Professors.

A year's sabbatical in 2010–2011 allowed an extended research period in Italy. Residing in Padua, I made regular visits to Venice for archival research. Since the train I took used to arrive prior to the opening of the archive, located in the former monastery of the Frari's Franciscans, I spent the time becoming reacquainted with the church. The visits revealed that many of the same families who had commissioned its art works were also supporters of Beolco's theater. The archival research revealed the network among them and the Beolco family's long-standing connections to them, while work with the Diaries of Marin Sanudo divulged particular connections with and new information about the *compagnia della calza* (patrician festive society) Triumphanti. At the conclusion of the year, I visited the Bodleian Library of the University of Oxford to study a little-known manuscript of the Canonician collection that Professor Carlo Dionisotti, with whom I had studied in graduate school, had identified as in the hand of Stefano Magno, who also copied a work of Ruzante's. The reading revealed the manuscript to have a number of unknown, anonymous works of great historical and cultural interest, though not uniformly of great literary merit. Thus was this volume conceived and given form.

The research presented here has received support from several sources. For a grant to study Ruzante's manuscripts I am grateful to the American Philosophical Society. The Georges Lurcy Faculty Research Fund and the Phase II Fund of Tulane University provided support for summer research travel in 2001 and 2006 respectively. And I am most grateful for being named a Suzanne and Stephen Weiss Presidential Fellow of Tulane University, as the research fund associated with it allowed me to follow the sources wherever they led.

Approaching Italy's vast and complex archives is a daunting task, in which the assistance of professional staff is indispensable. Scholars of Venice are fortunate to have expert guides to whom to turn in the Archivio di Stato; Dottoressa Michela Dal Borgo and Dottoressa Alessandra Sambo provided vital assistance to the present project. Also invaluable was the assistance of the staff of the Archivio di Stato in Padua, particularly in locating the Beolco family documents. I am grateful to the director of the Sezione Antica of the Biblioteca del Seminario Vescovile in Padua, the Reverend Riccardo Battocchio, and to its librarian, Dottoressa Giovanna Bergantino, for their assistance in identifying manuscripts of interest. The late Reverend Pierantonio Gios of the Biblioteca Capitolare of the Diocese of Padua provided constant and illuminating guidance to its collections.

Scholars do not live by documents and texts alone, but also require lodging and sustenance. The former was provided by the excellent faculty guest house of the Università di Padova under the auspices of the Fondazione Ing. Aldo Gini, superbly managed by Signora Monica Galuppo. The latter was provided during archival work in Venice especially by the Bar ai Nomboli, whose Signora Mirella handles the requests of the abundant clientele with intelligence, grace, humor, and kindness.

My most important and heartfelt thanks are reserved for my husband, Bruce Boyd Raeburn, whose constant encouragement and support have been invaluable. Among his many virtues is the generosity with which he agreed to spend our honeymoon in the newly-opened Czech Republic, where I researched the Conti di Collalto in the archive in Brno. His 'oceanic' (as one scholar characterized it) knowledge of New Orleans jazz, its creators, and its role in the city's culture has provided constant points of comparison and stimulus for my thinking about Ruzante and his relationship with the *compagnie della calza* of Venice. For this and so much more I am grateful to him.

Abbreviations

Institutions

ASPd	Archivio di Stato, Padua
ASVe	Archivio di Stato, Venice
PACV	Archivio della Curia Vescovile, Padua
PBC	Biblioteca Civica, Padua
PBUC	Biblioteca Universitaria Centrale, Padua
PSVBA	Seminario Vescovile, Biblioteca Antica, Padua
VBMC	Biblioteca del Museo Correr, Venice

Archival *Fondi*

AGB	ASVe, Archivio Grimani Barbarigo
AGRM	ASVe, Archivio Gradenigo Rio Marin
AO, ASC	ASPd, Archivio dell'Ospedale, Archivio della Scuola della Carità

Reference Works

DBI	*Dizionario biografico degli italiani*

General

m.c.	*more comune*
m.v.	*more veneto*
s.v.	*sub voce*

Introduction: Mercury, Venus, and the Muses

Commerce, Peace, and the Arts in Renaissance Venice

Summary

Explored in the three case studies that compose the present volume are intertwining phenomena that developed in Venice in the short distance between the last quarter of the fifteenth century and the first third of the sixteenth century: a strategy developed by some members of the patriciate to cope with their and the Republic's loss of commerce and international influence by cultivating the economic potential of mainland holdings and of ecclesiastical benefices, their utilization of a dense web of connections in pursuit of their strategy, and their announcement and promotion of it through patronage of the arts.

Between 1490 and 1530, the Most Serene Republic was transformed by the rising nation-states and empires from an independent, expanding empire richly financed by lucrative international commerce into a bounded and shrinking dominion strapped by heavy war debts and leanly financed by reduced commercial and agricultural income. Portuguese competition made unavailable to Venetian merchants most Asian luxury goods at the same time that wars between the northern European states to which Venice had exported them closed those markets to them. Turkish expansion up the Balkan peninsula into imperial and Venetian territory and along the eastern coast of the Mediterranean and the north coast of Africa, as well as increasing raids along the coast of the Italian peninsula, both interfered with galley commerce and posed a grave risk to the supply of foodstuffs and raw materials required by Venice's large population, dependent on importation from the eastern Mediterranean. While research has established that in the late sixteenth century Venice recouped some Asian trade, it is important not to anticipate that development. In the period in question it was drastically reduced, as is documented in the present study.[1] In response, Venetians intensified their previously sporadic investment of commercial profits in industrial and agricultural properties on the mainland permitted by the earlier expansion of the Venetian state as far

---

1 The magisterial work on relations between European states and the Turkish empire is Kenneth M. Setton, *The Papacy and the Levant*, 4 vols, Memoirs of the American Philosophical Society vols 114, 127, 161–2 (Philadelphia, 1976–84); for this period see vol. 2 *The Fifteenth Century* (127) and vol. 3 *The Sixteenth Century to the Reign of Julius III* (161).

west as Crema in Lombardy. They developed new and existing industries; particularly lucrative were printing and woolworking in Padua with its book-hungry university and local wool supply and artisans. Silk production was added when Syrian sources were prohibited from exporting to Italy.[2]

At the same time, Venice's patricians turned increasingly from commercial and governance responsibilities to cultural endeavors, including those that are the focus of the present work. Some of these endeavors, in which they might involve non-patricians and foreigners to introduce new trends or state difficult truths without loss of patrician dignity and authority, had connections to or were attempts at aligning public policy decisions in Venice's governing councils with patrons' personal or small-group interests. The three moments chosen for study exemplify three important points of these developments. Art works in the Frari demonstrate the increase in the late fifteenth century of commissions by private donors of large works in venues that, while under private control, were open to public viewing and thus potentially influential. Taken collectively, they warn of the dangers of Turkish aggression and promote relations with Venice's mainland dominion and other Italian states. The research from new, chiefly primary, sources confirms the art historians' sense that connections existed among the patrons. The early sixteenth century phase following on the wars of the League of Cambrai—that lasted from 1509 to 1517, devastating the mainland state, the Republic's finances, and patrician commerce—is exemplified by the subject of the second case study, a young patrician's detachment from his family's earlier involvement in commerce and governance in favor of collecting literary works and writing the history of

---

2   See especially Achille Olivieri, "Capitale mercantile e committenza nella Venezia del Sansovino," in *Investimenti e civiltà urbana. Secoli XIII–XVIII*, ed. Annalisa Guarducci (Florence, 1991), pp. 531–69; Lesley A. Ling, "La presenza fondiaria veneziana nel padovano (secoli XIII–XIV)," in *Istituzioni, società e potere nella Marca Trevigiana e Veronese. Sulle tracce di G.B. Verci*, ed. Gherardo Ortalli and Michael Knapton (Rome, 1988), pp. 305–16; Aldo Stella, "Bonifiche benedettine e precapitalismo veneto tra Cinquecento e Seicento," in *S. Benedetto e otto secoli (XII–XIX) di vita monastica nel Padovano* (Padua, 1980), pp. 171–93; Gian Maria Varanini, "Proprietà fondiaria e agricoltura," in *Storia di Venezia dalle origini alla caduta della Serenissima*, 8 vols (Rome, 1992–98), vol. 5 *Il Rinascimento. Società ed Economia*, ed. Alberto Tenenti and Ugo Tucci (1996), pp. 807–79; Angelo Ventura, "Considerazioni sull'agricoltura veneta e sull'accumulazione originaria del capitale nei secoli XVI e XVII," in *Agricoltura e sviluppo del capitalismo*. Atti del convegno organizzato dall'Istituto Gramsci (Rome 1968) (Rome, 1970), pp. 519–60. For weathervane families: Giuseppe Gullino, *I Pisani dal Banco e Moretta. Storia di due famiglie veneziane in età moderna e delle loro vicende patrimoniali tra 1705 e 1836* (Rome, 1984); Giuseppe Gullino, *Marco Foscari (1477–1551): l'attività politica e diplomatica tra Venezia, Roma, e Firenze* (Milan, 2000), esp. pp. 13–20. For printing see Antonio Barzon, ed., *Libri e stampatori in Padova*. Miscellanea di studi storici in onore di mons. G. Bellini (Padua, 1959). For Venetians inscribed in the Padua wool guild see PBC, B.P. 801 V Giovanni Lazara, *Memorie di famiglie nobili di Padova descritte nel Collegio dell'arte della lana e di famiglie nobili applicate all'esercizio di banchiere e cambista, raccolte dal c. Giovanni Lazara* (hereafter Lazara, *Memorie*). See also Linda L. Carroll, "Introduction," in Angelo Beolco (Il Ruzante), *La prima oratione*, ed. and trans. Linda L. Carroll, MHRA Critical Texts vol. 16 (London, 2009), pp. 5–74, and consult the volume's Bibliography. For silk, see Luca Molà, *The Silk Industry of Renaissance Venice* (Baltimore and London, 2000), esp. pp. 57–67, 215–23.

Venice and its patrician families. The third case study explores a 1525 semi-public Carnival festivity sponsored by the patrician *compagnia della calza* ('company of the hose', a patrician festive society) Triumphanti as a highly articulated example of the intersection of economic, policy, and artistic issues, a convergence that has been attracting increasing scholarly interest of late.[3] New information on the Triumphanti, their families, and the government officials attending the performance will support the hypothesis that the performance was connected with the efforts of certain patricians to influence decisions in the Venetian Senate about the direction of the international warfare and negotiations in which the Republic was then engaged. The fourth essay, a coda to the others, presents new material on relations between Niccolò Machiavelli and the Republic through the Venetian impresario Zuan (Giovanni) Manenti, who ran some of Venice's state lotteries, as well as documenting the extent to which the Republic used the lotteries to pay for war expenses in the 1520s.

Historical Background: The Fifteenth Century

Venice had enjoyed a number of victories in the phase preceding the one at issue. The papal throne had been occupied by one of its patrician families for much of the fifteenth century: Gregory XII (Angelo Correr; reigned 1406–17 in rivalry with Benedict XIII), his nephew Eugenio IV (Gregorio Condulmer; reigned 1431–47), and Eugenio's nephew Paolo II (Pietro Barbo; reigned 1464–71). Already possessed of a significant maritime state (*stato da mar*), the Republic had by the early fifteenth century created a hinterland state (*stato di terraferma*) by overcoming local lords. As magnificently demonstrated by Margaret King, the consolidation of mainland governance during the fifteenth century co-occurred with the development of a Venetian humanist culture favoring a rather severe Roman style, a form of learning from the ancients to manage the transition from republic to empire.[4]

With the peace of Lodi of 1454 came a period in which the relative lack of war freed resources to be devoted to cultural and artistic endeavors, including the new medium of print. The flowering is represented by the grand late Gothic *palazzi*, the architecture of Codussi, the sculptures of the Lombardo, the paintings of the Bellini and Carpaccio; and literature which, despite the epithet *secolo senza poesia*, was distinguished by the lyric poetry of Leonardo Giustinian. University texts, Bibles, humanistic treatises, literary works of ancient and modern authors flowed continuously from printing presses, machines that, in the early days, were borrowed from their chief function of winemaking.[5]

---

3 See *e.g.* Valerie Forman, *Global Economics and the Early Modern English Stage* (Philadelphia, 2008); Jan Bloemendal, Peter G.F. Eversmann, and Elsa Strietman, eds. *Drama, Performance and Debate: Theatre and Public Opinion in the Early Modern Period* (Leiden and Boston, 2013).

4 Margaret L. King, *Venetian Humanism in an Age of Patrician Dominance* (Princeton, 1986).

5 The scholarly literature on all of the preceding topics is too vast to summarize; some important studies concerning this last are Antonio Sartori, "Documenti padovani sull'arte della stampa nel secolo XV,"

Toward the end of the century, Venice's pacific state was truncated by a cluster of threats: the invasion of the peninsula by Charles VIII, a wave of Turkish aggression that resulted in humiliating naval defeats such as that at Zonchio with the loss of some important colonies, wars among northern European states that disrupted trade, the snatching of the bulk of Asian trade goods by the Portuguese, Spanish aggression on the Italian peninsula with the consolidation of a Neapolitan-Sicilian state, and Spanish ascendance to the papal throne with Alexander VI. Venice's wellbeing and the threats to it inform a number of the Frari art works discussed in Chapter 1. The earlier ones especially emphasize the importance of defending navigation from Turkish aggression, navigation whose fruits included the funding for the devotional works themselves. The later Frari works emphasized especially the need to cultivate the mainland state and ecclesiastical benefices as alternate sources of provisions and profits, facilitated by good relations with the dominant European powers.

Maritime commerce with the north, already in decline earlier in the fifteenth century, faced serious threats in its final two decades. Profitability decreased because fewer goods were available in the north for the return voyage, warring states increasingly interfered with the convoys, and potential investors were diverted by the attractive rates of Venice's funded war debt.[6] As recorded in a chronicle by Stefano Magno, whose literary endeavors are the subject of Chapter 2, the 1485 round was afflicted by grave misfortunes, including corsairs and sequester by the French king, with the loss of some goods. The 1487 round not finding investors, the Senate ameliorated the terms, but also required significant bank and investor backing. In addition to the chief backers, Agostino and Francesco Foscari, the Venetian patrician merchant investors included the Bernardo, the Capello, the Pesaro, the Garzoni, the Grimani, the Gritti, the Gussoni, the Lippomano, the Pisani, and the Marcello, among others. A few months later, although previously their books had shown only Venetian investors, the Foscari report that they sought support from foreigners, on the recommendation of Piero Trevisan writing to the Milanese "ser Zuan de Beolco e co[m]pagni" (Zuan de Beolco and associates) for financial support.[7] The galleys having reached London, two of them were

in *Libri e stampatori in Padova*, pp. 111–228; Martin Lowry, *The World of Aldus Manutius. Business and Scholarship in Renaissance Venice* (Ithaca, 1979); the numerous relevant articles in Girolamo Arnaldi and Manlio Pastore Stocchi, eds, *Dal Primo Quattrocento al Concilio di Trento*, Vol. 3.1 *Storia della Cultura Veneta* (Vicenza, 1980).

6 Frederic C. Lane, "Venetian Shipping," in *Venice and History* (Baltimore, 1966), pp. 3–24, 15–16; Raymond de Roover, *The Rise and Decline of the Medici Bank 1397–1494* (New York, 1966), pp. 5, 16, 195–6; Reinhold C. Mueller, *The Venetian Money Market. Banks, Panics, and the Public Debt, 1200–1500*, Vol. 2 of *Money and Banking in Medieval and Renaissance Venice* (Baltimore, 1997), pp. 230–51, 431–2; Gullino, *Marco Foscari*, p. 19; VBMC, ms. Cicogna 3533, Stefano Magno, *Annali Veneti*, fols 4ᵛ–5ʳ, 14ᵛ–15ʳ, 34ʳ, 60[bis]ᵛ–61[bis]ʳ ['bis' has been added because of a repeat numeration], 70ᵛ–71ʳ, 84ᶠ⁻ 101ᵛ, 111ᵛ, 126ʳ, 151ᵛ, 152ʳ⁻ᵛ.

7 The source for much of the information concerning the western and northern galleys in the mid 1480s is the account book of Agostino and Marco Foscari, one of three from the period found in the Archivio di Stato, Venezia, *Archivio Gradenigo Rio Marin*, busta 250, the second in chronological sequence that the *busta* contains, here termed 'second *vacchetta*', fols 7ʳ, 8ʳ, 9ᵛ, 26ᵛ, 35ᵛ–6ʳ.

prevented from loading goods and departing by the lack of funds to pay increased duties; moreover, the crews complained that they were not being paid. The Senate responded by requiring investors to increase their contribution. In this period the Foscari wrote numerous additional times to Beolco for support. Several of these transactions also involved the Genoese Salvago and Lomellino banking families, with whom Zuan de Beolco, one of the richest men in Milan, conducted other business.[8] In a sign of how extreme the threats to the voyage were, the Foscari brought additional foreigners, the Florentine Frescobaldi and the German Fugger, into the financing of the voyages.

The subsequent northern voyage headed by the Foscari benefitted not only from further investments by "Zuan de Beolcho e nipotti" (Zuan de Beolco and nephews) but by numerous other foreign investors whose first-time status and Lombard names possibly indicate recruitment by them. Zuan de Beolco together with his brother Lazaro had developed their financial interests in Venice and its mainland dominion in the second half of the fifteenth century. A financier to the Sforza and other important Milanese families and holder of key offices, Zuan remained in Milan while Lazaro moved first to Vicenza and then to Padua and Venice. By 1487, subsequent to Lazaro's death, the family business was represented in Venice by Lazaro's son Zuan Jacopo (Giovanni Giacomo), while Lazaro's older son Zuan Francesco (Giovanni Francesco) was undertaking a university career in Padua. He would later become the father of Angelo, the 'famosissimo' (very famous) Ruzante. In 1521 Stefano Magno would make the only known copy of Ruzante's *Pastoral* while his father was *capitanio* of Padua.[9]

8 The wealth and nobility of the Milanese Beolco family were discovered and published by Emilio Lovarini, "Notizie sui parenti e sulla vita del Ruzzante," in *Studi sul Ruzzante e sulla letteratura pavana*, ed. Gianfranco Folena (Padua: Antenore, 1965), pp. 3–60. An important source was a group of archival documents that Lovarini termed 'Eredità Beolco'; the reorganization of Padua's archives shortly thereafter made them difficult to locate, and they have not been consulted by subsequent scholars. I am deeply grateful to the staff of the Archivio di Stato, Padova for their assistance in helping me identify them as *Archivio dell'Ospitale, Archivio della Scuola della Carità*, buste 231–5. For this paragraph, see busta 231, fols 45–6. See also Patrizia Mainoni, "L'attività mercantile e le casate milanesi nel secondo Quattrocento," in *Milano nell'età di Ludovico il Moro*, Atti del convegno internazionale, Milano 28 febbraio–4 marzo 1983, ed. Giulia Bologna, 2 vols (Milan, 1983), 2: 575–84, esp. 582–3; Paola Venturelli, *Gioielli e gioiellieri milanesi. Storia, arte, moda (1450–1630)* (Cinisello Balsamo [MI], 1996), p. 72; Letizia Arcangeli, "Esperimenti di governo: politica fiscale e consenso a Milano nell'età di Luigi XII," in *Milano e Luigi XII: ricerche sul primo dominio francese in Lombardia, 1499–1512*, ed. Letizia Arcangeli (Milan, 2002), pp. 253–339, esp. pp. 312–28; Maria Nadia Covini, *"La balanza drita." Pratiche di governo, leggi e ordinamenti nel ducato sforzesco* (Milan, 2007), pp. 288, 319, 325 (Covini is the only scholar of Milan to note the family connection with Ruzante, though with some inexactitude in the details of the Veneto branch of the family); Beatrice Del Bo, *Banca e politica a Milano a metà Quattrocento* (Rome, 2010), pp. 105–106, 212. I am grateful to Luca Zenobi for the Milanese references.
9 ASVe, *AGRM*, busta 250, second *vacchetta*, fols 37ᵛ–52ʳ; ASPd, *AO, ASC*, busta 231, esp. fols 11, 17–22; busta 235, printed history, pp. 2–4; Lovarini, "Notizie," esp. pp. 5–7; Marino Sanuto [Marin Sanudo], *I diarii*, ed. Rinaldo Fulin et al., 58 vols (Venice, 1879–1902), 2: 1096–7; Paolo Sambin, *Per le biografie di Angelo Beolco, il Ruzante, e di Alvise Cornaro*, restauri di archivio

As Ugo Tucci and Gaetano Cozzi observed, by the early sixteenth century the prolonged period of mainland peace and the lengthy disruptions to trade had accustomed patricians of the younger generations to a pleasant life at home in contrast with the uncertain profits and stark discomforts, even dangers, of merchant life abroad. At the same time, their access to government office was restricted by a growing number of detailed requirements for maintaining patrician status and the prerequisite of a large loan to the state for candidacy in elections. It was in this period that young men increasingly cultivated a taste for art and turned to cultural endeavors such as poetry and song along with the requisite inspiration for them, love.[10]

Thalia (and Melpomene) in the Service of Cupid, Mercury, and Clio

Theatrical works articulated many of these developments. Previously confined to religious plays and some seasonal rituals, drama in the early fifteenth century had received an infusion of new life with the discovery of twelve lost Plautine comedies. Culturally authoritative because of their Roman origin, the works also displayed a refreshing streak of irreverence in their frank description and sometimes derision of the defects of authority figures, typically the father or other senior males. Such a tantalizing duality and its reflection of real social tensions created a compelling dynamic that catalyzed a vibrant, evolving theatrical tradition in Italy. At first Plautine and Terentian comedies were staged in Latin; later they were performed in vernacular translations in private settings by princely families, including women. Original plays began to be composed in Latin. Finally, original plays written in the vernacular and exploring contemporary issues began to appear. The epicenter of these developments was Ferrara and the matched-set marquisate of Mantua; however, the much-debated 1504 date of a first version of the *Mandragola* may hint that similar developments were occurring in Florence, where sacred theater flourished.[11]

In Venice, comedy developed somewhat late. The last years of the fifteenth century saw the first original plays written in Latin. While most playwrights were outsiders resident in Venice who dedicated their works to patricians, their number included one of the first members of a leading patrician family to turn from governance to the arts, Tommaso Mezzo.[12] In addition to a new comic

rivisti e aggiornati da Francesco Piovan (Padua, 2002), esp. "Lazzaro e Giovanni Francesco Beolco, nonno e padre del Ruzante (Relazioni e aspetti di famiglia, lavoro e cultura)," pp. 7–57, 8–27.

10 Ugo Tucci, "The Psychology of the Venetian Merchant in the Sixteenth Century," in *Renaissance Venice*, ed. J.R. Hale (London, 1973), pp. 346–78; Gaetano Cozzi, "La donna, l'amore e Tiziano," in *Tiziano e Venezia* (Vicenza, 1980), pp. 47–63.

11 For sacred theater, see *e.g.* Antonia Pulci, *Florentine Drama for Convent and Festival*, seven sacred plays annotated and translated by James Wyatt Cook, edited by James Wyatt Cook and Barbara Collier Cook (Chicago, 1996); Elissa Weaver, *Convent Theatre in Early Modern Italy. Spiritual Fun and Learning for Women* (Cambridge and New York, 2002).

12 Graziella Gentilini, "Mezzo, Tommaso," *DBI*, 74 (2010).

form, the playwrights presented a new theme: a young patrician man who, after overcoming paternal opposition, marries for love a young woman who, while at first seeming to be of low station, is discovered to be well-born and whose family supplies a significant dowry providing the couple with effort-free income. Art thus explored a real contemporary development, the reconciling of apparently conflicting norms. On the one side there was the norm, well established in literary and popular culture, that the heart does what it will, which, as Guido Ruggiero observed, over the previous two centuries had taken the shape of the vogue for love.[13] On the other was the norm, well established in historical usage, that fathers designated their children's spouses with families' economic and social status in mind, a practice that over the fifteenth century had given rise to dowry inflation. The two norms found congenial shared ground with the groom's need to find an income that would substitute for abandoned commerce and the dowry's availability to him long before his paternal inheritance. Useful to the resolution of the conflict between youthful love and mature insistence on maintaining the family's social status was the revived classical theatrical device of agnition. Through agnition, the lovable young woman who at first appeared to be of a lower class, was eventually discovered—often by the fortuitous arrival of a wealthy, high-ranking man recognizing her as a long-lost relative—to be of high birth and generous dowry.[14]

Typical works are Tommaso Mezzo's *Epirota*, Giovanni Antonio Marso's *Stephanium* and Bartolomeo Zamberti's *Dolotechne*.[15] In the *Dolotechne*, a wealthy young woman, kidnapped in a Greece assailed by the Persians, is brought to Italy. There her youthful beloved does battle with Cupid rather than Mars, while Venus settles conflicts. The eschewal of business for pleasure is exemplified by Niceratus of the *Stephanium,* who sloughs off his father's urging to join the family commercial enterprise and plans to use his beloved's dowry to spare himself all travail. The occurrence of similar events and values in the lives of the dedicatee of the *Stephanium* and his family of merchants and art patrons, the Pasqualigo, is explored in Chapter 1.

---

13 Guido Ruggiero, *The Boundaries of Eros. Sex Crimes and Sexuality in Renaissance Venice* (New York, 1985).

14 On dowries, see Stanley Chojnacki, "La posizione della donna a Venezia nel Cinquecento," in *Tiziano e Venezia*, pp. 69–70; the present study revisits Linda L. Carroll, "'Who's on Top?': Gender as Societal Power Configuration in Italian Renaissance Drama," *Sixteenth Century Journal* 20 (1989): 531–58. Linda L. Carroll and Anthony M. Cummings, "Historical Introduction," (Rome, 2014).

15 Texts: Graziella Gentilini, ed., *Il teatro umanistico veneto: La commedia: Tommaso Mezzo, 'Epirota', Giovanni Antono Marso 'Stephanium', Bartolomeo Zamberti, 'Dolotechne'* (Ravenna, 1983). For Marso's extensive influence on Venetian vernacular culture, see Pietro Bembo, *Lettere*, edizione critica a cura di Ernesto Travi, 4 vols (Bologna, 1987–93), 1: 101–102, lett. 110; Linda L. Carroll and Anthony M. Cummings, "Historical Introduction," in Antonio Molino (Il Burchiella), *Delightful Madrigals for Four Voices . . . , Newly . . . Composed and Brought to Light . . . First Book . . . 1568*, edited by Linda L. Carroll, Anthony M. Cummings, Zachary W. Jones, and Philip Weller (Rome, 2014), pp. X–LIII, X–XIV.

The Most Serene Republic suffered disastrous afflictions in the early sixteenth century in the military-political sphere. The soul-wrenching defeat of its army at Agnadello by the arrayed forces of Europe was followed by the ignominious flight of the army and Venetian mainland governors to the shores of the lagoon.[16] The rout brought about the Republic's subjugation to the papacy through the conditions required by the pope for the alliance with him that Venice desperately needed to reverse its fortunes. They included the loss of exclusive control of the Adriatic with its important shipping lanes and the ceding of the jewels of St. Mark as collateral for the loan from the pope necessary to the reinforcing of Venice's army.[17]

Contemporaneously, and especially in the developing vernacular comedy and the first tragedies, came a new taste for brutal candor, often displacing high-culture rhetoric. Reflecting the remorseless self-examination of Venetians recorded by diarists Marin Sanudo and Girolamo Priuli brought on by the defeat, these plays, though written and largely performed by outsiders, were staged by patricians. Signally among the hosts was the rising patrician generation organized into the festive societies known as *compagnie della calza* (companies of the hose) for the colorful and distinctive hose that they wore. Among the entertainers invited by *compagnie*, often under the guise of Carnival revelry, were non-patricians whose critiques of the established generation and proposals of new directions corresponded with the younger generation's (financial) interests. Young patricians thus could accomplish the pronouncement of unpleasant truths in such a way as to distance themselves from and, if expedient, cast off the pronouncers.

The most famous of the guests and the most extreme in his proposals, though along a well-travelled trajectory, was Angelo Beolco, known by the name of the peasant character that he created and played, Ruzante. His first named performance in Venice occurred in 1520 at a spectacular festivity staged by the *compagnia della calza* Immortali (Immortals) to induct Federico Gonzaga, a consolation prize to the new young marquis of Mantua after the failure of his bid to be hired by Venice as a *condottiero*. Ruzante may have performed even earlier, at a private 1518 festivity for visiting Roman cardinals held by their confrère Venetian Marco Corner.[18] Other barbed comedies included *La veniexiana*, formally anonymous but convincingly linked by Giorgio Padoan to the circle of Zuan Francesco Valier, an ecclesiastic and the illegitimate son of a Venetian patrician who shared with his father ties to the Gonzaga; Bibbiena's *Calandria*,

---

16 See the ever-valuable overview in Kenneth M. Setton, *The Sixteenth Century to the Reign of Julius III*, vol. 3 of *The Papacy and the Levant*, 4 vols, Memoirs of the American Philosophical Society (Philadelphia, 1976–84); subsequent references will be to this volume unless otherwise specified. See also Linda L. Carroll, "Giorgione's *Tempest*: Astrology is in the Eyes of the Beholder," *Reconsidering the Renaissance. Papers from the Twenty-First Annual Conference*, ed. Mario Di Cesare (Binghamton, 1992), pp. 125–40.

17 Felix Gilbert, *The Pope, His Banker, and Venice* (Cambridge, 1980).

18 See Linda L. Carroll, "Venetian Attitudes toward the Young Charles: Carnival, Commerce, and *Compagnie della Calza*," in *Young Charles V, 1500–1529*, ed. Alain Saint-Saëns (New Orleans, 2000), pp. 13–52; Carroll, "Introduction," in Beolco, *La prima oratione*.

whose plot is set in motion by the Venetian loss of two ancient maritime possessions, Modon and Coron; and Machiavelli's *Mandragola* with its critique of the impotent French king and Florentine doctor and its anxiety about Turkish invasion (Act II, scene 6; Act III, Scene 4).[19] The *Mandragola* was staged by recently-arrived former courtiers of Leo X in 1522, who also likely brought the satirical works on the election of his successor that found their way into the manuscript studied in Chapter 2. Occurring thirteen years after Machiavelli's visit to a Verona under enemy domination, the performance had connections to the Venetian *cittadino* and former member of the Leonine court Zuan (Giovanni) Manenti. Manenti was charged by Venice at the same time with running lotteries to finance its wars and by Machiavelli with conveying intelligence to the Doge. These complicated connections are discussed in all four of the chapters.[20]

Numerous plays, including Ruzante's *Pastoral*, were transcribed or collected by Stefano Magno, whose father Andrea held important mainland governance positions, including *capitanio* of Padua, in the first decades of the sixteenth century. During those years, Andrea acquired properties on the mainland, concentrating on well-chosen adjacent agricultural parcels. Just as Stefano was reaching maturity, the limits and dangers of commerce were impressed upon the family by a shipwreck that cost a Magno cousin his life when inadequately-repaired galleys were sent out too hastily to resume the trade interrupted by the Cambrai wars. Stefano, like Niceratus, eschewed such demanding tasks, postponing even Venice-based offices until late. Supported by his wife's large dowry and the estates prudently acquired by his father, he devoted himself to cultural pleasures. He composed historical accounts of Venice centered on the patriciate, including many who figure in the present volume, and collected various literary works, including some satirizing identifiable Venetian and foreign figures. His various literary assemblages dating to these years, including the *zibaldone* manuscript Bodleian Canonician Ital. 36 that contains the works on the papal election, are the subject of Chapter 2.

Comedies with elements of political satire continued to be staged during the post-Cambrai period through most of the third decade of the century, as the politico-military sphere saw a perfect storm of threatening changes. The Ottomans extended their rule over the entire eastern shore of the Mediterranean and into north Africa, including the port of Alexandria so crucial to Venetian commerce, and were soon

---

19 *La Veniexiana. Commedia di anonimo veneziano del Cinquecento*, Testo critico, tradotto ed annotato da Giorgio Padoan (Padua, 1974); Giorgio Padoan, *La commedia rinascimentale veneta* (Vicenza, 1982), pp. 140–53; Linda L. Carroll, "Dating *La Veniex[ia]na*: The Venetian Patriciate and the Mainland Nobility at the End of the Wars of Cambrai, with a Note on Titian," *Annuario dell'Istituto Romeno di cultura e ricerca umanistica* (Venice) 5 (2003): 511–19. While Padoan only links the play with Valier's *ambiente*, the data point to Valier's having been a prime mover of the play or even its author.

20 Sanuto, 32: 458; for a political interpretation of a letter written during that visit, see Linda L. Carroll, "Machiavelli's Veronese Prostitute: *Venetia Figurata*?" in *Gender Rhetorics: Postures of Dominance and Submission in History*, ed. Richard C. Trexler (Binghamton, 1994), pp. 93–106.

planning an invasion of Italy. Charles, by an election to the imperial throne contracted by his grandfather Maximilian in the summer of 1518 although not accomplished until the following summer, acquired much of the coast along which the northern galleys sailed. He soon allied himself with the sovereigns of the remainder of it, Henry VIII and Francis I. He even pressed east from Spain across the north African coast. While his expansion there helped Venetian merchants by quelling the local population and extending a single rule over what had been a swarm of statelets, it subjected their voyages to a much more powerful and better-financed sovereign. This set of obstacles arose just as the galleys had resumed their rounds after the eight-year suspension caused by the wars of Cambrai. While many Venetian patricians were blind to the implications of Charles's election, the best-informed and most perspicacious immediately realized that, as diplomat Marin Zorzi declared in the Senate, Charles had become 'il primo re del mondo' (the greatest king in the world).[21] Venice was thereby required to reassess its strategy of international alliances, especially in light of the struggle for control of the peninsula, principally wealthy Milan and its Lombard state, that all knew would erupt between Charles and Francis.

Reassessment of relations with Charles clove the patriciate into three groups. Some wished to remain with the traditional Venetian loyalty to France which, being more distant and having little or no historical claim to territories that had become the mainland state, represented the lesser threat. Others, at least during some moments of this phase, frankly preferred an alignment with Charles. As investors in the African or northern galleys they needed his approval for their passage, or as owners of property to which he did or could lay some claim they wanted to cultivate his favor, or they sought benefices from a Church increasingly influenced by him, or, like Don Abbondio of Alessandro Manzoni's *Promessi Sposi*, they simply preferred the stronger power. Other patricians, often the ones still engaged in commerce and contemplating new ports and routes, continuously modified their preference so as to remain in the good graces of as many external powers as possible, an expansion of what Frederic Lane termed Venice's "double balancing act."[22] What united almost all, however, was the desire to avoid active warfare or at least to prevent it from penetrating the bounds of their state. The core Venetian strategy of the Lombard and Cognac wars of the third decade of the century was to keep troops and fighting out of the mainland state at all costs. The reason is immediately obvious in the secret policy deliberations of the Senate and in the hair-raising descriptions of the damages to Padua and its territories wrought during the Cambrai wars both by the foreign soldiers overrunning Venetian territory and by their own troops defending it that are contained in declarations made during the 1518 Estimo (state recording of real estate holdings for tax purposes).[23]

21 Sanuto, 27: 455.
22 Frederic C. Lane, *Venice. A Maritime Republic* (Baltimore, 1973), p. 246.
23 The reality behind the *fiacca strategia* described by Robert Finlay, "Fabius Maximus in Venice: Doge Andrea Gritti, the War of Cambrai, and the Rise of Habsburg Hegemony, 1509–1530," *Renaissance Quarterly* 53 (2000): 988–1031.

It was precisely at this time that invitations to perform in Venice were extended to Angelo Beolco, with whom and with various relatives of whom numerous patricians had had private connections for at least forty years. In 1523, at the moment in which the Republic was constrained by Charles to join him in an alliance that included Milan, Beolco's father renewed the business agreement with the Milanese branch of the family.[24] Such considerations cast fresh light on the emphasis given by Emilio Lovarini and renewed by Emilio Menegazzo on the Beolco family's status as imperial feudatories and on their connections with other supporters of the empire.[25] They also raise the issue of what functions in addition to entertainment Angelo might have provided the Republic or his patrician supporters.

Early in 1525, French and imperial forces battled near Pavia while Venice, still formally committed to Charles but secretly pledged to Francis, kept its own forces aloof from the fighting. The Senate, in the meanwhile, was debating the three alliance possibilities. Senators representative of the more prudent or commercially-invested patricians wanted to refrain from antagonizing the strong outside parties because of the need to promote commerce, which had recently seen the failure of a desperate initiative to reimport Asian goods from Lisbon. They also recognized the importance of preserving the mainland from fighting because of the foodstuffs, wood, and other goods it produced, including the silk needed to replace that previously obtained from sources now forbidden to them by the Turkish conquest of Syria. The need to preserve the mainland from harm had become all the more pressing because patricians had increased their ownership of land in the early 1520s through purchases from state sales of property confiscated from imperial rebels and defeated nobles to reduce the war debt.[26]

In the midst of the debate, some of the leaders of important governmental bodies abandoned their deliberations to attend instead a Carnival festivity with the theme of concord, the subject of Chapter 3. It was sponsored by the *compagnia della calza* Triumphanti and featured three plays, including one by Beolco in which dirty language and wifely infidelity scandalized the audience. In choosing

24 ASPd, *Notarile*, busta 1056, fols 188ᵛ–9ᵛ; *AO, ASC*, busta 231, fols 17–22; Lovarini, "Notizie sulla vita e sui parenti del Ruzzante," p. 4; Cesare Cantù, *Storie minori*, 2 vols (Turin, 1864), 1: 458–9, note 11; Sambin, "Lazzaro e Giovanni Francesco Beolco," p. 26, note 73. The renewed connection did not have time to bear fruit, as both died in 1524.

25 See Emilio Menegazzo, "Ricerche intorno alla vita e all'ambiente del Ruzante e di Alvise Cornaro," in *Colonna, Folengo, Ruzante e Cornaro. Ricerche, testi e documenti*, ed. Andrea Canova (Padua, 2001), pp. 223–66, esp. 252–7. See also Arcangeli, "Esperimenti," p. 325. For the family's noble status, see G.B. di Crollalanza, *Dizionario storico blasonico delle famiglie nobili e notabili italiane estinte e fiorenti*, 3 vols (1886; Bologna, 1965), 1: 418.

26 The properties did not include any of the Beolco probably because, although rebels Zuan Jacopo and the illegitimate half-brother Melchiorre were confined to Venice, Zuan Francesco was a loyalist. However, the Beolco were later denied the tax exemption usually granted to their property formerly belonging to the Este. For exemption, ASPd, *Estimo 1418*, busta 26, fols 252–6; *Estimo 1518*, busta 35, fol. 56ʳ⁻ᵛ.

Beolco for the performance, the Triumphanti, a number of whose family members had invested in the voyages assisted by the Milanese Beolco, were calling again upon the family. This time they may have been seeking a cultural assist to their interests, if the open marriage proposed by the play is read as a metaphor for avoiding dangerous conflict through alliances or agreements with all of the threatening external powers. Beolco himself, however, may have been expressing with the *outré* material a feeling of abandonment or even betrayal as Venice and its major trade partner England moved away from alliance with Charles and toward alliance with France. Indeed, he would have only one more invitation to perform in the capital, in 1526, weeks prior to the announcement of the League of Cognac formed by France and Venice, when he staged a play at a festivity at which the captured Francis I was mocked by the release onto the table of a rooster whose comb and crest had been cut.

With the defeat of the League and the ascent of Charles, sealed by the Peace of Bologna and his coronation (1529–30), history and culture took another turn. The patriciate had managed to retain the shell of its independence, although surrounded on all sides by the empire or imperial client states.[27] Some patricians even made their affiliation with the empire more overt, such as the Pasqualigo and Bernardo with the eagles atop their Frari tombs.

Formal structure and hierarchy returned as social and cultural values, while literary and theatrical authors occupied themselves increasingly with entertainment rather than social assessment. Vernacular literary genres flourished in manuscript and increasingly in print, a development facilitated by the codification of Tuscan grammar by Leo X's Venetian patrician secretary, Pietro Bembo, and by the diffusion of small private schools teaching a widening proportion of the population to read, including girls, as in a small school located in a building owned by the Pasqualigo.[28] The expansion of printing and especially, somewhat later, of theatrical entertainment would provide the patriciate with new sources of income.[29] In the political sphere, the patriciate strengthened its monopoly over the social, economic, and political framework of the Republic through increasingly exclusive bloodline requirements for patrician status.[30] At the same time, it introduced variety or superficial innovation to cultural life through the inclusion of short-term contributions, especially by members of certain categories on its fringes (pretenders to patrician status such as Alvise Cornaro, illegitimate sons, *cittadini*, foreigners). For a brief period in the seventeenth century, the two strands were joined when descendants of

27 See Linda L. Carroll, "A Newly-Discovered *Charles V with Dog*," *Ateneo Veneto* ser. 3, 4.2 (2005): 43–77.

28 See Pasquale Sabbatino, *La "Scienza" della scrittura: Dal progetto del Bembo al manuale* (Florence, 1988); Sanuto, 26: 131.

29 See especially Ellen Rosand, *Opera in Seventeenth-Century Venice. The Creation of a Genre* (Berkeley, 1991).

30 See Victor Crescenzi, *"Esse de Maiori Consilio": legittimità civile e legittimazione politica nella Repubblica di Venezia (secc. XIII–XVI)* (Rome, 1996).

compagni della calza who had invited Ruzante took on the role of critics of the establishment themselves.[31]

Festivities and the Creative Arts in Venice: Structures and Uses

Venice's *compagnie della calza* offered an unusual platform on which social and political values could be displayed and even negotiated.[32] Like the Carnival krewes of New Orleans, Venice's *compagnie della calza* were not simple festive societies but brotherhoods promoting the careers and other life accomplishments of their members in coordination with one another with the collective goal of consolidating as much power, wealth, and status as possible in members and their families. Composed mostly of Venetian patricians, they could also include a few mainland nobles of importance to the Republic (usually *condottieri*), and the most open (*e.g.* Ortolani) enrolled even the occasional *cittadino* (Alvise di Piero Martini, *popolano*) or foreigner (Besalù). *Compagni* might group together at public events even when not formally attending as a *compagnia*, as demonstrated by an analysis of patricians answering the call to greet foreign dignitaries.[33] Such episodes illuminate the bivalent status of the *compagni*. On the one hand young and acting in concert, they were, on the other hand, the scions of leading families preparing for future leadership roles often then held by senior male relatives. Operating in the interstices of private and public life, the *compagnie* organized exclusive celebrations for life events of their members such as weddings but also Carnival and other festivities either held in public places or allowing some public attendance (often for a fee). The members' youth allowed them a little license to express themselves, a license that could be further pressed in the direction of a specific value or multiple values by the choice of works staged, the non-*compagni* staging them, the costumes and other theatrical elements, and even the venue (whose *palazzo*, which public space). Their festivities, however, required governmental approval and when it was felt that the private activity encroached too much on the public sphere or the predominant public interest, approval was denied or withdrawn.

A close look at the specific individuals and groups sponsoring theatrical performances and commissioning works of art reveals additional functions that artistic products served, particularly in the relationships between the *compagni* and the many non-patricians who swirled around them. As the content of

---

31 Linda L. Carroll, "Venetian Literature," in *A Companion to Venetian History, 1400–1799*, ed. Eric Dursteler (Leiden; Boston, 2013), pp. 615–49, 636 commenting on Edward Muir, *The Culture Wars of the Late Renaissance* (Cambridge, 2007), pp. 111–48. For the transition from *compagnie della calza* to Commedia dell'Arte, see Peter Jordan, *The Venetian Origins of the Commedia dell'Arte* (New York, 2014).

32 For more detail, see Chapter 3; Carroll, "Venetian Attitudes."

33 Carroll, "Venetian Attitudes."

Ruzante's plays well demonstrates, theatrical and other public performances such as those by groups of peasant singers offered Venetians means of understanding and connecting with the mainland, its inhabitants, and their customs at the close of the Cambrai wars, as Venetians reclaimed and repaired their properties and rebuilt their relations with the peasants who farmed them.[34] This was neither a casual timing nor a trivial contribution, given the increasing need for Venetians to derive income, supplies, and troops from the mainland state as the impending conflict between Charles and Francis loomed. As is demonstrated with specific examples in the present studies, the non-patrician figures were not only clients of the patricians but also helped them to move into new worlds of income-making and associated tasks. Alvise Cornaro, for example, witnessed a petition to Federico Gonzaga along with the membership of the Immortali, invited a number of them on a hunt, was assisted in a dispute by the Immortale Pietro Pasqualigo qu. Marco who resided in Padua, and acquired land for a Triumphante who was the brother of ecclesiastic Gaspare Contarini.[35] These extensions of the theatrical relationship open the way for the question of whether or not Beolco, who as an illegitimate son could not inherit a proportional share of the patrimony or even enjoy the civic responsibilities entrusted to his illegitimate uncle and whose plays demonstrate a personal distaste for figures resembling his patron, was attempting through them to find other work such as captain of a *cernida* or manager of peasant women cultivating silk worms or assistant to patricians in other agricultural endeavors. If so, demonstrating to his audience that he shared goals and concerns with them and was able to solve related problems would be an effective way of cultivating them.

The inclusion of military officers in *compagnie* is another mixing that could appear incongruous to modern eyes but that instead is rooted in their origins. As has been more clearly recognized of late, the *compagnie* began as urban imitations and adaptations of military *compagnie*, an origin reflected, for example, in their doublet and hose.[36] It might not be too romantic a notion to see the connection between the military roots of the *compagnie* and their sponsorship of the performing arts as a distant echo of the Indo-European tradition of declaiming in and after battle, with Venetians then in contact with several still-living examples (*e.g.* Albanian populations). And the conjoining of the military with the

34   For peasant performances, see Sanuto, 16: 206–7; ASVe, *AGRM*, busta 28, fol. 10ᵛ; see also Mario Baratto, "L'esordio del Ruzante," in *Tre studi sul teatro* (Vicenza, 1968), pp. 11–68.
35   Mantua, Archivio di Stato, *Archivio Gonzaga*, busta 1454, fols 326–7; Sanuto, 26: 397; ASPd, *Notarile*, busta 1116, fol. 433ʳ⁻ᵛ; busta 2727, fols 516ʳ–19ʳˑ Paolo Sambin, "Altre testimonianze (1525–1540) di Angelo Beolco," in *Per le biografie*, pp. 59–77, 69; Paolo Sambin, "Briciole biografiche del Ruzante e del suoi compagno d'Arte Marco Aurelio Alvarotti (Menato)," in *Per le biografie*, pp. 87–114, 90; and for Triumphante status see Chapter 3. Cornaro would later make substantial proposals to the Republic concerning engineering and the lagoon: Alvise Cornaro and Cristoforo Sabbadino, *Scritture sopra la laguna*,repr. Venice, 1987).
36   See especially Matteo Casini, "The 'Company of the Hose': Youth and Courtly Culture in Europe, Italy, and Venice," *Studi Veneziani* 63 (2011): 1217–37.

performing arts was not limited to those years, as indicated by Antonio Molino's dedication of his book of madrigals to the Pesaro *capitanio* of Vicenza, his inclusion in it of military themes, and his self-identification as a *stradioto* (member of the swift light Albanian cavalry hired by Venice and other states as shock troops). Nor was it peculiar to Venice, as is demonstrated by a composition detailing Milanese events of 1521 by a Mantuan author, the heads of whose state (Isabella d'Este Gonzaga and her son Federico II) personified the union of artistic and military interests.[37]

Mainland governance duties brought some patricians into contact with courtly traditions in the creative and performing arts, whose intertwining relationships were complicated by divisions between nobility and peasantry. Specific subgenres were even created thereby, such as the peasant *mariazo*[38] appropriated by students at the University of Padua for inclusion among their ribald entertainments. Needing to establish a *modus vivendi* with nobility and peasants, Venetian mainland governors became familiar with the courtly love lyric and tragedy of the former and the earthy songs and comedies of the latter, as is demonstrated by the works that attracted the attention of Stefano Magno while he accompanied his father to his mainland offices. Mainland performances and festivities could also have dual effects. While offering some insights into local culture, they reinforced the status of those governing, keeping them from identification with locals by stressing their cultural and social distance.[39]

Some Observations on Primary Sources

Some observations on primary sources are warranted by the wealth of them so vast as to allow scholars to construct an intimate portrait of exactly how various political, economic, and cultural shifts occurred, which patrician families and individuals were most deeply involved, who led, and who followed. With regard to real estate owned in the mainland dominion, of great value are the 1514 Redecima (land-owning records collected after the destruction of the records office by the great fire of Rialto) and the 1518 Estimo of land holdings in Padua and the *padovano*. While the latter is limited to that dual geopolitical entity, its record in the Archivio di Stato of Padua is especially valuable not only because it unites in a single volume all Venetian landholders (unlike the Redecima records, which are divided into separate volumes by parish), thus permitting easy comparisons, but because the exemption from tribute for those who had held the land since before 1446 induced many owners to include detailed histories of when and how the land was acquired. Many also provide details of the income that it produced and

---

37 Molino; Alessandro D'Ancona, *Origini del teatro italiano*, 2nd ed., 2 vols (Turin and Rome, 1891), 2: 23–30.

38 Marisa Milani, "La tradizione del mariazo nella letteratura pavana," in *Convegno internazionale di studi sul Ruzante*, ed. Giovanni Calendoli and Giuseppe Vellucci (Venice, 1987), pp. 105–15.

39 Cf. Sanuto, 56: 264–5.

the peasants who cultivated it. The vast notarial *fondo* of the Archivio di Stato in
Padua provides an almost limitless record of Venetian presences and transactions
in that city because when one party was an inhabitant of Padua or its territory, as
was often the case, a copy was retained there.

Other government documents providing extensive information are the records
of the secret Senate deliberations (*Senato Secreta*). Kenneth M. Setton's thorough use of them in conjunction with other *fondi* and Marin Sanudo's *Diarii*
instructs. Especially if a sufficiently extensive account of a Senate debate is
available in Sanudo's entry, the Senate records of bills and their sponsors permit
the tracing of the political positions, mutations, and pivots of individual leading
patricians through their detailed account of which committees and even which
members of committees proposed bills and modifications of bills and their nota-
tions of individuals' absences and the reasons. The range of this last goes from
recording without comment (*i.e.* the list of committee members proposing the
bill is missing one or more names but there is no overt statement of absence), to
a simple statement that a given member is absent, to a statement of absence with
an exculpatory reason such as illness, to a statement of absence out of dissent.
Scholars can thus see, for example, that a member of a committee who supported
an early strong wording of a bill is 'silently' absent when the wording is weak-
ened rather than actively placing himself in opposition. Information given by
Sanudo may then explain why he preferred the earlier wording but was reluctant
to oppose the preferences of others. Senate records are particularly revealing
in the period prior to the 1525 performance, when one may compare sponsors
or co-sponsors of bills or letters favoring good relations with France and the
Turks, ones favoring peace with all Christian princes, ones favoring good relations with the pope, ones favoring good relations with the empire, and pragmatic
ones expressing fears of insufficient French support. While in many instances the
same names recur and the need for peace among Christians is a common theme,
one can note those patricians who joined the group favoring the empire only until
France showed strength, as well as the very telling absence of the *savi dil consejo*
as *en bloc* sponsors in early 1525 until their effort in mid February to bring peace
between Francis and Charles. When, ten days later, Charles's troops captured
Francis I, nine of them by name co-sponsored the letter of congratulations to
the emperor. Four of the nine had been the officials leading the way to the 1525
performance (of whom one was the father of a Triumphante and two others had
kinsmen in the Triumphanti).[40]

The most telling information is often given in diaries, chronicles, and family
papers. An impressive example of what can be obtained from them is Giuseppe
Gullino's work with the family archive of the Gradenigo Rio Marin, a family

---

40 ASVe, Senato, *Secreta*, reg. 50, see as examples respectively fols 14^v–15^r, 16^v, 17^r, 18^v–19^v, *e.g.*
72^v–3^r, 130^v–32^r, 122^r–30^v; while the *savi* as a united committee did no sponsoring in those months,
specific members did. Details concerning the patricians involved are presented in Chapter 3.

fondo of nearly four hundred *buste* recently made available in the Archivio di Stato of Venice and provided with a partial but extensive catalogue. Gullino's resulting study of Marco Foscari catalyzed the work with that *fondo* contained in the present volume. The Archivio di Stato of Venice also possesses numerous other family archives (Tiepolo, Grimani Santa Maria Formosa, Grimani-Barbarigo, Bernardo, etc.), each with its own riches. In Padua the manuscript collections of the Biblioteca Universitaria Centrale and the Biblioteca Antica of the Seminario Vescovile contain a number primary sources of great relevance to scholars of Venice as well as scholars of Padua. They include chronicles and diaries written by Venetians, some of them patricians, who were involved in or close to the events described and who explain motivations and give details found nowhere else. These last include the perception of Venetians by locals, such as Antonio Monterosso's detailed accounts of Venetian governors and bishops, which merit publication. The Biblioteca Capitolare holds detailed records of the bishopric and other ecclesiastical institutions including the cathedral canon chapter.

The difficulties for work with such sources, posed by the enormous amount of heterogeneous detail that most contain, their sedimentary organization, and difficulty of access have been somewhat reduced by digitized documents and by the capacity of computers to organize large amounts of information. By starting with matrices such as the membership rolls of *compagnie della calza* and cross-referencing those individuals and families with information provided by Sanudo and other primary sources, scholars can construct reasonable hypotheses of the goals of *compagnie* and the strategies that they employed to achieve them, as the present work attempts to do. The quantity of detail given here is directed toward the triple goal of building a portrait of the complex systems of relationships characterizing Venetian patrician life in the Renaissance, of elucidating the numerous and intimate connections between civic life and patronage of the arts, and of providing scholars at large with a map of the riches of the primary sources cited. Because of the unpublished and often previously-uncited nature of much of the primary source documents and texts utilized here, the scholarly endeavor at large is best served by more information being given from them than would otherwise be the case. Work on the many interconnections of Venetian patrician families being still in its early stages, the detail on the intermarriages, ascendants, and descendants of the figures mentioned serves to increase knowledge of their very dense and complex network.

A Note on Language

As part of the effort to present as historically accurate an account of the people and events described as possible, contemporary Venetian spelling is reproduced here. It is important to note several characteristics of Venetian language use at the time. Spelling was not standardized and was influenced both by indigenous traditions and by aulic ones including Latin and Tuscan. Therefore names and terms may occur in several variant spellings. Latin and Tuscan also exerted broader influence on Venetian linguistic use, including in the areas of lexicon, morphology, and syntax. In the view of the present author, it is important to an understanding of the Venetians of the Renaissance to hear them speak at least occasionally in their own voices.

1 Twelve Monuments, Five Altarpieces, Five Chapels, and a Fresco

Frari Patronage and Renaissance Venetian Political Economy

Introduction

While the many important works of art present in the basilica of Santa Maria Gloriosa dei Frari (fig. 1.1) have been studied individually and in small clusters, the web of links among the patrons of a sweeping arc of them awaits elucidation. The works in question were supported by and expressive of an equally encompassing network of commercial and political endeavors through which a group of Venetian patrician families attempted to achieve and maintain the strongest possible international position for themselves and the Republic during the multiple grave challenges of the late fifteenth and early sixteenth centuries. In particular, the works warn of the dangers posed to Venice's lucrative Mediterranean commerce and *stato da mar* by recent waves of Turkish aggression; they propose, as a response, the cultivation of relations with Venice's mainland dominion, other Italian states including the papacy, and even the Holy Roman Empire. From its starting point in the right transept's monument to Jacopo Marcello (fig. 1.2), the arc continues with the monument to Benedetto Pesaro over the sacristy entrance (fig. 1.3), the frescoes and Bellini *sacra conversazione* (fig. 1.4) of the sacristy's Pesaro Chapel, the Bernardo Chapel with its Vivarini altarpiece (fig. 1.5), the funeral monuments of Doges Francesco Foscari (fig. 1.6) and Nicolò Tron (fig. 1.7) and the magnificent Titian *Assunta* at the high altar that they flank, the chapel of the Scuola dei Milanesi with its Vivarini-Basaiti altarpiece (fig. 1.8), the Corner Chapel with its Vivarini altarpiece (fig. 1.9), funeral plaques of the wife and son of Luca Zen and of Alvise Foscarini, the funeral monument of Bishop Giacomo Pesaro (fig. 1.10), Titian's *Madonna di Ca' Pesaro* (fig. 1.11), the no-longer-extant tombs of Raphael and Francesco Besalù (Bexalù), the now-transferred chapel of the Scuola dei Fiorentini, and, flanking the main entrance, the tombs of Alvise Pasqualigo (fig. 1.12), and Piero Bernardo.

Numerous primary sources documenting the extent and thrust of the network and the identity of its participants, many of which are preserved in family archives as yet little explored by scholars, will be presented here. They demonstrate the extent to which the families' enormous wealth was generated by Venice's lucrative traditional trade routes involving the eastern Mediterranean

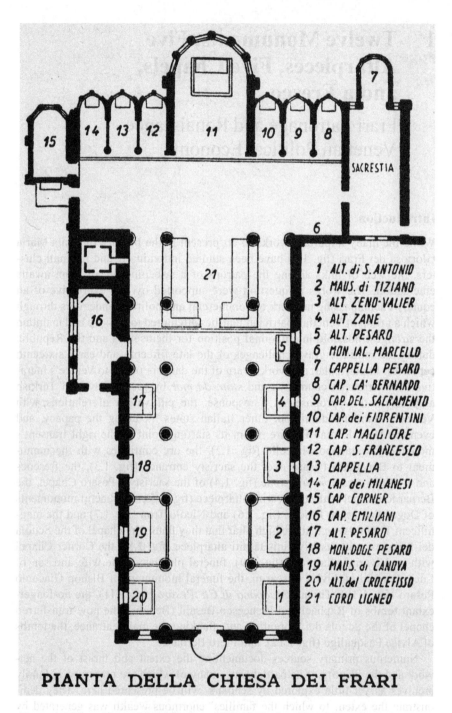

SACRESTIA

1 ALT. di S. ANTONIO
2 MAUS. di TIZIANO
3 ALT. ZENO-VALIER
4 ALT ZANE
5 ALT. PESARO
6 MON. IAC. MARCELLO
7 CAPPELLA PESARO
8 CAP. CA' BERNARDO
9 CAP. DEL SACRAMENTO
10 CAP. dei FIORENTINI
11 CAP. MAGGIORE
12 CAP. S. FRANCESCO
13 CAPPELLA
14 CAP dei MILANESI
15 CAP CORNER
16 CAP. EMILIANI
17 ALT. PESARO
18 MON. DOGE PESARO
19 MAUS. di CANOVA
20 ALT. del CROCEFISSO
21 CORO LIGNEO

PIANTA DELLA CHIESA DEI FRARI

Figure 1.1 Plan of Santa Maria Gloriosa dei Frari, Venice. (Photo: Naya-Böhm)

Figure 1.2 Funeral Monument of Jacopo Marcello, Santa Maria Gloriosa dei Frari, Venice. (Photo: Böhm)

Figure 1.3 Lorenzo Bregno and Baccio da Montelupo, Funeral Monument of Benedetto
Pesaro, Santa Maria Gloriosa dei Frari, Venice. (Photo: Naya-Böhm)

with its Asia connections, extending along the coasts of southern Italy, northern
Africa, and Sicily, and continuing on to Spain, Portugal, England, and Flanders.
This international trade faced increasing difficulties in the late fifteenth and early
sixteenth centuries with the aggressive expansion westward of the Ottoman

Figure 1.4 Giovanni Bellini, *Frari Triptych: Madonna and Child with Saints Peter, Nicholas, Benedict and Mark*, Santa Maria Gloriosa dei Frari, Venice. (Photo: Böhm)

Turks, Portuguese dominance in Asian trade, the Aragon-Habsburg-Valois wars for control of the Italian peninsula, and the increasing power of the papal state. As a result, the Frari families began re-directing their wealth-generating strategies to new opportunities. To substitute declining Asian commerce, they imported grain to feed Venice's burgeoning population; fostered European commerce both south and north of the Alps including through increased contacts with Milan; and consolidated their control of the mainland state and exploitation of its agricultural and industrial potential.

The new financial strategy called for an adjustment to their preferences in international relations. Numerous defeats of the Venetian armada having demonstrated

Figure 1.5 Bartolomeo Vivarini, *Bernardo Triptych*, Santa Maria Gloriosa dei Frari, Venice. (Photo: Cameraphoto Arte, Venice / Art Resource, NY)

Figure 1.6 Funeral Monument of Doge Francesco Foscari, Santa Maria Gloriosa dei Frari, Venice. (Photo: Böhm)

Figure 1.7 Antonio Rizzo, Funeral Monument of Doge Nicolò Tron, Santa Maria Gloriosa dei Frari, Venice. (Photo: Böhm)

Figure 1.8 Alvise Vivarini and Marco Basaiti, *St. Ambrose and Saints*, Santa Maria Gloriosa dei Frari, Venice. (Photo: Erich Lessing / Art Resource, NY)

that the Ottoman Empire wielded a vastly greater naval force, Venice (largely) relinquished war with the Turkish Porte in favor of peace. The new preference for increased trade with and through other Italian states motivated a preference for cooperation with them. Emphasis on the mainland state as a source of revenue and materials resulted in greater involvement in its governance and defense, as well as

Figure 1.9 Bartolomeo Vivarini, *Triptych of St. Mark with Sts. John the Baptist, Jerome, Nicholas and Paul,* Santa Maria Gloriosa dei Frari, Venice. (Photo: Alinari / Art Resource, NY)

Figure 1.10 Funeral Monument of Bishop Jacopo Pesaro. (Photo: Böhm)

Figure 1.11 Titian (Tiziano Vecellio), *Ca' Pesaro Madonna*, Santa Maria Gloriosa dei Frari, Venice. (Photo: Cameraphoto Arte, Venice / Art Resource, NY)

Figure 1.12 Giammaria Mosca (Padovano), Funeral Monument of Alvise Pasqualigo, Santa Maria Gloriosa dei Frari, Venice. (Photo: Böhm)

an increasing amount of property owned there. All of the new strategies would be favored by good, or at least peaceful, relations with the major European powers: the papacy, France, Spain, and the Holy Roman Empire. The conflicts between and among them, however, created difficulties in Venice's achieving peaceful relations with all of them simultaneously.

What was astutely described by Frederic Lane as a "double balancing act" now became a triple-quadruple one.[1] Some of the families favored developing a relatively cooperative relationship with the Aragonese and the Habsburgs, a stance that included opposition to the Turks. Others, instead, favored supporting the French, who united the advantages of hostility to the Aragonese and Habsburgs, threat-reducing distance from Venice, and friendly relations with the Turks with whom Venice still conducted important trade. Yet others adapted their preferences to changing circumstances. All were concerned with the ability to conduct trade with and through Milan. While the families participated in the warfare necessary to defend these endeavors, often in leadership roles, their principal interest was to maintain the peace that fostered favorable economic conditions.

A critical element was introduced into their calculations by the election of Charles of Spain as Holy Roman Emperor. The union of Habsburg and Spanish realms that it achieved gave him control of large parts of the litoral along the profitable western galley routes, which Charles augmented through alliance with the Portuguese and English kings, who controlled two of the routes' terminus points. The latter, with the lucrative London market, was so important to certain Venetian families, including some Frari ones, that they were known as 'da Londra' (of London).[2]

Beyond their connections in commerce and the figurative arts, the Frari families had a theatrical one that further illuminates the political as well as artistic ramifications of their patronage. They figured among the patricians inviting Angelo Beolco (Il Ruzante) to perform in Venice between 1520 and 1526, and had benefitted financially from connections to his wealthy Milanese family of financiers established two generations earlier.

The following material will first follow the arc of the Frari works, indicating for each the interests of the patron family, and then detail the family's connections with the Beolco family and with Angelo's artistic, social, and political program.

The Works and their Patrons

Heroic in style, the first monument under consideration memorializes Jacopo Marcello as commander of the Venetian armada fighting the Turk, in which role he died in 1484 (fig. 1.2). The year was also one in which his family, of the San Tomà branch whose family palazzo was known as 'dei Leoni' (of the lions), was deeply involved in trade with northern Europe.[3] The Marcello were heroic also in

1   Frederic C. Lane, *Venice. A Maritime Republic* (Baltimore, 1973), p. 246.

2   For alliance, see Peter Gwyn, *The King's Cardinal. The Rise and Fall of Thomas Wolsey* (London, 1990), pp. 147–57.

3   For an overview of this trade, see Peter Stabel, "Venice and the Low Countries: Commercial Contacts and Intellectual Inspirations," *Renaissance Venice and the North. Crosscurrents in the Time of Bellini, Dürer, and Titian*, ed. Bernard Aikema and Beverly Louise Brown, for the Ministero per i Beni e le Attività culturali, and Giovanna Nepi Scirè (Milan, 1999), pp. 30–43; ASVe, *AGRM*, busta 250, second *vacchetta*. For Donà di Antonio, Zuan Francesco, Marco Antonio, and Piero qu. Jacomo Marcello, see fols 3ᵛ, 5ʳ, 6ᵛ, 7ʳ, 10ᵛ and 40ʳ. Another account of some voyages of the late fifteenth century is found in Magno, *Annali*, fols 4ᵛ–5ʳ, 14ᵛ–15ʳ, 34ʳ, 70ᵛ–71ʳ, 60bisᵛ–61bisʳ [a series

the defense of the mainland, to the governance of which they contributed many *rettori* (large towns had two *rettori*, a *podestà* with general governance duties and a *capitanio* charged with military and financial matters; in smaller towns the two offices were combined), to the defense of which they contributed *provveditori* (civilian overseers of the army), and where they owned large properties, including the quarry of Monselice.[4] The family had particular connections to Padua, where Pietro served as bishop and others held canonries and other benefices, and a family member joined the wool guild.[5] A further family member, Bernardino the archpriest of Piove di Sacco, designated burial in the Frari in 1520 with the tomb to be paid for by Paduan properties.[6]

The impressive Pesaro and Corner chapels anchor the basilica's right and left corners respectively.[7] The Pesaro patrons were a group of brothers belonging to the

of folios with repeat numeration, here termed 'bis', occurs in the manuscript at this point], 84^{r-v}, 101^{r}–2^{r}, 111^{v}–12^{r}, 125^{v}–6^{r}, 151^{r}–2^{v}. For later commerce see ASVe, *Archivio Grimani Barbarigo*, busta 30, unnumbered folios.

4 Andrea Gloria, *Il territorio padovano*, 4 vols (Padua, 1862), 1: 278–2; 3: 155; Padua, Seminario Vescovile, Biblioteca Antica, ms. 555, Antonio Monterosso, *Reggimenti di Padova dal 1459 sino al 1533* (hereafter Monterosso, *Reggimenti*), vol. 4, fasc. XI, fols 1–2; Biblioteca Civica Padua, B.P. 3159, Zuan Antonio da Corte (Cortivo), *Historia di Padova, 1509–1530 (Diario degli avvenimenti padovani dal 13 giugno 1509 al 12 ottobre 1529)* (hereafter da Corte), fols 146^{r}, 150^{r}, 160^{r}; Marino Sanuto (Marin Sanudo), *I diarii*, ed. Rinaldo Fulin et al., 58 vols (Venice, 1879–1902), 2: 178; 9: 377; 10: 429; 11 *s.v.* Giacomo di Marino Marcello; 14: 639; 17: 248–9; 25: 400; 27, 28: *s.v.* Pietro Marcello qu. Marin; 30: 14; Pietro Bembo, *History of Venice*, edited and translated by Robert W. Ulery, Jr., 3 vols, The I Tatti Renaissance Library 28, 32, 37 (Cambridge, 2007–9), Book 4, pars 25, 40, 42, 48; Book 5, pars 21, 25; Book 7, par. 44; Book 9, pars 38, 44, 57; Book 10, par. 9; Book 12, par. 30; Vittorio Lazzarini, "Beni carraresi e proprietari veneziani," in *Studi in onore di Gino Luzzatto*, 2 vols (Milan, 1949), 1: 274–88, 277, 280, 283; ASVe, *Archivio Bernardo*, busta 1bis, unnumbered item dated 1527; ASPd, *Estimo 1518*, busta 352, fols 80^{v}, 106^{v}, 257^{v}–8^{v}, 262^{v}–3^{r}, 313^{v}; busta 354, fols 41^{r}–2^{r}, 113^{v}; busta 358, fol. 111^{r}; ASPd, *Notarile*, busta 1760, fols 106^{r}–7^{r}; ASPd, *Notai d'Este*, busta 648, fol. 246^{r-v}; ASVe, *AGB*, busta 4, unnumbered folio dated 1522.

5 PSVBA, ms. 385, Antonio Monterosso, *Vite dei vescovi di Padova* (hereafter Monterosso, *Vite*), fol. 117^{v}; Gloria, 1: 195; 2: 77, 125; da Corte, fols 119^{v}–20^{r}, 121^{r}, 154^{r}, 195^{r}, 203^{r}; Francesco Scipione Dondi Dall'Orologio, *Serie cronologico-istorica dei canonici di Padova* (Padova, 1805), pp. 121–4; Francesco Scipione Dondi Dall'Orologio, *Dissertazioni sopra l'istoria ecclesiastica padovana*, 9 vols (Padua, 1802–17), 9: 3, 14, 16, 21, 45; Pierantonio Gios, *L'attività pastorale del vescovo Pietro Barozzi a Padova (1487–1507)* (Padua, 1977), p. 117; Pierantonio Gios, "Nomine canonicali a Padova durante l'episcopato di Pietro Barozzi (1487–1507)," *Studia Patavina. Rivista di Scienze Religiose* 54 (2007): 189–211, 199; PACV, *Acta capitularia*, vol. 11, fol. 96^{r}, 69^{r}; vol. 12, fols 4^{v}–5^{r}, 76^{r}–7^{r}; da Corte, fols 121^{r}, 154^{r}, 195^{r}, 203^{r}; ASPd, *Notarile*, busta 2796, fols 539^{v}–40^{r}; busta 1309, fols 190^{v}–91^{r}, 309^{v}–10^{r}, 369^{r}; Lazara, *Memorie*, unnum. fol dated 1408; ASPd, *Estimo 1418*, busta 418, fol. 220^{v}; busta 67, fol. 18^{r}; *Estimo 1518*, busta 352, fols 110^{v}, 116^{r}, 145^{r}, 238^{v}, 338^{v}; *Notarile*, busta 1116, fols 287^{v}–8^{r}; busta 1309, fol. 488^{v}; ASVe, *Ufficiali alle Rason Vecchie*, reg. 48, fols 24^{v}–6^{r}; ASPd, *Notarile*, busta 1117, fol. 12^{r}; busta 1309, fol. 407^{v}; busta 2679, fol. 316^{v}; busta 2906, fols 133^{r}–4^{r}, 146^{r-v}; busta 2907, fols 206^{r}, 370^{r}; busta 4889, fol. 201^{r}; Sanuto, 33: 491.

6 ASVe, *Santa Maria Gloriosa dei Frari, Atti*, busta 106, filza 33, doc. 5d; busta 118, unnumbered fascicle dated 1520, unnumbered fascicle dated 1525; ASPd, *Notarile*, busta 2733, fols 154^{r-v}, 593^{v}–5^{v}, 628^{r}–30^{r}, 631^{r}–3^{r}, 679^{r}–82^{v}.

7 See Rona Goffen, *Piety and Patronage in Renaissance Venice. Bellini, Titian, and the Franciscans* (New Haven, 1986), pp. 24, 30–72; Gino Fogolari, *Chiese veneziane: i Frari e i SS. Giovanni e Paolo* (Milan, 1931), pp. vii–xc.

'da Londra' branch.[8] Entrance to their chapel passes through a portal surmounted by the monument to one of them, Benedetto (fig. 1.3). It glorifies the contribution that he made to family prowess in the naval warfare that protected the *stato da mar* and Mediterranean commerce, when, after a period active in the London trade, he was elected *capitanio generale* in the war against the Turk in 1500. The campaign also had financial benefits: his cousin supplied the force with biscuit.[9] The family participated in the trend toward investment in mainland agricultural, rental, and industrial properties and in the governance and defense necessary to protecting those interests.[10] In the late fifteenth century Fantin became *capitanio* of Padua, a member of the family married the daughter of a *stradioto* (a member of the Albanian light cavalry serving as shock troops for the Republic) in Padua, and another joined Padua's wool guild.[11] This involvement would seem to be reflected in the choice of Paduan artists, including Jacopo da Montagnana, for the chapel's frescoes (though its best-known work is Giovanni Bellini's s*acra conversazione*, *Frari Triptych: Madonna and Child with Saints Peter, Nicholas, Benedict and Mark*, fig. 1.4). Family trends continued with Benedetto's son Girolamo, the

8   ASVe, *AGRM*, busta 250, first *vacchetta*, fol. 17^r; second *vacchetta*, fols 18^v, 21^r, 28^v, 23^v, 24^r, 30^r, 31^r, 33^r, 43^v, 55^r; ASVe, *AGRM*, busta 333, Famiglia da Pesaro pp. 3, 5; Sanuto, 3: 137–8; Louis Gilliodts-van Severen, *Cartulaire de l'ancienne estaple à Bruges. Recueil de documents concernant le commerce intérieur et maritime, les relations internationales et l'histoire économique ce cette ville*, 4 vols (Bruges, 1904–6), 2: 813; Joseph Marechal, "Le Départ de Bruges Des Marchands Etrangers (XVe–XVIe Siècles)," *Handelingen Van Het. Genootschap Voor Geschiedenis "Société d'Emulation" / Annales de la Société d'Emulation, Bruges*, 88 (1951): 26–74, 55.

9   For overview of the anti-Turkish effort, see Setton, pp. 516–35; for Pesaro, see Marco Barbaro, *Arbori dei patritii veneti*, copied by Tommaso Corner and Antonio Maria Tasca (1743), ASVe, *Misc. Codici I, Storia Veneta* 17 (hereafter Barbaro), 6, 83; Bembo, *History*, Books 5 and 6; Goffen, pp. 62–4.

10 Mueller, p. 349 Table 8.8, p. 352 Table 8.10; Monterosso, *Reggimenti*, vol. 4, fasc. XI, fols 11–12, 25–6 for Francesco and Paolo Pesaro and ASVe, *AGRM*, busta 251 for Francesco's wife's wish to be buried in the Frari; Capi del Consiglio di Dieci, *Lettere di Condottieri di gente d'armi*, buste P.V. 307, 308; Padua, Biblioteca universitaria centrale, ms. 996, Marin Sanudo, *Itinerario* (hereafter Sanudo, *Itinerario*), fol. 4^v, 53^r and see now Marino Sanuto, *Itinerario per la Terraferma veneziana*, edizione critica e commento a cura di Gian Maria Varanini, Cliopoli 1 (Rome, 2014); *I libri commemoriali della Repubblica di Venezia. Regesti*, Monumenti storici publicati dalla R. Deputazione Veneta di Storia Patria, Serie Prima, Documenti (Venice, 1876–1914) (hereafter *Libri commemoriali*), Vol. XI, tome 6: 159, 169; Sanuto, 2: 221; 4: 414, 424; 10: 404; 12: 162; 17: 249; 24: 327–30, 329, 551, 586; 25: 471; 26: 500; 28: 324; 29: 139–40, 186, 333, 564; 30: 54, 116–17, 154, 282–3, 284; 31: 375; 32: 191; 34: 456; 35: 197, 400; 36, 37, 38, 39, 40, 41 *s.v.* Piero Pesaro qu. Nicolò; Bembo, *History*, Book X, par. 78; Book XI, par. 45; PSVBA, ms. 609, fols 144^r, 147^v; Girolamo Priuli, *I diarii*, ed. Arturo Segre et al., *Rerum Italicarum Scriptores*, 2nd edition (Città di Castello and Bologna, 1912–33), vol. 24, fasc. 326, pp. 204–5; Bembo, *History*, Book 12, par. 91; ASVe, *AGRM*, busta 234 unnumbered fascicle; busta 352; busta 366, unnumbered fascicle, La Redecima 1537; ASPd, *Notarile*, busta 1291, fol. 3^{r-v}; busta 2991, fols 451^r–2^v; ASPd, *Estimo 1518*, busta 352, fols 141^v, 160^v, 273^{r-v}, 303^{r-v}, 315^{r-v}; busta 356, fol. 119^v; ASPd, *Notarile*, busta 2793, fol. 182^{r-v}; ASPd, Notai d'Este, busta 648, fol. 34^v; PACV, *Mensa vescovile*, vol. 95, fol. 92^v.

11 ASPd, *Notarile*, busta 247, fol. 634^{r-v}; busta 2683, 606^{r-v}; Lazara, *Memorie*, unnumbered folio, dated 1483.

patron of his father's monument as well as his own. Having witnessed the crushing Portuguese competition in spices in London in 1503 as captain of the Flanders galleys, he redoubled commitment to the mainland through numerous defense and governance offices including the *capitaniato* of Padua in 1515. He would later lead the Venetian armada against Turkish forces including Barbarossa.[12]

A more singular commitment to commerce and the banking derived from it characterized the Bernardo family. Having contributed to the construction of the belltower of the Frari in the fourteenth century, they commissioned the Bartolomeo Vivarini altarpiece in their chapel when the family flourished in the peace of the latter fifteenth century.[13] Dedicated to Saints Jerome and Lawrence, it also bears images of family name saints Andrew, Nicholas, Paul and Peter above and Francis and Sebastian below (fig. 1.5). Andrea, the father of Hironimo (Girolamo, Jerome), with his brothers Nicolò, Polo and Piero, formed the core of the family business, succeeded by Polo's son Francesco and Hironimo's son Sebastiano, but with much of the banking turned over to their partners the Garzoni.[14] Banking activities included financing endeavors in Padua such as the purchase of a large house by a member of the Foscari family.[15] Although the interruptions to commerce at the turn of the century caused by Portuguese competition and Turkish aggression resulted in losses to their investments in Venetian, Milanese, and Florentine endeavors, the Bernardo managed to prosper by intensifying their commitment to western and northern trade. This was especially true of Mafio, of whom Sanudo observed that, starting with very little, he amassed a fortune through northern trade.[16] He acquired influence great enough that his son put an end to a trade-interrupting war between the English and the French kings, resulting in his knighting by both.[17] The Bernardo immediately invested their profits in large amounts of real estate on the mainland, especially Padua, to which they also provided *rettori* and a law professor.[18] They helped to take the city and its territory

---

12 ASVe, Barbaro, 6, 83; Goffen, p. 136; Sanuto, 5: 28; 17, 18, 20–24 *s.v.*; Rawdon Brown ed. and trans., *Four Years at the Court of Henry VIII. Selection of Despatches Written by the Venetian Ambassador, Sebastian Giustinian, and Addressed to the Signory of Venice, January 12th 1515, to July 26th 1519*, 2 vols (London, 1854; reprint New York, 1970), 2: 76 note 1; PBUC, ms. 874, *Cronaca di Venezia dalle origini fino all'a. 1552*, 3 vols, 3: 133ᵛ–5ᵛ. Further references will be to volume 3 unless otherwise specified.

13 Pietro Selvatico, *Sulla architettura e sulla scultura in Venezia dal medio evo sino ai nostri giorni* (Venice, 1847), p. 123, note 1 (I am grateful to Jan-Christoph Rössler for this reference); ASVe, *AGRM*, busta 250, second *vacchetta*, fols 6ᵛ, 9ʳ, 11ʳ, 12ʳ, 13ᵛ, 14ʳ, 16ᵛ, 18ᵛ, 22ʳ, 24ʳ, 25ʳ, 25ᵛ, 26r, 32ʳ, 41ʳ, 48ᵛ, 52ᵛ, 53ᵛ, 54ᵛ, 57ʳ, 66ʳ⁻ᵛ, 68ᵛ, 69ʳ, 84ᵛ, 85ᵛ; ASVe, *AGB*, busta 40, unnumbered folio dated 1478; Sanuto, 22: 34.

14 Sanuto, 3: 96–8, 758; 4: 304; Mueller, pp. 60–61, 195, 219–20.

15 ASPd, *Notarile*, busta 2683, fols 474ʳ–5ᵛ, 502ʳ⁻ᵛ.

16 Sanuto, 24: 307; 26: 17; 30: 125, 256–9; 31: 182–3 (quotation); 33: 288, 341; 34: 10; 36: 34, 78, 146, 148–9, 203, 344, 349, 399–400, 401; 39: 43–5, 338; 40: 639–40.

17 PBUC, ms. 874, 3: 182ʳ–3ʳ.

18 ASPd, *Estimo 1518*, busta 352, fol. 137ʳ, 140ʳ, 143ʳ, 252ᵛ–3ʳ; busta 358, fols 57ᵛ–8ᵛ, 114ʳ; ASVe, *Archivio Bernardo*, busta 8, unnumbered item dated 1433; PACV, *Acta capitularia*, vol. 15, fol. 229ʳ⁻ᵛ; Monterosso, *Reggimenti*, vol. 3, fasc. VII, 32ʳ⁻ᵛ.

back from the empire in 1509, continuing their efforts for the duration of the war by making frequent large loans to the state and holding positions of responsibility in the governing councils.[19]

Between the Bernardo chapel and the high altar lies the chapel containing what is the church's first documented art work sponsored by a patron, the 1336 tomb of Duccio degli Alberti, the Florentine ambassador to Venice. He wished to be buried there rather than in the Franciscan church of Santa Croce in Florence with which his family was associated. This site was later designated as the Cappella dei Fiorentini, transferred from its original location to the left of the main door (see below).[20]

Commitment to western trade, mainland investment and governance, and international diplomacy characterized the careers of the Foscari, as detailed in the research of Dieter Girgensohn, Giuseppe Gullino, and Dennis Romano.[21] It is the Foscari account books that provide the details of the western and northern galleys cited here.[22] They also contributed a bishop and *rettori* to Padua, where they acquired the palazzo at the Arena and a variety of other properties, among which were episcopal feuds.[23] The monumental tomb occupying the right wall of the sacristy memorializes the leading figure in the family, Doge Francesco, known for his commitment to the mainland state (fig. 1.6).

Dominating the high altar is the splendid *Assunta* or *Santa Maria Gloriosa* (*gloriosa* being the attribute expressing assumption), commissioned in 1519 probably by Bishop Jacopo Pesaro.[24]

Facing Foscari's monument is that of Doge Nicolò Tron (fig. 1.7), whose distant relative Franceschina, the mother of Benedetto Pesaro, was honored by the sacristy chapel.[25] Nicolò himself had raised his small clan to prominence through enormous successes in grain commerce with the Mediterranean. One of his sons died at Negroponte,[26] while another followed in Nicolò's footsteps as *rettore* of

---

19 Sanuto, 8: 522–5, 528–9, 534; 9: 66, 71, 241, 281; 10: 167, 185, 248, 260–62, 408–9, 469, 659, 827; 11–41 *s.v.* Nicolò Bernardo qu. Pietro; 12: 167; 13: 217; 16: 247; 17: 252, 283; 19: 75; 20: 458, 538, 539, 555, 556; 21: 158, 173–4, 176, 318.

20 Goffen, p. 7.

21 See Dieter Girgensohn, *Kirche, Politik und adelige Regierung in der Republik Venedig zu Beginn des 15. Jahrhunderts*, 2 vols (Göttingen, 1996), 2: 756–83 (I am grateful to Jan-Christoph Rössler for this reference); Giuseppe Gullino, *Marco Foscari (1477–1551): l'attività politica e diplomatica tra Venezia, Roma, e Firenze* (Milan, 2000); Dennis Romano, *The Likeness of Venice. A Life of Doge Francesco Foscari* (New Haven, 2007).

22 See also ASVe, *AGRM*, busta 333, Famiglia Foscari, p. 57; Sanuto, 1: 722, 906; 20: 264–8, 33: 257–8.

23 Gloria, 1: 195, 251, 273, 274, 280; Dondi, *Dissertazioni*, 9: 45, 64–6; ASVe, *AGRM*, busta 66, fasc. 15; busta 225, unnumbered fascicle dated 1520; busta 315; busta 355, unnumbered fascicle; busta 360, unnumbered *pergamena* of Feb. 13, 1518; ASPd, *Estimo 1518*, busta 352, fol. 95[r-v]; busta 126, fol. 123[r]; ASVe, Dieci Savi alle Decime, *Redecima 1514*, busta 46.

24 See esp. Goffen, pp. 94–106.

25 Goffen, pp. 186–7, note 14.

26 This paragraph informed by Robert Finlay, *Politics in Renaissance Venice* (New Brunswick, 1980), pp. 231–4; Sanuto, 5: 78–9.

Padua, where he maintained ties with other Venetians from his parish of San Beneto and where other family members owned property and belonged to the wool guild.[27] Nicolò's nephew Luca, a procurator of San Marco, advocated forceful mainland defense in the early sixteenth century, when at least one family member was a *rettore* in a militarily important town.[28]

The second chapel to the left of the high altar is graced by the tomb of Melchiorre Trevisan. A great military hero, Melchiorre served as *podestà* of Padua and *provveditore generale* of the army, bringing Cremona into the mainland state.[29] His successes there led to his being made *capitanio generale* of the Venetian armada in the 1499–1500 maritime war with the Turks. Even he was unable to prevent their capture of Modon, one of Venice's most ancient colonies; shortly after the loss he died.[30] Involved in northern commerce,[31] the Trevisan had shops in Padua and property in the *padovano*, which they augmented with purchases of confiscated rebel properties after the Cambrai wars.[32] They contributed numerous *rettori* to Padua and took other leading roles in the defense of the mainland.[33]

Flanking that chapel is the Cappella dei Milanesi, with its large altarpiece celebrating Milan's patron St. Ambrose (fig. 1.8). The Scuola dei Milanesi, which fostered commerce between Milan and Venice, had been founded in 1361[34]; its chapel was originally located farther left, where the Corner chapel now stands. Beginning with its renewal in 1420, the Scuola enjoyed a long period of growth, with patents given by Doge Francesco Foscari in 1454 and by Duke Francesco Sforza of Milan in 1461. The Scuola's members had connections with other Frari

27 Monterosso, *Reggimenti*, vol. 3, fasc. VII, 32[r–v], 34[r–v]; ASVe, *AGRM*, busta 86, fasc. 5, fol. 1; ASPd, *Notarile*, busta 1292, fols 475[r]–6[v]; busta 2908, fol. 348[r]; busta 4884, fol. 276[r]–7[v]; ASPd, *Estimo 1518*, busta 352, fols 178[v]–9[r], 304[v]; busta 356, fol. 98[r–v]; Lazara, *Memorie*, unnumbered folio dated 1486.

28 Sanuto, 9: 183; 12: 460; Sanudo, *Itinerario*, fols 14[v]–15[r].

29 Monterosso, *Reggimenti*, vol. 3, fasc. VIII, fols 12[r]–14[v]; PBUC, ms. 392, fol. 1[r]–3[r]; Bembo, *History*, Book 2, par. 39; Book 3, pars 34, 37–9; Book 4, par. 62; Book 5, pars 14, 24, 28–32; Sanuto, 2 *s.v.*

30 Anne Markham Schulz, *Giammaria Mosca called Padovano: A Renaissance Sculptor in Italy and Poland*, 2 vols (University Park, PA, 1998), 1: 52–3.

31 ASVe, *AGRM*, busta 250, first *vacchetta*, fols 2[v], 22[r]; second *vacchetta*, fols 7[r], 8[r], 9[r], 11[r], 15[r], 16[v], 17[r], 18[v], 22[v], 23[r], 26[v], 53[v], 55[r], 56[v], 57[v], 60[r], 61[v], 84[v], 85[v].

32 ASPd, *Estimo 1518*, busta 352, fols 81[v], 84[v], 94[r–v], 136[v], 154[v], 163[v], 164[v], 172[v]–3[r], 182[v], 212[v]–13[r], 243[r–v], 287[v]–8[r]; busta 358, fols 81[v]–2[r], 114[r]; busta 1290, fols 317[r]–18[v]; ASPd, *Notarile*, busta 1315, fol. 223[r]; busta 1335, fols 57[r], 174[r], 260[r]; busta 4010, fol. 197[r]; ASVe, Dieci Savi alle Decime, *Redecima 1514*, busta 56; ASVe, *AGRM*, busta 189, fasc. 1; busta 242, unnumbered fascicle; ASVe, *AGB*, busta 51; Gloria, 3: 245; Ling, pp. 305–16, 312; ASVe, *Ufficiali alle Rason Vecchie*, reg. 48, fols 1, 11[v]–12[r], 41[v]–2[r]; Sergio Zamperetti, *I piccoli principi. Signorie locali, feudi e comunità soggette nello Stato regionale veneto dall'espansione territoriale ai primi del '600* (Venice, 1991), pp. 278–9.

33 Monterosso, *Reggimenti*, vol. 3, fasc. VII, 29[r–v]; vol. 3, fasc. VIII, 16[r]–17[r]; vol. 4, fasc. IX, fol. 21[v]; Gloria, 1: 74, 273–80; Sanuto, 18: 9, 203, 270–71; 12: 276, 421; 22: 270; 23: 543; 28: 26, 592; 32: 323–4.

34 ASVe, Dieci, *Miste*, reg. 5, fol. 95[r]; reg. 10, fol. 28[r]; Goffen, p. 26 and p. 181 note 103.

patron families; they drew on Francesco Pesaro, for example, as their advocate before a Venetian magistracy.[35] As Sanudo records, the Milanese ambassador was routinely invited to the chapel on Ambrose's feast, which gave rise to delicate issues when the Lombard city was under divided imperial and French control, as in 1524, or retaken by imperial forces, as in 1525.[36] Its altarpiece was begun by Alvise Vivarini and completed by Marco Basaiti in the early years of the sixteenth century.[37]

A particular jewel of the Frari is the external chapel constructed by the Corner (Cornaro). Federigo Corner commissioned its first work, his cenotaph, of the sculptor Jacopo Padovano.[38] The altar is further graced by the 1474 tryptich by Bartolomeo Vivarini depicting family name saints Mark, John the Baptist, Jerome, Paul, and Nicholas (fig. 1.9).[39] The importance of the family to the commercial and political life of Venice is almost impossible to overstate.[40] It may be glimpsed, however, in their marriages into the Byzantine imperial family and the Paduan Scrovegni (patrons of Giotto's Arena Chapel, later owned by the Foscari); their holdings on Cyprus where Caterina was queen; their trade with the north in wine, sugar, and fruit and with Barbary and Spain in wool[41]; their relations with Florentine merchant-bankers[42]; their numerous *rettori* of Padua and their participation in mainland defense[43]; their land holdings in and near Padua as well as membership in the wool guild and a

35 ASVe, *Santa Maria Gloriosa dei Frari*, busta 100, esp. fols 52ʳ, 68, 69ʳ, 71ʳ⁻ᵛ.
36 Sanuto, 37: 291–2; 40: 429.
37 Rodolfo Pallucchini, *I Vivarini (Antonio, Bartolomeo, Alvise)*, Saggi e studi di storia dell'arte 4 (Venice, n.d. [1961]), p. 141 cat. no. 278; John Steer, *Alvise Vivarini: His Art and Influence* (Cambridge, 1982), pp. 84–7.
38 ASVe, *Santa Maria Gloriosa dei Frari, Atti*, busta 106, filza 33, doc. 5l: 1378 will of Ferigo Corner; 1382 publication of will; 1417 assignment of location; 1421 construction; 1473 will of Pietro Corner fu Ferigo; Juergen Schulz, "The Testamento of Federigo Corner 'Il Grande'," in *From Florence to the Mediterranean and Beyond. Essays in Honour of Anthony Molho*, ed. Diogo Ramada Curto, Eric R. Dursteler, Julius Kirschner, and Francesca Trivellato with the assistance of Niki Koniordos, 2 vols (Florence, 2009), 2: 683–94; Goffen, p. 24.
39 Pallucchini, cat. no. 169, pp. 121–2.
40 For individual family members see Giuseppe Gullino, "Corner, Andrea"; "Corner, Giacomo"; "Corner, Giorgio"; "Corner, Giorgio"; "Corner, Giovanni"; "Corner, Marco," "Corner, Marco," "Corner, Marco," in *DBI*, 29 (1983). For an overview, see Linda L. Carroll, "Introduction," in Angelo Beolco (Il Ruzante), *La prima oratione*, ed. and trans. Linda L. Carroll, MHRA Critical Texts vol. 16 (London, 2009), pp. 5–74.
41 ASVe, *AGRM*, busta 250, second *vacchetta*, fols 8ʳ, 13ᵛ, 14ʳ, 19ʳ, 25ᵛ, 55ʳ, 67ᵛ; Guillodts-van Severen, 1: 635–6; 2: 12; Stabel, p. 36; Nella Giannetto, *Bernardo Bembo umanista e politico veneziano*, Civiltà veneziana Saggi 34 (Florence, 1985), pp. 400–401.
42 Mueller, pp. 99, 196, 283, 502–3.
43 Gloria, 1: 274, 278, 279, 282; Monterosso, *Reggimenti*, vol. 3, fasc. 7, fols 20ʳ–21ʳ; vol. 4, fasc. 9, fols 15ʳ, 18ʳ⁻ᵛ; Sanudo, *Itinerario*, fols 8ᵛ, 35ᵛ, 64ᵛ; Bembo, *History*, Book 1, pars 37–41; Book 7, pars 23–6, 29, 32–3, 35, 37, 39–40, 42, 64, 83; Book 8, pars 3, 36, 45; Book 10 pars 27, 49, 70.

monopoly on paper there[44]; their holding of the Paduan bishopric and various other ecclesiastical offices.[45]

On the wall to the left of the chapel entrance is what remains of the tomb of Alvise Foscarini, a humanist who served the Republic with distinction in offices that included embassies to the duke of Milan and to the marquis of Mantua. He also held numerous mainland governorships; his work as *podestà* of Padua was praised by Mario Filelfo, who also wrote poetry in praise of the Corner.[46] While *podestà* in Verona, he became acquainted with Isotta Nogarola, one of the first women humanists. His family invested in the northern galleys and in property in Padua and the *padovano*, his son served as *capitanio* in Padua and *provveditore generale in Lombardia*; the family supplied *podestà* to Rovigo and to Asolo.[47] Other relatives were buried in the Frari cloister.[48]

Also on that wall, opposite the Cappella dei Milanesi, is the funeral plaque of the wife of procurator Luca Zen, Generosa Orsini, and their son Maffeo, topped by a double-headed imperial eagle. Generosa belonged to the family of Niccolò Orsini, Count of Pitigliano, a *condottiero* for the Republic defending Brescia against the Milanese on the western border in 1498. In that year Zen, related by marriage to the Corner, was elected *capitanio* of Padua and his only son died; the following year he was nominated *provveditore generale* in Brescia but lost to

44 Sartori, pp. 133–4; Neri Pozza, "L'editoria veneziana da Giovanni da Spira ad Aldo Manuzio. I centri editoriali di terraferma," *Dal primo Quattrocento al Concilio di Trento*, ed. Girolamo Arnaldi and Manlio Pastore Stocchi, Vol. 3 of *Storia della Cultura Veneta* (Vicenza, 1980), pp. 215–44, 242; ASVe, *Archivio Grimani Santa Maria Formosa*, busta 3, file labeled "Acquisti di folli C[arta], fol. 1ʳ; ASPd, *Notarile*, busta 247, fol. 170ᵛ; busta 250, fol. 41ᵛ–2ʳ; busta 254, fols 182ᵛ–3ᵛ, 259ᵛ–60ʳ; busta 1757, fol. 44ʳ; busta 1762, fol. 350ᵛ; busta 2679, fol. 311ᵛ; busta 2682, fol. 50ʳ, 115ʳ; busta 2787, fol. 561ʳ; ASVe, *Ufficiali alle Rason Vecchie*, reg. 48, fols 32ᵛ–3ʳ, 41ᵛ–2ʳ; Bruno Rigobello, "Modi di intervento del capitale veneziano nel polesine e l'insediamento agricolo dei Loredan, dei Corner, dei Badoer, e dei Grimani," in *Palladio e palladianesimo in Polesine* (Rovigo, 1984), pp. 21–35, 24; Lazara, *Memorie*, unnumbered folio, at date of 1489.

45 Gullino, *DBI* entries; Carroll, "Introduction"; PBUC, ms. 320, Gerolamo da Potenza, *Cronica Giustiniana o annali del mon[astero] di s. Giustina dala edificat[ion]e de padova et Monast[ero]. Insino a questi tempi nostri 1604*, fol. 105ʳ; ASPd, *Notarile*, busta 1315, fol. 178ᵛ; Pietro Bembo, *Lettere*, ed. Ernesto Travi, 4 vols (Bologna, 1987–93), 2: 113 lett. 368, 293 lett. 590, 298 lett. 598, 352–3 lett. 669, 369 lett. 691, 376 lett. 696.

46 See Barbaro, 3: 541; Margaret L. King, *Venetian Humanism in an Age of Patrician Dominance* (Princeton, 1986), *s.v.* and esp. pp. 374–7; Vatican City, Biblioteca Apostolica Vaticana, Cod. Urb. Lat. 804, fols 30ᵛ–36ʳ, 141ᵛ–8ʳ.

47 ASVe, *AGRM*, busta 250, first *vacchetta* fol. 17ʳ, second *vacchetta*, fol. 70ᵛ; ASVe, *AGB*, busta 30, unnumbered folio; PBUC, ms. 865 *Galee del traffico, 1507–1508*, fol. 34; ASPd, *Estimo 1518*, busta 352, fols 111ᵛ, 128ᵛ, 146ᵛ, 147ʳ, 156ʳ, 158ʳ⁻ᵛ, 184ʳ, 191ᵛ, 195ʳ, 195ᵛ–6ʳ, 222ʳ⁻ᵛ, 230ʳ, 237ʳ⁻ᵛ, 273ᵛ–4ʳ; busta 358, fol. 113ᵛ, 121ᵛ, 214ʳ; ASVe, *Ufficiali alle Rason Vecchie*, reg. 48, fol. 17ʳ; ASPd, *Notarile*, busta 2733, fols 519ʳ–20ʳ; busta 1335, fols 529ʳ–30ʳ; ASPd, *Notai d'Este*, busta 64, fol. 48ʳ; Monterosso, *Reggimenti*, vol. 4, fasc. IX, 5ʳ⁻ᵛ; Bembo, *History*, Book 3, par. 64; Book 4 pars 34, 36, 68; Book 6, par. 59; Book 7, par. 7; PSVBA, ms. 568 *Memorie spettanti alla città di Asolo*, fol. 17ᵛ.

48 ASVe, *AGRM*, busta 369, unnumbered folio dated 1520; ASVe, *Santa Maria Gloriosa dei Frari, Atti*, busta 106, filza 33, doc. 5cc.

Melchiorre Trevisan and Marc'Antonio Morosini.[49] *Capitanio* and *vice-podestà* of Padua in the last years of the fifteenth century, Luca Zen was among the first proposers of its retaking in July 1509.[50] He also shared the strongly anti-Turkish stance of his kinsman Tomà, captain of the *galee grosse* under *capitanio generale di mar* Melchiorre Trevisan in the 1499–1500 campaign.[51] With his fellow procurators Tommaso Mocenigo and Domenico Trevisan, he appears in a devotional work by Giovanni Bellini.[52] Family members were early and important acquirers of property in Padua and the *padovano*. Two joined the Paduan wool guild in the second half of the fifteenth century.[53] The family acquired ecclesiastical offices and episcopal feuds especially through Antonio, vicar to Bishop Pietro Donà, and Jacopo, bishop from 1460 to 1481.[54] Jacopo was recorded as being generous toward the poor, making an inventory of diocesan records, recovering much of the diocese's agricultural and other real estate, dowering numerous female relatives, distributing church offices to the worthy, and consecrating the tomb of St. Anthony. The family's most illustrious ecclesiastic was Cardinal Bishop Giovanni Battista Zen.[55] Although the family's trade orientation favored the eastern Mediterranean and they had not been involved in the Foscari galley rounds, they participated in the lucrative Barbary galleys of the 1520s.[56]

Pesaro family monuments glorify the next segment of the wall, signally the tomb of Bishop Jacopo Pesaro (fig. 1.10) and the family funerary chapel, whose altarpiece, the *Madonna di Ca' Pesaro*, Bishop Jacopo commissioned of Titian in 1519 (fig. 1.11).[57] Alluded to in the painting are both a familial devotion to Sts. Francis and Anthony of Padua and Jacopo's participation in the family's glorious military tradition in the war against the Turks. In that campaign, in an unusual family pairing with his kinsman Beneto as *generalissimo da mar* of the Venetian armada, Jacopo commanded the papal

49   Monterosso, *Reggimenti*, vol. 3, fasc. VIII, fol. 30ʳ; Sanuto, 1: 742; 2: 42, 418, 962–3; 32: 433; 37: 73; for Morosini, see below.
50   Gloria, 1: 279; Monterosso, *Reggimenti*, vol. 3, fasc. VIII, fols 30ʳ–31ʳ; Sanuto, 8: 507–8; 9: 544.
51   Sanuto, 3, *s.v.*
52   Rona Goffen, *Giovanni Bellini* (New Haven, 1989), p. 99; Lorenzo Finocchi Ghersi, *Il Rinascimento veneziano di Giovanni Bellini* (Venice, 2003–4), figs 65, 66.
53   ASPd, *Estimo 1518*, reg. 352, fols 82ʳ, 93ʳ, 115ʳ–16ʳ, 167ʳ, 198ᵛ–9ᵛ, 208ʳ, 259ᵛ, 261ʳ, 301ʳ, 306ᵛ, 322ᵛ, 352ʳ; ASPd, *Notarile*, busta 1389, fols 92ʳ–ᵛ, 136ʳ–8ᵛ, 288ʳ–9ᵛ; busta 1531, fol. 179ʳ–ᵛ; busta 1532, fols 224ʳ–5ʳ; busta 2679, fol. 9ᵛ; ASPd, *Notai d'Este*, busta 648, fols 110ʳ–11ʳ; PACV, *Mensa vescovile*, vol. 95, fol. 91ᵛ. Guild: Lazara, *Memorie*, unnumbered folio at 1453 and 1462.
54   Monterosso, *Reggimenti*, vol. 3, fasc. V, fol. 33ʳ–ᵛ; Alfredo Viggiano, *Governanti e governati. Legittimità del potere ed esercizio dell'autorità sovrana nello Stato veneto della prima età moderna* (Treviso, 1993), p. 196; for Bishop Jacopo see ASPd, *Notarile*, busta 1755, fol. 179ʳ–ᵛ; busta 2682, fol. 50ʳ; ASVe, *AGRM*, busta 1bis, fasc. 9; busta 21bis, fasc. 8; busta 119 fasc. 10; busta 126, fascs. 4 and 7; busta 148, fasc. 9; busta 247; busta 355; ASVe, *AGB*, busta 13.
55   See King, *s.v.* and esp. pp. 447–9; Dondi, *Dissertazioni*, 9: 52–64; Monterosso, *Vite*, fols 119ʳ, 123ᵛ–4ʳ. On Giovanni Battista, see James S. Grubb, *Provincial Families of the Renaissance. Private and Public Life in the Veneto* (Baltimore, 1996), pp. 132, 211; Gaetano Cozzi and Michael Knapton, *Storia della Repubblica di Venezia dalla Guerra di Chioggia alla riconquista della terraferma* (Turin, 1986), p. 250.
56   Sanuto, 27: 528; 29: 333; 30: 100.
57   See the extensive treatment in Goffen, *Piety*, pp. 107–37.

armada, whose galleys were financed by Cardinal Giovanni Battista Zen.[58] Their forces, conjoined with those of Spain, were victorious in the 1502 battle of Santa Maura.[59] Rona Goffen has identified the painting's other figures as four of Jacopo's brothers (Antonio, Fantin, Francesco, and Zuan) and one of their sons (Francesco di Fantin). This branch of the family, too, became deeply involved in the mainland and especially Padua, where Fantin was briefly *capitanio*. They purchased extensive properties in the city and its *territorio* including some from the Foscarini in Bovolenta and its Contrada Polverara.[60] Their distinguishing epithet, in its full form 'Dal Carro di Lizzafusina' but often shortened to 'Dal Carro', referred to their 1514 purchase of the lucrative 'carro' at Lizzafusina, the mechanism at the edge of the lagoon that transferred goods from land means to water ones and vice versa. The parcel of land and businesses, which they purchased in the midst of the Cambrai wars for 11,800 ducats from a Venetian government desperate for income, included a tavern and industrial complex that, as the Pesaro ensured through the purchase agreement, had a monopoly not only on the *traghetto* (ferry) but on the sale of wine, bread, and meat and on the washing of wool in Mestre. It also extended a similar monopoly to their butcher shops there, purchased in 1483. The rental of these services brought in 1,200 ducats per year. The Pesaro brothers purchased 22 of the 24 *carati*; the others were purchased by Silvano Capello and Antonio and Luca Vendramin. The magistracy charged with auctioning the property, the *governadori di l'entrade* (governors of revenue), was composed of Marco Orio, Andrea Magno (for whom see Chapter 3), and Nicolò Venier.[61] Antonio Pesaro was expert enough in land dealings that the *condottiero* Bernardino da Martinengo contracted with him in 1494 to manage his properties in the *padovano*; this connection was likely made when Fantin was *podestà* in Brescia, the Martinengo family seat, in 1483.[62] Such expertise contributed to his election as *capitanio* of Vicenza and *podestà-capitanio* of Treviso.[63] Antonio married his daughter Bianca to the son of the fabulously wealthy Zaccaria Contarini, who had inherited the Carrara land in Padua and the *padovano*. Antonio's only son was married to the daughter of Carlo Valier, who, being his only legitimate child, inherited his entire fortune.[64] The Valier family's importance to literary, ecclesiastical, and political developments will be discussed in Chapter 2.

Continuing along the wall toward the *rio*, one encounters the spot, at the Altar of the Crucifix near the joining of the nave wall with the wall of the facade,

58 Jacopo and Beneto were first cousins once removed; see Goffen, *Piety*, p. 155.
59 Setton, pp. 516–34.
60 ASPd, *Estimo 1518*, busta 356, fol. 58ʳ; busta 352, fol. 117ʳ; ASVe, *AGRM*, busta 352, unnumbered fascicle; Sanuto, 1: 629.
61 ASVe, *AGRM*, busta 139, fasc. 21; busta 234, unnumbered fascicle; PUBC, ms. 380, fols 29–30; PUBC, ms. 198 *Sentenza arbitrale pubblicata in Trento (a. 1535) per le controversie tra l'Imperatore e la Rep. di Venezia*, fols 26ᵛ–7ʳ; Sanuto, 19: 243, 276–7; 46: 500.
62 ASVe, *AGRM*, busta 356, unnumbered *pergamene*; Sanudo, *Itinerario*, fol. 53ʳ.
63 Sanuto, 26: 377; 40: 838.
64 Sanuto, 37: 440–1, 449, 462, 549; 46: 500; the daughter's name was kindly provided by Jan-Christoph Rössler. For the Contarini insistence on maintaining the Carrara tax exemptions and other privileges, see PBUC, ms. 311, *Privilegi della Famiglia Contarini rispetto ai beni posseduti pel matrimonio di Francesco Contarini con Maria figlia di Jacopo da Carrara*.

where the tombs of Raphael and Francesco Besalù were located. Presumably also entombed there was their affine Zuan Beltrame, buried on the same day in the Frari as the famed courtesan Agnola Caga-in-Calle, for whom a character in Beolco's *Betia* had worked.[65] Financiers of Sephardic Jewish origin who had served the interests of the Spanish crown in Venice, they participated in the papal loan to the Republic during the wars of the League of Cambrai secured with the jewels of San Marco that saved the Republic but that also subjected it to the papacy on some important issues. Expressions of the Republic's gratitude to them also included the granting of citizen status to Raphael's son Gaspare despite a law forbidding it to those of his background.[66]

The Besalù tomb was originally flanked by the chapel of the Scuola dei Fiorentini, the merchants of the Tuscan city that had first hosted them. In 1435, shortly after Cosimo de' Medici had returned to Florence from his exile in Venice, the Council of Ten approved the community's request to found a *scuola* at the Dominican church of San Zanipolo (Santi Giovanni e Paolo). The community's leaders included the Bardi, the Altoviti, and especially the Martelli, who were agents of the Medici bank in Venice and other cities. At the time, Francesco Foscari was doge and the pope, Eugenio IV, was Venetian. The year 1435 also saw a treaty joining Venice, Florence, the papacy, and Milan. Cosimo's sojourn in Venice may have impressed upon him the size and international scope of Venetian banking and provided him with the opportunity to forge contacts not only with bankers and clients but with leaders in the government, especially Doge Francesco Foscari, who assisted him in obtaining his return to Florence. Cosimo, who continued to run his business while in Venice, made loans both to the Venetian government and to individual patricians and was later asked to contribute to the work on the *scuola*'s chapel.[67] In 1443, the *scuola* was transferred to the Frari, which had already been chosen as the site of its chapel in 1436.[68] In these years patricians including Bernardo Zane, Andrea Zen, the Capello, the Lippomano and the Garzoni (Bernardo) were doing business with the Medici bank.[69] Like other Florentine banks, it had a branch in Milan, opened in 1452 at

65 Sanuto, 17: 541; 19: 25; Angelo Beolco (Il Ruzante), *Betia* V, vv. 791, 1120; VBMC, ms. Grimani-Morosini 4, Angelo Beolco (Il Ruzante), *Betia*, fols 97^r, 104^v [Angelo Beolco (Il Ruzante), *Betia*, in *Teatro*, ed. and trans. Ludovico Zorzi (Turin, 1967), hereafter *RT*, pp. 465, 485)].

66 Felix Gilbert, *The Pope, His Banker, and Venice* (Cambridge, 1980); Linda L. Carroll, "Venetian Attitudes toward the Young Charles: Carnival, Commerce, and *Compagnie della Calza*," in *Young Charles V, 1500–1529*, ed. Alain Saint-Saëns (New Orleans, 2000), p. 49 and note 97.

67 Amalgamating information in Goffen, *Piety*, p. 26 and the extensive note 104 on p. 181; Alessandro Parronchi, *Donatello e il potere* (Florence; Bologna, 1980), pp. 93–9; Raymond de Roover, *The Rise and Decline of the Medici Bank 1397–1494* (New York, 1966), p. 8; Reinhold C. Mueller, *The Venetian Money Market. Banks, Panics, and the Public Debt, 1200–1500*, Vol. 2 of *Money and Banking in Medieval and Renaissance Venice* (Baltimore, 1997), pp. 257–8, 279–80, 284–5; Vittore Branca, *Poliziano e l'umanesimo della parola* (Turin, 1983), p. 7; Romano, pp. 119–21, 147.

68 ASVe, *Santa Maria Gloriosa dei Frari, Atti*, busta 103, fasc. 16; Mueller, pp. 257–8, 277–86, 354, 441; de Roover, pp. 42–3, 47, 51, 53, 55, 66, 69, 70–71, 73, 82, 101, 111–12, 128–9, 141, 196–8, 243–51, 337; Sanuto, 1: 613, 712, 715, 724, 726, 935.

69 Cf. Mueller, pp. 75, 196–7, 327, 354, 441.

the invitation of Duke Francesco Sforza. In this period, Venetian merchants purchased Florentine cloth for export to the eastern Mediterranean, while Florentines bought Venetian silks for export to Milan and elsewhere.[70] By the latter half of the fifteenth century, the most important Venetian clients of the Medici bank (and often other Florentine banks) were the Corner and the Contarini[71]; late in the century, the list extended to the Bernardo and Federico Priuli.[72] Other Florentines also conducted banking in Venice, continuing to do so after the Medici bank closed at the end of the fifteenth century; their clients included Mafio Bernardo and Francesco Grimani.[73]

Several funeral monuments occupy the interior of the facade wall; of particular interest to this study are the cenotaph of Alvise Pasqualigo (fig. 1.12) and the tomb of Piero Bernardo, whose families were neighbors in death as in life.[74] Pasqualigo wished a monument in the Frari "per memoria" (in order to be remembered) despite being buried on Murano on the family tomb. He commissioned the Paduan Giammaria Mosca, who repeated in the Pasqualigo monument decorative details of the Trevisan and Foscarini tombs and topped it with the double-headed eagle demonstrating Alvise's status as imperial count.[75] Padua, which their kinsman Nicolò defended in the Cambrai wars and where the Immortale Pietro Pasqualigo qu. Marco lived, was the location of family-owned shops, millwheels, and homes; their commercial dealings there included Jewish merchants. They had agricultural holdings and a home in Piove di Sacco and a holding in Codevigo; they purchased more land in the area through the Monte Nuovo sales held after the wars of the League of Cambrai.[76]

The properties were purchased with the proceeds of the family's northern commerce, widely known through the letter that Alvise's brother Lorenzo wrote from London in the late fifteenth century regarding Giovanni Cabotto (John Cabot).[77] Alvise himself had been the *patron* (financier) of a Flanders galley.[78] Lorenzo continued to send frequent reports from England, where he remained until 1519.[79] Toward the end of the Cambrai wars, Alvise was elected a *capo di dieci* (Head of the Council of Ten) and, after holding a number of other offices

70 De Roover, pp. 261–74; 184, 190.
71 ASVe, *AGB*, busta 27, unnumbered folio.
72 Sanuto, 2: 391–2, ASVe, *AGB*, busta 40, unnumbered folio dated 1478; de Roover, pp. 267, 337; cf. Mueller, pp. 99, 174–5, 220, 502–3.
73 Sanuto, 26: 17; probably Francesco di Pietro Grimani.
74 ASVe, *Santa Maria Gloriosa dei Frari, Atti*, busta 106, filza 33, docs 4, 5a; *Archivio Bernardo*, busta 8, unnumbered item; Sanuto, 26: 131.
75 Sanuto, 54: 152 (quotation); Schulz, *Mosca*, 1: 52–3; see also Barbaro, 6: 17.
76 ASPd, *Estimo 1518*, busta 352, fol. 80ᵛ; busta 353, fol. 37ʳ; busta 354, fol. 107ʳ; busta 358, fol. 114ʳ; *Notarile*, busta 1335, fol. 330ʳ; busta 2787, fol. 44ʳ; VBMC, mss. Provenienze Diverse c, 833, XIII; ms. 1324 (1; Pasqualigo's will); ASVe, *Ufficiali alle Rason Vecchie*, reg. 48, fols 34ᵛ–5ʳ, 42ᵛ–3ʳ, 43ᵛ–5ᵛ; Sanuto, 8: 522; 12: 438; 14: 557; 17: 279.
77 Sanuto, 1: 806.
78 Sanuto, vols 2, 3 *s.v.*
79 Sanuto, esp. 14–19 *s.v.*; 28: 45.

and much electioneering, a procurator.[80] Lorenzo had more difficulty obtaining a procuratorship subsequent to his return. His offer was accepted only in 1526 when the Republic, aligned with the French against the empire in the League of Cognac, was facing another expensive war. Given the retaliation against Venetian merchants and goods that Charles V and Henry VIII had unleashed in the early 1520s to force Venice into an alliance, probable factors favoring a patrician so completely identified with England were the acceptance of the League of Cognac by Henry, whose marital complications had by then set him against Charles, and the proposal to use land routes (including French) for northern trade made then by Francesco Corner.[81] As Sanudo noted, Lorenzo's success meant that two brothers occupying the same house were elected procurators.[82] The diarist no longer expressed shock at the overturning of the old norms preventing such a concentration of power and authority in close relatives.

Another brother, Pietro, was a distinguished humanist who had studied philosophy in Paris, though completing his degree in Rome after escaping the French capital in servant's dress when Charles VIII banished all Venetians after the Republic's victory over him at Fornovo (1495).[83] As noted in the Introduction, Giovanni Antonio Marso dedicated his comedy *Stephanium* to a Pietro Pasqualigo,[84] most likely this one. Like many Venetian patrician university laureates, he served as ambassador, in his case to Portugal, Spain, and England, where he witnessed the overwhelming Portuguese competition in the spice trade. Later he was sent to Hungary, where his secret mission was to obtain Venice's inclusion in the truce with the Turkish Porte; he was also sent to France during the delicate negotiations dividing control of Lombardy toward the end of the Cambrai war.[85] In the postwar period another Pietro Pasqualigo added to his properties near Padua, where his sister was the abbess of the monastery of San Giorgio.[86]

Lives of relevant Bernardo family members were outlined above. The most active in the effort to return Padua from imperial to Venetian rule were the brothers Sebastiano and Piero, whose investments in the city and *territorio* were extensive enough to require a *gastaldo* (resident manager).[87] That fact and the

---

80 Sanuto, 22 *s.v.*; 33 *s.v.*, esp. 300.
81 Retaliation: Sanuto, 32: 405–7, 444–5, 33: 127, 140, 145, 278, 295, 341, 376, 390, 407, 416, 424, 475, 478, 542, 629; for Henry, Gwyn, p. 455; land routes Sanuto, 33: 407, 424; 37: 505.
82 Sanuto, 41 *s.v.*, esp. 612.
83 Bembo, *History*, Book 2, par. 60; Bruno Nardi, "Letteratura e cultura veneziana del Quattrocento," *Saggi sulla cultura veneta del Quattro e Cinquecento*, ed. Paolo Mazzantini (Padua, 1971), pp. 3–43, 41–2.
84 Laura Riccò, *"Su le carte e fra le scene." Teatro in forma di libro nel Cinquecento italiano* (Rome, 2008), pp. 26–7.
85 Bembo, *History*, Book 6, pars 1, 15; Book 9, par. 22; Book 10, par. 62; Brown, *Four Years*, 2: 82, note 6; Sanuto, 5: 129–31, 133–4, 840–43; 6: 26–8, 55–7, 65–6, 86–8; ASVe, Senato, *Secreta*, reg. 43, fols 178ᵛ–9ᵛ; reg. 46, fol. 92ᵛ–3ᵛ, 89ᵛ–90ᵛ; Sanuto, 9: 241. He died while on the mission to France.
86 ASPd, *Estimo 1518*, busta 352, fol. 80ᵛ; Bembo, *Lettere*, 4: 303–4, lett. 2185.
87 Sanuto, 8: 522–5; 32: 31; ASVe, *Capi del Consiglio dei X, Lettere*, filza 13, fol. 293; ASPd, *Estimo 1518*, busta 352, fols 137ʳ, 253ᵛ; PACV, *Acta capitularia*, vol. 15, fol. 229ʳ⁻ᵛ.

effort of the family member who held the most important government offices, Nicolò qu. Pietro qu. Pietro qu. Francesco (their second cousin), to accommodate not only to the empire but to the French, whose advantages included land routes for northern commerce, may explain the single-headed eagle atop Piero's tomb, more ambiguous in its political reference than the double-headed one. Sebastiano and Piero later sought a favorable legal decision from the empire, an important motivation for maintaining good relations.[88] Their actions thus reveal a specific "double balancing act": regaining Padua from direct imperial control while simultaneously cultivating good relations with the empire to retain a feudatory status or avoid further imperial aggression.

Connections of Frari Patron Families with the Beolco

An additional set of connections is shared by the Frari families, ones that interweave financial issues, and probably political ones, with theatrical patronage. When the western galleys that produced their fortunes encountered difficulties in the 1480s, they received financial assistance from Zuan de Beolco, a Milanese noble and financier to the Sforza and other important Milanese families, who invested personally in the voyages and seems also to have been the catalyst for investments by numerous other Lombards.[89] Zuan's agents in Venice were his younger brother Lazaro and Lazaro's younger son Zuan Jacopo, both of whom resided in Venice while serving in this function; in Lazaro's case residence in Venice became permanent. Lazaro's other son, Zuan Francesco, was beginning a career at the Università di Padova that culminated in two terms as prior and that put him in contact with numerous important Venetian patricians.[90]

88 Barbaro, 2: 13–14; ASVe, *Archivio Bernardo*, busta 8, unnumbered item; for Nicolò: Sanuto, 8–18, 21–38, 41–2 (41: 216 relations with French), 44–58, *s.v.*; empire: Sanuto, 58: 137.

89 See also Introduction; ASVe, *AGRM*, busta 250, second *vacchetta, passim*, esp. fols 7^r, 8^r, 9^v, 18^v; the information here adds to Gullino, *Marco Foscari*, p. 19. For the Beolco in Milan, see Patrizia Mainoni, "L'attività mercantile e le casate milanesi nel secondo Quattrocento," in *Milano nell'età di Ludovico il Moro*, Atti del convegno internazionale, Milano 28 febbraio-4 marzo 1983, ed. Giulia Bologna, 2 vols (Milan, 1983), 2: 575–84, 582–3; Letizia Arcangeli, "Esperimenti di governo: politica fiscale e consenso a Milano nell'età di Luigi XII," in *Milano e Luigi XII: ricerche sul primo dominio francese in Lombardia, 1499–1512*, ed. Letizia Arcangeli (Milan, 2002), pp. 253–339, 300, 302–3, 312–14, 316, 320, 325, 327–8; Beatrice Del Bo, *Banca e politica a Milano a metà Quattrocento* (Rome, 2010), pp. 105–6, 212.

90 See Emilio Lovarini, "Notizie sulla vita e sui parenti del Ruzzante," in *Studi sul Ruzzante e sulla letteratura pavana*, ed. Gianfranco Folena (Padua: Antenore, 1965), pp. 3–60; ASPd, *AO, ASC*, buste 231–5. Additional archival discoveries were published by Paolo Sambin and Emilio Menegazzo in articles gathered into Paolo Sambin, *Per le biografie di Angelo Beolco, il Ruzante, e di Alvise Cornaro*, restauri di archivio rivisti e aggiornati da Francesco Piovan (Padua, 2002), esp. "Lazzaro e Giovanni Francesco Beolco," pp. 8–34; Emilio Menegazzo, *Colonna, Folengo, Ruzante e Cornaro. Ricerche, testi e documenti*, ed. Andrea Canova (Padua, 2001), esp. "Ricerche intorno alla vita e all'ambiente del Ruzante e di Alvise Cornaro," pp. 223–66, 225–40. For University career, see PBC, B.P. 938, Francesco Dorighello, *Memorie di professori e letterati di Padova, particolarmente di medici*, fol. 41; PBC, B.P. 143, Francesco Dorighello, *Notizie storiche delli collegii d'artisti e medici in Padova*, fols 393^v–4^r, 395^r, 426^r, 429^v.

In about 1495, he became the father of an illegitimate son, Angelo, better known later as Ruzante.[91]

The Frari families directly participating in the voyage assisted by the Beolco were the Foscari, Marcello, Pesaro, Bernardo, Trevisan, and Corner. The financial interactions among the Venetian families went beyond the voyages; when Nicolò Foscari qu. Jacopo had a complicated transaction in Padua in 1479, for example, the funds were entrusted to the Bernardo bank in Venice.[92] The families had proximities to the Beolcos in Padua and its territory, and were prominent among those inviting the playwright to entertain in Venice.[93] Because the Beolcos' connections to the Corner and the Foscari were the strongest, they will be presented first, followed by a tracing of the playwright's connections with other patrons along the arc described in the church possibly alluded to in his comedy *Betia* in the phrase "[Ver]zene maria glurioxa" (Glorious Virgin Mary).[94]

The first time that Ruzante was recorded by name as performing in Venice occurred in 1520, in a lavish festivity sponsored by the Immortali and hosted by Immortale Zuan qu. Agostin Foscari, whose father and uncle had organized the 1480s voyage. Zuan also owned the Arena in Padua, whose chapel was decorated with Giotto's splendid frescoes. It had been purchased by Bishop Pietro Foscari, who, among his other accomplishments, had named as prior of Padua's Collegio Pratense Alvise Anzelieri. Anzelieri founded the real estate fortune further developed by his nephew the land magnate and Ruzante patron Alvise Cornaro.[95] Zuan's cousin Francesco Foscari qu. Alvise as *podestà* of Padua had turned the city over to local imperialist nobles after the defeat of Agnadello. According to one chronicle, he and the other Venetian officials fled to Venice to avoid being hanged. Justice was exacted from the Paduan rebels by the Council of Ten when, after the recapture of the city, it sentenced four Paduan imperial leaders to be hanged in Piazza San Marco.[96] In 1511, prior to his departure for Rome as ambassador, Francesco saw the marriage of his daughter to another Immortale, Fantin Corner qu. Hironimo; their son Zuan would later marry the daughter of Alvise

91 In addition to the works cited in the Introduction, notes 8, 9, and 25, see Francesco Piovan, "Tre schede ruzantiane," *Quaderni Veneti* 27–8 (1998): 93–105.

92 ASPd, *Notarile*, busta 2683, fols 474^r–5^v.

93 The general issue of Venetian patrician purchase of mainland agricultural properties and the connection with their interest in Beolco was first raised by Mario Baratto, "L'esordio del Ruzante," in *Tre studi sul teatro* (Vicenza, 1968), pp. 11–68; see also Carroll, "Introduction."

94 Beolco, *Betia*, Act V, scene 1, v. 4; VBMC, ms. Grimani-Morosini 4, fol. 81^r; see also the other manuscript version of the play, Venice, Biblioteca Marciana, Ital. XI, 66 [=6730], fol. 185^r, "la vergene gioriosa"; *RT*, p. 413.

95 On 1520, see Carroll, "Venetian Attitudes"; the first to explore Zuan Foscari's more extensive connections with Angelo was Andrea Calore, "Giovanni Foscari, un amico veneziano di Angelo Beolco," in *III Convegno Internazionale di Studi sul Ruzante*, ed. Giovanni Calendoli (Padua, 1993), pp. 21–7, 22; for Anzelieri, Menegazzo, "Ricerche," pp. 228–32.

96 Zuan and Francesco were first cousins once removed; Sanuto, 8: 336, 340, 354–5; PBUC, ms 874, 3: 16^r.

Cornaro.[97] In 1518, Marco Corner, the new bishop, invested Zuan's branch of the Foscari with certain episcopal feuds that they had enjoyed under Bishop Pietro.[98] A few months after Ruzante's performance, Zuan Foscari and his brother bought a large piece of agricultural property in the Polesine di Rovigo, the rich territory between the Adige and Po rivers that Venice had taken from Ferrara in the 1480s and fought hard to retain in the Cambrai wars.[99] A few months later, their kinsman Francesco Foscari qu. Nicolò was elected *podestà-capitanio* of Rovigo and became involved in early preparations for the subsequent war, during which he would serve as *capitanio* of Brescia on the western border of the mainland state.[100] In the mid 1520s when the war in Lombardy intensified, Alvise Foscari qu. Nicolò served as *podestà-capitanio* of Crema on the western front, where Immortale and mainland noble Taddeo di la Volpe was serving.[101] Zuan Foscari's continued contacts with Alvise Cornaro and Ruzante are demonstrated by his witnessing of a property document for Cornaro in Padua in 1525 together with the playwright.[102]

Turning to the other families involved in the arc of patronized work, it should be noted that Nicolò Marcello, who was elected doge in 1473 shortly after Lazaro Beolco became a resident of Venice, had the meeting room of the Maggior Consiglio in the Ducal Palace adorned with the paintings of the Venetian fight against Barbarossa on behalf of Pope Alexander that Ruzante describes in the Venetian Prologue of the *Betia*.[103] Ferigo Marcello qu. Piero qu. Antonio, probably the nephew of one of the numerous Marcello invested in the 1480s voyage, was a member of the Immortali. In 1524 he was among the purchasers of agricultural properties confiscated from the Paduan rebels and auctioned by the Venetian state to pay its war debt.[104] His holding was located in Legnaro, near Sant'Angelo di Piove di Sacco, whose *pieve* (rural church) Ruzante would later serve as *fattore* (manager).[105] Ferigo's kinsman Hironimo bought a mill near Montagnana, where his kinsman Piero qu. Giacomo, who had invested in the 1486 voyage, had farms and a mill.[106] Motta di Montagnana was the location of a large feud of the

97 Sanuto, 13: 259; Barbaro, 3: 17.
98 ASVe, *AGRM*, busta 21bis, fasc. 8; busta 360, unnumbered pergamena; Gullino, *Marco Foscari*, pp. 39, 43.
99 ASVe, *AGRM*, busta 225, unnumbered fascicle; Gullino, *Marco Foscari*, p. 27.
100 Sanuto, 30: 12, 445; 36: 110; 38: 297.
101 Sanuto, 35: 209–10; 36: 82, 190, 246–7, 317, 318–19.
102 ASPd, *Notarile*, busta 5031, fol. 62; published in Paolo Sambin, "Altre testimonianze (1525–40) di Angelo Beolco," in *Per le biografie*, pp. 59–86, 60.
103 Cf. Vatican City, Biblioteca Apostolica Vaticana, Cod. Urb. Lat. 512, fol. 274ʳ; ASPd, *AO, ASC*, busta 231, fol. 10. The play has two distinct prologues, one for performances in *pavana* (the Paduan countryside) and one for performances in Venice; the description of the paintings is found solely in the latter.
104 ASVe, *Ufficiali alle Rason Vecchie*, reg. 48, fols 17ᵛ–18ʳ, 41ᵛ–2ʳ.
105 Lovarini, "Notizie," pp. 57–9; Lovarini, "Nuovi documenti sul Ruzzante," in *Studi*, pp. 61–80, 66–7.
106 ASPd, *Estimo 1518*, busta 352, fol. 106ᵛ; ASVe, *AGRM*, busta 250, second *vacchetta*, fol. 5ʳ and cf. Sanuto, 2: 730–31.

Este family purchased by the Venetian state that had been sold to the Beolcos' Milanese Isella relatives, who in 1488 sold it to Ruzante's father and uncle. They would continue to add to it. The Beolcos' purchase of the property may have had a hidden link to the ill-fated voyage: their payment of 1,600 ducats was to be deposited in a Venetian bank that was first designated as the bank of Francesco Pisani. A later interlinear modification, however, added the bank of Andrea Garzoni, *i.e.* Bernardo. Even more curiously, the deposit was "ad risichum dicti d. Nicola [the seller]," who was forbidden to spend it on anything but land. Such stipulations raise the possibility that the sum, deriving partly from the recent sale of Lazaro Beolco's property in Vicenza, was functioning as a loan to Francesco Pisani, a principal investor in the troubled galley round then underway; Andrea Garzoni may have been added because he was not then invested in the voyage. Those troubles made the prudence of land investment imperative; the purchase proved providential, as crippled commerce combined with great war expenditures caused a banking collapse in 1499–1500.[107]

Additional members of the Marcello family had both involvements in Padua and proximity to Beolco's circle. As recorded in a document of 1496, a property held by Alvise Marcello in the *padovano* bounded land of Zuan Francesco and Zuan Jacopo. The Marcello added to their holdings in the early sixteenth century, including a property purchased from Zuan Batista Castegnola, a member of the Paduan noble family of an actor in Ruzante's group.[108] The grandmother of Beolco's acting partner Marc'Aurelio Alvaroto (Menato) was a Russian *sclava* sold to Alvaroto's noble grandfather by a Marcello. Piero Marcello, who had served as *provveditore* of the army before and during the wars of Cambrai (when he presided over the disastrous loss of the Polesine), was *capitanio* of Verona and then *podestà* of Padua in the late 1510s and early 1520s, overlapping with Andrea Magno as *capitanio*.[109] During Magno's governorship, his son Stefano made the only known copy of Beolco's *Pastoral* (see Chapter 2). Andrea Marcello di Bernardo was a member of the *compagnia della calza* inviting Ruzante in 1525, as revealed by the recently-discovered complete roll of the Triumphanti (see Chapter 3). The performance, which drew so many high government officials that it drained the Senate and the Council of Ten, was of a play whose *outré* content caused great scandal. In 1533, Andrea Marcello qu. Antonio as *capitanio* attended the Paduan performance of Ruzante's *Vaccaria*, his only play to mention Monselice, where the Marcello had large amounts of land and a lucrative quarry. Like the Beolcos,

107 For Isella, Sambin, "Lazzaro"; for Motta property, ASPd, *Notarile*, busta 1758, fols 294r–6v; *AO, ASC*, busta 231, fols 37, 53, 84–5, 86; ASPd *AO, ASC*, busta 231, fol. 11; ASPd, *Notarile*, busta 2684, fols 598r, 610r; Francesco Pisani: ASVe, *AGRM*, busta 250, second *vacchetta*, fols 5r, 6r, 6v, 7r, 10v, 11r, 13r, 13v, 18v, 19r, 19v, 20r, 22r, 24r, 25v, 26r, 38r, 43v, 53v, 54v, 55r, 60r, 69v, 80r; Garzoni: fol. 41r; ASPd, *Notarile*, busta 1758, fol. 510r; on banking crisis, Mueller, esp. pp. 236–43; cf. Gullino, *Marco Foscari*, pp. 17–19.

108 ASPd, *AO, ASC*, busta 231, fols 49–50; ASPd, *Estimo 1418*, reg. 67, fol. 18r.

109 Sanuto, 3: 107; 9: 356; 10: 213, 338–40, 360, 364, 366, 377–81, 688; Monterosso, *Reggimenti*, vol. 4, fasc. XI, fols 1–2; Sanuto, 27, 31–4 *s.v.*

Andrea also had land in Arquà. Andrea's property in Noventa was worked by the peasant Perduocimo, the original name of the character Ruzante.[110] Of the members of the Pesaro family associated with the sacristy, the one with the most important links to the Beolco was Pietro, the son of Nicolò. Nicolò's investment in the 1480s voyage for the *fraterna* was funded in part by Francesco and Zuan Pisani and by Nicolò Bernardo.[111] In 1483, Alvise qu. Luca procurator became a member of the wool guild in Padua, where his son Antonio had married the daughter of an important *stradioto*, the knight Ladislas of Bosnia. Alvise lived in the parish of Santa Maria in Vanzo, near the woolen mills and San Daniele, where the Beolco lived.[112] As a young man, Pietro served as a *patron* of the Flanders galleys and later continued to invest in them. He owned extensive property in Padua and its territory, the income deriving from it including profits from his extensive pasturage near Este at the foot of the Euganean Hills, where there was a large Venetian garrison.[113] The material for the bows that he exported to England likely came at least in part from these properties, whose trees and the products made from them are praised by Beolco in the *Prima oratione*.[114] Pesaro's large house in Padua was located in the *contrada* of Santa Sofia, near the Speroni-Alvaroto. In Este, where the Beolco owned several *campi*, Pesaro had another large house where one of the town's notaries conducted business.[115] Among the notary's clients was Alvise Cornaro, who also had a house in Este and whose notarial acts in Este were witnessed by Angelo Beolco among others.[116]

Pesaro's connections with Paduan leaders were numerous. He was a *compare* (godfather) of the Paduan noble loyalist Antonio Caodevaca, apparently to be interpreted literally (*e.g.* as Caodevaca's baptismal sponsor or possibly co-sponsor with Caodevaca of a baptism) because the relationship resulted in Pesaro's exclusion from a Senate vote on Caodevaca's case.[117] Before the wars, Pietro Pesaro had given credit to the Paduan Bertucci Bagarotto, who had previously acted as a Pesaro agent in buying land and in selling a horse to *condottiero* Carlo Malatesta.[118] Bagarotto participated in the 1509 rebellion. He was one of the four hanged, although he proclaimed his innocence and his son claimed that Pesaro had convinced his father, who had wanted to go to Venice

110 ASPd, *Estimo 1518*, busta 352, fol. 145ʳ, 257ᵛ–8ᵛ.
111 ASVe, *AGRM*, busta 37, unnumbered folio, *Arbore Pesaro*; ASVe, *AGRM*, busta 250, second *vacchetta*, fols 18ᵛ, 23ᵛ, 24ʳ, 30ʳ, 31ʳ, 33ʳ, 43ᵛ, 55ʳ.
112 Lazara, *Memorie*, unnumbered folio; ASPd, *Notarile*, busta 2683, fol. 606ʳ⁻ᵛ; busta 247, fol. 634ʳ⁻ᵛ; busta 1291, fol. 3ʳ⁻ᵛ.
113 ASPd, *Notarile*, busta 352, fol. 303ʳ⁻ᵛ; ASPd, *Estimo 1518*, busta 352, fol. 315ʳ⁻ᵛ.
114 Sanuto, 11: 276; 12: 162; Bembo, *History*, Book 10, par. 78; Book 11, par. 45.
115 ASPd, *Notarile*, busta 1759, fols 146ʳ–7ᵛ and Sambin, "Lazzaro," p. 25; ASPd, *Notai d'Este*, busta 648, *passim, e.g.* fols 34ᵛ, 42ᵛ–3ʳ; busta 649, *passim, e.g.* fols 11ʳ, 120ʳ, 136ʳ, 219ʳ.
116 Menegazzo, "Ricerche," pp. 223–5, 236–47, 263–4.
117 Sanuto, 4: 414, 424; 24: 327–30; 26: 500; 27: 427.
118 ASPd, *Notarile*, busta 1292, fols 5ᵛ–6ᵛ; busta 2793, fol. 182ʳ⁻ᵛ. Marco Bagaroto witnessed a document for other members of the Pesaro family in 1508 in Este: ASPd, *Notai d'Este*, busta 4, fasc. 7, fols 78ᵛ–9ʳ.

when Padua passed to imperial control, to stay in Padua and gather military intelligence for Venice. After the war Pesaro advocated relative clemency in the treatment of the rebels.[119]

In international affairs, Piero Pesaro supported strong defense against the Turks including large *cernide*, the local peasant militias that supported the professional soldiers.[120] He favored good relations with the French when they had the upper hand in the ongoing wars, while still seeking to protect Venetian interests.[121] On more than one occasion Pesaro opened his Venetian home in the parish of San Beneto for Carnival festivities with connections to current events. During the latter phase of the Cambrai wars (1515), he hosted a performance of Plautus's *Miles gloriosus* by the Immortali whose *intermezzi* referring to contemporary entertainers may have inspired some scenes in the *Betia*.[122] In 1521, when he was attentive to the rekindling of the war in Lombardy brought about by the end of the three-year truce of 1518, he hosted the first festivity of the Ortolani at which Ruzante is named as performer. The guest of honor was an inductee, noble and *condottiero* Antonio da Martinengo of the knightly family of Brescia, on the Venetian state's western frontier. Contacts between the Pesaro and the Martinengo stretched back to the early years of Brescia's entrance into the Venetian dominion, as Fantin Pesaro was among its first *podestà* at a time when Antonio's father Bernardino was a leading citizen.[123] Later in 1521, as war on the Lombard plain was heating up, Piero Pesaro was elected *provedador sopra lo armar* (in charge of recruitment), an office that he had solicited, and then *podestà* of Brescia. Uncharacteristically, Sanudo does not give a list of candidates for the latter election, likely indicating that Piero had solicited it as well, in his family's tradition of commitment to defense. Piero chose as *compagno di spada* (who accompanied a patrician to a state ceremony shortly before the latter's departure to assume a governance office) Hironimo Marcello qu. Antonio. The latter was the kinsman of Jacopo Marcello, the *generalissimo da mar* buried in the Frari. Piero's cousin Hironimo Pesaro qu. Beneto, whose father's funeral monument frames the portal of the sacristy, was then serving in Brescia as *provveditore generale in terraferma* (chief civilian overseer of mainland forces).[124] Such an intertwining was typical of the cousins' lives. Hironimo too had captained Flanders galleys, in 1508, when he learned of the crushing Portuguese competition.[125] He too, just prior to the Cambrai wars,

119   Antonio Bonardi, "I padovani ribelli alla repubblica di Venezia (a. 1509–1530), studio storico con appendice di documenti inediti," *Miscellanea di storia veneta a cura della Deputazione veneta di storia patria* ser. 2.8 (1902): 303–612, 397–403, 578–9, 602–4; Sanuto, 9: 358–9; 28: 203.
120   Sanuto, 28: 555, 559; 31: 437, 443, 490–91.
121   Sanuto, 31: 145, 251, 264.
122   Lovarini, "La *Betia*," in *Studi*, pp. 293–317, 295–6.
123   Sanudo, *Itinerario*, fol. 53ʳ.
124   Sanuto, 32: 10, 191, 281; for Hironimo Pesaro, originally also buried in the Frari, see Goffen, esp. pp. 69–72, 136; Barbaro, 6: 83.
125   Sanuto, 5: 28, 680, 980, 1043, 1064–5; Brown, 2: 76 note 1.

had utilized Bertuzi Bagaroto as his agent in selling a horse, this one to the Paduan noble Artusio Conte.[126] Toward the wars' conclusion and after serving as *provveditore* in Treviso, he was elected *capitanio* of Padua.[127] Moreover, their cousin Francesco qu. Marco, who had been delegate to the truce negotiations with the empire in Verona in 1519, held numerous mainland governance offices in this period including the *capitaniato* of Verona; his wife, a daughter of Francesco Foscari, stipulated burial in the Frari in her will.[128]

In 1524, Piero Pesaro was elected *provveditore generale in campo* (chief civilian field overseer) for the Lombard war.[129] Upon his return to Venice, he hosted a supper for the new *capitanio general*, Francesco Maria della Rovere, with entertainment by famed comedian Zuan Polo, with whom Ruzante had performed earlier in the year.[130] Three months later, on a very short ballot that also included his cousin Hironimo, Piero was again elected *provveditore generale in campo*; it was noted by Sanudo that he was a great friend ('molto amico') of the *capitanio general*. As *provveditore*, Piero was the first to report the capture of Francis I at Pavia on February 25, 1525 (see Chapter 3). He later presided over the loss of Cremona, which an anonymous Venetian author attributed in large part to his facile assumptions of Venetian strength, his departure from the field with the excuse of illness when his assumptions proved false, and his appropriation of army draft animals from the transport of artillery to the transport of his personal goods.[131] Pesaro's final term as *provveditore generale*, at the 1528 siege of Naples, concluded shortly after the Franco-Venetian defeat with his death.[132]

Might Pesaro have had reasons beyond simple entertainment for his hosting of Ruzante's 1521 performance? If one accepts the Lovarini-Menegazzo theory of Beolco connections with imperialists, it could have sent a friendly signal to the empire that would have facilitated the Pesaro family's continued involvement in the western galleys. Such a function was conducted for the Triumphante Vicenzo Contarini by his brother Gaspare, the future ecclesiastic, who was the Venetian ambassador to the emperor during an important galley round in which the Contarini were involved.[133] Given Pesaro's commitment to mainland defense, another potential reason may have been the consideration of Beolco as a director of *cernide*, the peasant forces useful to the predicted conflict between Charles V

---

126 ASPd, Archivio *Notarile*, busta 2794, fol. 278ʳ.
127 Sanuto, 17–18, 20–23 *s.v.*
128 *Libri commemoriali*, 6: 159; Sanuto, 26–8 *s.v.* Pesaro, Piero, and see Ennio Concina, *La macchina territoriale. La progettazione della difesa nel Cinquecento veneto* (Bari: 1983), p. 17; Sanuto, 24–41 *s.v.* Pesaro, Francesco; Monterosso, *Reggimenti*, Vol. 4, fasc. XI, fols 11ʳ–12ᵛ; he would be *podestà* of Padua together with Nicolò Venier as *capitanio* in 1523; ASVe, *AGRM*, busta 251, unnumbered item dated 1520.
129 Sanuto, 35: 400, 417 and 35, 36 *s.v.*
130 Sanuto, 35: 393; 36: 431, 450, 460; ASVe, *AGRM*, busta 28, fols 10ᵛ, 17ʳ.
131 Sanuto, 37: 64–5, 66, 648 and 37–43 *s.v.*; PSVBA, ms 609, fols 144ʳ–7ᵛ.
132 Sanuto, 49: 91.
133 *Libri commemoriali*, tomo VI, p. 169; Sanuto, 28–33 *s.v.* Alessandro qu. Nicolò; Sanuto, 29 *s.v.* Pesaro, Antonio qu. Alvise qu. Angelo; for the Triumphanti, see Chapter 3.

and Francis I for control of the peninsula. Emilio Menegazzo many years ago noted the title *strenuus* (soldier) applied to Beolco in a document of 1526; connecting that with his conspicuous absence from known documents between 1526 and 1528 and his realistic description of war in the *Reduce* (The Veteran; also known as *Parlamento* or Speech and *Primo dialogo* or First dialogue), Menegazzo theorized that Beolco had spent the two years as a soldier in Lombardy.[134] If so, it would have been under Pesaro as *provveditore generale*. The scene in *Betia* in which Zilio (Beolco's character) and Nale (Alvaroto's character) direct a fighting force of peasant neighbors to take Betia back from her mother seems to be a kind of rehearsal for or advertisement of Beolco's capacity to direct a *cernida* (Act IV, scene 1).[135] The document in which he is termed *strenuus* is dated June 2, 1526, precisely the time at which Venice publicly declared its adherence to the League of Cognac.[136] Through it, "strenuus dominus Angelus de Beolcho" (soldier sir Angelo de Beolco) gives power of attorney to Alvise Cornaro to pay the debt that Beolco had incurred with Zuan Corner qu. Hironimo, the Immortale and Alvise's future father-in-law, for a horse.

In discussion of the document, much has been made of Beolco's hypothesized passion for horses and, with the exception of Menegazzo's remarks, little has been made of the possibility that Beolco needed the horse and the power of attorney because he was leaving for war. Unnoticed have been the markers of Beolco feudatory status in his name (*dominus* and *de*). As Lovarini pointed out, connecting the surname to Castel Beolco in the Brianza, the family belonged to the Lombard feudal class. Lovarini's views are supported by the particle 'de' regularly included in the early recordings of Lazaro's name and other family documents such as the will that rebel Zuan Jacopo made in Venice that was witnessed by a Lipomano.[137] The inclusion of linguistic markers of feudal status in the 1526 power of attorney was appropriate for a mission to the Beolcos' native Lombardy, where their confrères such as the Martinengo continued their defense function. A following notarial act, dated June 14, involves Antonio Martinengo and Alvise Cornaro; a notarial act on the preceding folio involves an in-law of Cornaro's and a member of the company of Jacomo Vicoaro, a *capitano* of *stradioti* then leaving to serve

---

134 Emilio Menegazzo, "Stato economico-sociale del padovano all'epoca del Ruzante," in *Colonna*, pp. 304–37, 330 note 76.

135 VBMC, ms. Grimani-Morosini 4, fols 65ʳ–70ᵛ (*RT*, pp. 361–75).

136 ASPd, *Notarile*, busta 5031, fol. 202; see also fols 201, 207; Sambin, "Altre testimonianze," pp. 61–2, 78.

137 See, *e.g.* ASPd, *Notarile*, busta 477, fols 120ʳ, 122ʳ–3ᵛ, 132ʳ–3ᵛ, 348ʳ, 370ᵛ, 398ʳ–400ʳ (published Sambin, "Lazzaro," pp. 43–4), 398ʳ, 411ʳ–14ᵛ, 418ʳ; for family members termed 'dominus' or 'nobiles': ASPd, *Notarile*, busta 1056, fols 188ᵛ–9ᵛ; busta 1762, fol. 437ᵛ; busta 4078, fol. 268ʳ; busta 1756, fol. 246ʳ; busta 2788, fols 263ʳ–4ᵛ; and in busta 3969, fols 15ᵛ–16ᵛ, in the will made while he is confined to Venice, Zuan Jacopo provides the full "nobilis mediolanensis dominus" and see fols 126ʳ–7ʳ for the same phrase for his Milanese cousin; ASPd, *AO*, *ASC*, busta 231, fols 39, 44; busta 232, fol. 189ʳ; busta 235 printed family history and additional documents; for similar nominatives for the Martinengo, see *e.g.* Sanuto, 1: 248; 2: 1308; 3: 392; 8: 320; 15: 474, 501; 36: 537–8; 38: 258; 39: 467.

near Pavia under Pesaro and Marc'Antonio Martinengo, a cousin of Antonio.[138] This additional information supports Menegazzo's hypothesis that Beolco, like others, was making the legal preparations necessary prior to departure for the front and an uncertain future.

Connections between the Beolco and the Bernardo and their partners the Garzoni chiefly involved banking matters. All did business with the same Florentine bankers: the Medici (the Bernardo bank served as the bank of deposit for a transaction involving a Lombard investor, the ambassador of the duke of Milan, and Lorenzo de' Medici), the Nerli, and, when the Medici bank closed, the Frescobaldi who took their place and who were influential at the Burgundian court.[139] The Beolco and their in-laws utilized the Bernardo-Garzoni bank to transfer funds between Padua and Venice and, as mentioned above, possibly as a way of masking their profits from the voyages and investments by others to avoid charges of usury.[140] Nicolò Bernardo, whose great-grandfather was Doge Francesco Foscari and who owned land in Arquà, had invested heavily in the 1484 voyages.[141] He had been a member of the Zonta (Addition) of the Dieci in 1514 when Giacomo Alvaroto qu. Conte and his brother were pardoned for their participation in the imperial dedication of Padua and readmitted to the Venetian dominion.[142] The father of a Triumphante, he attended the 1525 performance.[143] The connection outlasted Angelo's lifetime; in 1543, the Garzoni were renting a home in Padua owned by Angelo's half-brothers.[144]

Foscari connections to the several generations of Beolco have been delineated above: their involvement in the Flanders galleys and contact with the Milanese Beolco for financing, their strong presence in Padua, their hosting of Angelo's first named performance in Venice at a spectacular festivity with military overtones. Their willingness to maintain connections with mainland feudal nobility and the emperor emerges in the marriage of Doge Foscari's great-granddaughter Lucia Mocenigo to a Conte of Collalto and her residence at the imperial court during the wars of Cambrai.[145] Francesco Foscari qu. Nicolò, whose additional

138 Sanuto, 31: 180, 232, 334, 345, 410; 32: 49, 64, 118 (Martinengo), 37: 55, 268, 287, 301, 552; 40: 136, 141, 163, 588; 42: 151, 225–7, 298, 483, 525. Joining the forces toward the end of the year was the company of the religious reformer Michael Gaismair, added to the Venetian garrison in Padua, whose pro-peasant sympathies were close to Beolco's: Sanuto, 43: 153; Giorgio Padoan, "La dimora padovana di Michele Gaismar e la richiesta di 'leze e stratuti nuovi'," in *Momenti del Rinascimento veneto* (Padua, 1978), pp. 239–48; Linda L. Carroll, "A Nontheistic Paradise in Renaissance Padua," *Sixteenth Century Journal* 24 (1993): 881–98, esp. 889–91.

139 ASPd, *AO, ASC*, busta 231, fols 17–22 (1484), 45–6 (1494–99); Sanuto, 2: 391–2; Mueller, p. 286; Stabel, p. 35; *AGB*, busta 40, unnumbered item dated 1478.

140 ASPd, *Notarile*, busta 1758, fol. 294^r–6^v; busta 1759, fols 436^r–7^r; busta 1760, fols 21^v, 23^v–4^v, 392^{r-v}, 393^r–5^r.

141 Barbaro, 2: 14; ASVe, *Archivio Bernardo*, busta 8, unnumbered item dated 1487.

142 Sanuto, 18: 56, 62, 232.

143 Sanuto, 21: 436; 37: 559–60 and see Chapter 3.

144 ASPd, *Estimo 1518*, Reg. 35, fols 46^r–7^r.

145 Brno (Czech Republic), Státní oblastní archiv, Antonio Rambaldo Conte di Collalto, *Genealogia Rectae, imperturbataeque Lineae Excellentissimi Principis Antonij Rambaldi Collalti Comitis*

proximities to Angelo Beolco included a house in San Giorgio di Torreselle of Padua near San Daniele and land in Sant'Angelo di Piove di Sacco, figured among the members of the Senate presenting the request for a *privilegio di stampa* for Ruzante's two Plautine plays in 1533.[146]

Nicolò Tron's proximities to the Beolco family were numerous. He served in the early 1460s as *capitanio* of Padua, where he owned property.[147] He was doge from 1471 until 1478, a period in which the Beolcos conducted business in Venice. The full-lira *tron*, which his monetary reform created and which bore his image during his lifetime, became the basic Venetian coin and is the coin most frequently mentioned in Beolco's plays.[148] Nicolò's son Filippo, who maintained a home in Padua, became the city's *podestà* in 1484, immediately after the Ferrara war. He presided over a period of peace during which his kinsman Santo qu. Francesco, whose wife owned a mill in Padua, joined the Padua wool guild.[149] Along with *capitanio* Alvise Bernardo and *condottiero* Roberto da San Severino, he organized a joust to honor the visiting son of Ludovico Sforza, the duke of Milan.[150] Another prominent family member, as noted by Robert Finlay, was Doge Nicolò's nephew Luca Tron who, with other family members of his generation, opposed the use of money to build political careers.[151] Luca was unusually outspoken in legislative bodies and paid particular attention to the western galleys and mainland defense.[152] Along with Nicolò Bernardo, he led the government officials attending Beolco's 1525 Triumphante performance. The next year, with war raging in Lombardy, Vicenzo Tron qu. Priamo, like Doge Nicolò of the San Beneto branch, became *capitanio* of Bergamo, serving until 1528. The *podestà* was Polo Valaresso, with a kinsman in the Triumphanti.[153] A different Filippo Tron would later figure indirectly in Beolco's life. In 1531, this Filippo Tron was among the *avogadori di comun* accused of appropriating jurisdiction of a crime committed by a member of the Guioti or Guidoti, the Montagnana family

ab anno aesti 930 usque ad annum 1729, fol. 16[r-v]. I am grateful to Jan-Christoph Rössler for the clarification of Lucia's exact relationship to Doge Francesco Foscari.

146 ASPd, *Estimo 1518*, busta 126, fol. 123[r]; ASVe, Senato, *Terra*, Reg. 27, 203[r] (old numeration 182[r]) Dec. 13, 1533; cf. Sanuto, 58: 520, 750.

147 ASPd, *Notarile*, busta 4889, fol. 200[r].

148 *Betia*, Prologue I, par. 6; Act II, v. 282; Act V, v. 325 (*RT*, pp. 150–1; 252–3; 434–5), *Seconda oratione*, par. 14 (*RT*, pp. 1214–15), *Parlamento* [also titled *Reduce*], Scene 5, par. 34 (*RT*, pp. 524–35; Zorzi, "Note al *Parlamento*," note 44 p. 1369), *Bilora*, Scene 4, par. 47 (*RT*, pp. 560–61), *Moscheta* Act IV, scene 8, par. 65 (*RT*, pp. 640–41), *Piovana* Act V, scene 2, par. 54; Act V, scene 5, par. 95; Act V, scene 11, par. 148 (*RT*, pp. 1000–1001; pp. 1008–9; 1020–21); *Vaccaria*, Act II, scene 1, pars 29–31; Act III, scene 4, par. 131 (*RT*, pp. 1072–3, 1116–17).

149 ASPd, *Notarile*, busta 1292, fols 475[r]–6[v]; Monterosso, *Reggimenti*, vol. 3, fasc. VII, 32[r-v]; ASPd, *Estimo 1518*, busta 352, fol. 304[v]; Lazara, *Memorie*.

150 Monterosso, *Reggimenti*, vol. 3, fasc. VII, fols 32[r-v].

151 Finlay, esp. pp. 231–4.

152 Sanuto, 29: 410–11, 456; 30: 154–5, 198, 199–200; 36: 86.

153 Sanuto, 21: 436; I am grateful to Jan-Christoph Rössler for the identification of Tron with the San Beneto branch.

of Beolco's step-mother, and of resolving the matter with a fine divided among themselves and various collaborators including Pietro Bernardo.[154] Tron was still in office in 1539 when Angelo's half-brother Ludovico was held in the *carcere forte* (fortified prison) of the Ducal Palace.[155]

Numerous Trevisan were involved in the 1480s voyage assisted by the Beolco, including Beneto who as *podestà* of Padua accepted a legal agreement involving Beolco in-laws that apparently resulted from it.[156] The Trevisan had property in several locations associated with the Beolco or Angelo personally: the Euganean hills, Piove di Sacco, and Pernumia, a location favored by Zuan Francesco Beolco.[157] In a 1509 episode to which Ruzante refers in the *Betia* (see also Chapter 3), the son of Melchiorre Trevisan, Marin, had accompanied his uncle Anzelo as *capitanio zeneral* of the Venetian armada that defended the Polesine di Rovigo. The armada was located near the fortress of Ficarolo, whose position on the Po River at the boundary with the Ferrarese state made it crucial to the defense of the rich agricultural Polesine that Venice had taken from Ferrara in that earlier war and whose farms had been eagerly snapped up by Venetian patricians—especially Beolco supporters—in the wave of mainland investment that took shape as commerce faltered. The 1509 defense failed badly, but a 1510 campaign recouped the losses.[158] A member of the Ortolani, Marin hosted their first known festivity at his home on the Giudecca. The *compagnia* had made its links with military leaders evident from the beginning; among the guests at the inaugural festivity was the infantry *capitano* Renzo da Cere Orsini, who later included Beolco among his trusted agents.[159] Domenego Trevisan, who was the grandson of a Paduan *cittadina* of likely Friulan origin and who frequented the mainland city in the 1460s when Lazaro Beolco first arrived, served as its *podestà* in the first years of the century and was honored for his wisdom, justice, and probity.[160] His wife was a member of another Frari patron family, the Marcello, the sister of Immortale Ferigo. Shortly after the 1520 Immortale

154 Sanuto, 55: 274, 276–8, 278, 324, 668; 58: 232, 265–6; while the father of this Filippo was also named Priamo, he appears not to have been the brother of Vicenzo, whose *fraterna* consisted of himself and brother Nicolò: Sanuto, 47: 568; on the Gui(d)otti: Linda L. Carroll, "Per un itinerario della Padova del Ruzante," *Padova e il suo territorio* 164 (Agosto, 2013): 6–9.

155 ASPd, *AO, ASC*, busta 232, fols 79^r, 81^v.

156 ASVe, *AGRM*, busta 250, second *vacchetta*, fols 7^r, 8^r, 9^v, 11^r, 15^r, 16^v, 17^r, 18^v, 22^v, 23^r, 26^v, 53^v, 55^r, 56^v, 57^v, 60^r, 61^v, 69^r, 84^v, 85^v; Monterosso, *Reggimenti*, vol. 3, fasc. VIII, 16^r–19^r; ASPd, *AO, ASC*, busta 231, fol. 43 and cf. *Notarile*, busta 1760, fols 392^r–5^r.

157 ASPd, *Estimo 1518*, busta 352, fols 81^v, 84^v, 94$^{r–v}$, 118^v, 136^v, 171^r, 212^v–13^r; busta 356, fol. 160^r; busta 358, fols 38$^{r–v}$, 81^v–2^r; *Notarile*, busta 1335, fol. 57^r.

158 For the two manuscript versions and analysis, see Linda L. Carroll, "'El g(h)e sa bon laorare': Female Wealth, Male Competition, Musical Festivities, and the Venetian patriciate in Ruzante's *pavan*," in *Sexualities, Textualities, Art and Music in Early Modern Italy. Playing with Boundaries*, ed. Melanie L. Marshall, Linda L. Carroll, and Katherine A. McIver (Farnham, 2014), pp. 155–83, 159–68; Sanuto, 9: 248, 310, 349–50, 393–6, 9: 545.

159 Sanuto, 19: 434; Lovarini, "Nuovi documenti," pp. 63–4; the document was subsequently lost or destroyed.

160 Barbaro, 7: 123; Monterosso, *Reggimenti*, vol. 4, fasc. IX, 8^r–10^v; ASPd, *Notarile*, busta 2907, fols 55^r, 125^r, 140^r, 173^r–4^r.

festivity, Domenego Trevisan hosted a private performance of Ruzante's Paduan play in his *procuratia*.[161] During this period, he and Antonio Tron served on the commission selling the appropriated land of Paduan rebels to pay Venice's war debt.[162] Another Trevisan, Nicolò, possibly the one invested in the northern voyage with the Beolco, attended the 1525 performance. Closing the circle, the house of Marin Trevisan that had hosted the first Ortolano festivity also hosted Ruzante's last performance in Venice, in 1526, at which the captured Francis I was mocked with a mutilated rooster.[163]

Despite the co-presence in Venice of the Beolco and the Scuola dei Milanesi, in the available records of the latter there is no evidence of the former. The Milanese names that recur in Scuola records are Osnaghi and Panigarola.[164] If, as it appears, the Beolco were not members, it may have been because, as Beatrice Del Bo has observed, they were not among the traditional Milanese bankers but among the new men with wealth based in commerce and agricultural products whose success was achieved in the latter 1450s with the rise of Francesco Sforza. Letizia Arcangeli has documented the extent to which, by around 1500, both the Sforza and other important Milanese were in debt to Zuan de Beolco, for a total of about 45,000 ducats. She also notes their imperial leanings.[165]

The importance of the Corner in Ruzante's connection to Venice and his performances there and elsewhere is almost impossible to overstate. Marco Corner, who with his brother Jacomo studied at the University of Padua when Zuan Francesco Beolco was prior, was the addressee of Ruzante's *Prima oratione* (*First Oration*). The *Seconda oratione* (*Second Oration*) is addressed to yet another brother, Cardinal Francesco. Ruzante's first performance in Venice may have been of the *Prima oratione* in 1518, when Cardinal Marco was visiting there incognito; he performed it multiple times in 1521 on the occasion of Marco's formal entrance as Bishop of Padua.[166] The Immortali included three members of the family: Marco's brother Zuan; Fantin qu. Hironimo, whose son's later marriage to the daughter of Alvise Cornaro provided Alvise's descent line with the official patrician status that he craved; and, from a further branch of the family, Zuan qu. Antonio qu. Nadal.

During the war with Ferrara, Zorzi, the father of Marco and Zuan, had served as *capitanio* at the fortress of Ficarolo, whose defense, as mentioned above, was the subject of an extended riff in Ruzante's *Betia*.[167] Zorzi, whose ascent line included the Paduan Scrovegni who were patrons of Giotto's frescoes in the Arena Chapel, went on to serve as *podestà* of Padua from 1503 to 1504. In 1520 at the private

161   Gloria, 1: 279; Sanuto, 28: 264.
162   Sanuto, 26: 494.
163   Marin was by then deceased: Sanuto, 26: 218; 40: 789–90.
164   ASVe, *Santa Maria Gloriosa dei Frari*, busta 106; Del Bo, *s.v.*; cf. Mueller, p. 275.
165   Del Bo, pp. 95–110; Arcangeli, "Esperimenti," pp. 324–5; one ducat at the time was worth approximately $1,000.
166   Carroll, "Introduction."
167   Monterosso, *Reggimenti*, vol. 4, fasc. IX, fols 17ʳ–19ʳ; Sanudo, *Itinerario*, fol. 35ᵛ.

Ruzante performance hosted by Domenego Trevisan, Zorzi was seated next to Trevisan, then serving on the commission to sell the Polesine land that had been created through a bill supported by Corner.[168] Soon after, Zorzi was elected to a commission to rebuild the walls of Padua, whose strength is referred to in the *Prima oratione* and the prologue of the *Anconitana* (*The Woman from Ancona* or *The Anconitan Play*).[169] Zorzi's branch of the family owned extensive properties in Padua and its *territorio* including a villa at Tencarola.[170] They were not lacking in a connection to Milan; Zorzi's father sold its duke his palazzo on the Grand Canal in 1460.[171] The Ortolani also included a Corner, Marco qu. Pietro. Davit qu. Pietro belonged to the wool guild in Padua and the line owned much property there, including at Ponte Corvo near Alvise Cornaro.[172]

Luca Zen had a kinsman (Carlo di Pietro) in the Ortolani; another (Marino) owned property in Arquà bounded by Beolco property and some in Este that paid a *livello* to the Pesaro. His daughter owned a small farm near Piove di Sacco.[173] Another kinsman, Carlo di Baccalario, married the sister of Immortale Zuan Corner qu. Antonio qu. Nadal in 1516 and invested in the Barbary galleys shortly thereafter.[174]

The Foscarini had extensive holdings in several locations associated with the Beolco or Ruzante plays: Bovolenta, near those of Alvise Cornaro and precisely in Polverara,[175] mentioned in Ruzante's *Fiorina*; Piove di Sacco,[176] the site of a Ruzante play; and Montagnana,[177] where the Beolco had land and which was the seat of Zuan Francesco's in-laws, the Guidotti, who provided fighting men and a trusted governmental secretary to the Republic. Antonio Foscarini di Nicolò, whose father had been *capitanio* of Padua, was at the university when Zuan Francesco Beolco was on the faculty.[178] He may also be the subject of a hand-written comment in the Correr manuscript of the *Betia*; the identity is rendered

168 Sanuto, 28: 681–2; Giuseppe Del Torre, *Venezia e la terraferma dopo la guerra di Cambrai. Fiscalità e amministrazione (1515–1530)* (Milan, 1986), pp. 153–60.

169 *Prima oratione*, par. 22 (*RT*, pp. 1190–91); *Anconitana*, Prologue II, par. 3 (*RT*, pp. 780–81). For walls see Sergio Polano, ed., *L'architettura militare veneta del Cinquecento* (Milan, 1988); Sanuto, 24: 75–6, 78, 398, 608, 684–8; 29: 632.

170 ASPd, *Notarile*, busta 2787, fol. 561ʳ.

171 VBMC, mss. Provenienze Diverse c, 599 / XXXIV.

172 Lazara, *Memorie*, at 1489; ASPd, *Notarile*, busta 250, fol. 493ʳ; busta 254, fols 182ᵛ–3ᵛ; busta 520, fols 236ʳ–7ʳ; busta 2682, fol. 115ʳ; busta 2683, fol. 276ʳ; *Estimo 1518*, busta 352, fol. 171ʳ.

173 ASPd, *AO, ASC*, busta 231, fol. 40ʳ; for Arquà: ASPd, *Estimo 1518*, busta 352, fols 82ʳ, 352ʳ; ASPd, *Notai d'Este*, busta 648, fols 110ʳ–111ʳ.

174 Barbaro, 7: 364; 29: 333, 417; 30: 100.

175 ASPd, *Estimo 1418*, busta 427, fol. 105ᵛ; *Estimo 1518*, busta 352, fols 146ᵛ, 147ⁱ, 156ʳ, 158ʳ⁻ᵛ, 191ᵛ, 222ʳ⁻ᵛ, 237ʳ⁻ᵛ, 273ᵛ⁻4ʳ; ASVe, *AGRM*, busta 352, unnumbered fascicle, Esenzioni sopra beni a Bovolenta.

176 ASPd, *Estimo 1518*, busta 352, fols 111ᵛ, 184ʳ, 195ʳ, 195ᵛ⁻6ʳ, 206ᵛ, 230ʳ, 243ʳ; busta 358, fol. 113ᵛ; *Notarile*, busta 2733, fols 20ʳ⁻ᵛ, 419ʳ⁻20ᵛ, 519ʳ⁻20ʳ; busta 1335, fols 529ʳ⁻30ʳ; busta 1336, fol. 32ʳ.

177 ASPd, *Estimo 1518*, busta 352, fol. 128ᵛ.

178 Barbaro, 3: 541; Monterosso, *Reggimenti*, Vol. 4, fasc. IX, fols 5ʳ⁻6ʳ; PBC, ms. B.P. 143, Dorighello, *Notizie*, fols 404ᵛ⁻5ʳ; PBC, ms. B.P. 938, Dorighello, *Memorie*, fol. 29; Nardi, p. 40.

uncertain by the obscuring of the final portion of the surname by the binding.[179]
The comment reads: "Al Mag.co m/. Ant.o Fosc . . . " Emilio Lovarini opined
that there was only space for three additional letters and thus read the surname
as 'Foscari' but the widespread use of nasal marks and the loss of final vowels
in Venetian could produce 'Foscari[n]' (*i.e.* Foscarini) even with three letters.
Padoan propended for Antonio Foscarini di Nicolò, who held offices in some key
rural areas including Rovigo and who subsequently invited Rovigotto entertainers to Venice.[180] The new evidence of Foscarini family holdings in the Polesine
throws fresh light on Antonio's preference for those offices and for his potential
interest in the peasant fighting force represented in the play.

A reference to the family's literary heritage may be found in the *Anconitana*'s
high-born women characters, whose names Isotta and Ginevra echo those of the
learned women of the noble Veronese Nogarola family with whom the humanist Alvise Foscarini had maintained a literary relationship. Alvise Foscarini also
had a connection with Ancona: it was there that he, as the ambassador of the
Republic, met Pope Pius II to discuss a cause to which he had a personal commitment, the Christian expedition that was to have sailed from the port city to attack
the Turks and that would have included forces led by Duke Philip of Burgundy,
the great-great-grandfather of Charles V. The Spanish garrison at Gaeta, from
which the *Anconitana*'s Isotta and Ginevra hail, protected the Aragonese court
in Naples that offered refuge, in Beolco's time, to a Nogarola imperial partisan
whose participation in the rebellion against Venice after Agnadello had resulted in
the confiscation of the family estate at Bagnolo and its sale to the Pisani.[181]

Of the Pesaro del Carro, Bishop Jacopo attended the last Venetian performance
of Ruzante recorded by Sanudo, that of Carnival 1526 (see Chapter 4). Sponsored
by Marin Grimani Patriarch of Aquileia who, when in Padua, lived in the Grimani
home on Pra' da la Valle near the Beolco, it was staged in Marin Trevisan's home
on the Giudecca.[182] And it may not have been the first Ruzante performance that
Bishop Jacopo attended, if indeed Ruzante recited a version of the *Prima oratione*
in Venice in 1518 at Cardinal Marco's festivity, which saw Bishop Jacopo in the
audience.[183] The patriarch's brother Marco was a member of the Ortolani and
maintained a personal relationship with Beolco (see Chapter 3). Antonio Pesaro,

179 VBMC, ms. Grimani-Morosini 4, guard folio.
180 Emilio Lovarini, "Per l'edizione critica del Ruzzante," in *Studi*, pp. 109–63, 137; Giorgio Padoan, "Angelo Beolco da Ruzante a Perduoçimo," in *Momenti*, pp. 94–192, 114 and note 73.
181 Giacomo Moro, "Foscarini, Ludovico," *DBI*, 49 (1997); on the Nogarola sisters, see Margaret
L. King and Albert R. Rabil Jr., eds, *Her Immaculate Hand: Selected Works by and about the
Women Humanists of Quattrocento Italy* (Binghamton, NY, 1983), pp. 16–18, 57–69; Anthony
Grafton and Lisa Jardine, *From Humanism to the Humanities* (Cambridge, 1986), p. 40; Margaret L. King, "Book-lined Cells: Women and Humanism in the Early Italian Renaissance," in
Renaissance Humanism: Foundations, Forms, and Legacy, ed. Albert R. Rabil Jr., 3 vols (Phila-
delphia, 1988), 1: 443; for play, Linda L. Carroll, "Dating the *Woman from Ancona*," *Sixteenth
Century Journal* 31 (2000): 963–85.
182 Sanuto, 40: 789–90; 25: 33.
183 Sanuto, 26: 53–4.

the senior brother in the collective portrait at the center of Titian's *Madonna di Ca' Pesaro*, acquired a connection to Ruzante through his daughter's marriage to the brother of an Ortolano and one to Zuan Francesco Valier through his son's marriage to Valier's half-sister.[184]

The Scuola dei Fiorentini moved from the original planned location of the Dominican church of San Zanipolo (Santi Giovanni e Paolo) to the Frari in 1443. Alessandro Parronchi has theorized that the move was prompted by Cosimo de' Medici's preference for the Franciscans, influential during the period of his exile spent in Venice shortly before.[185] The Martelli, who ran the Venice branch of the Medici bank and belonged to the *scuola* at the time of the move, were among the bankers with whom Zuan de Beolco worked in the last decade of the fifteenth century, in particular with their offices in Lyon and Florence and their colleagues the Spannocchi.[186] In the early sixteenth century, the Nerli—also among Zuan de Beolco's banking connections—along with their relatives and partners the Frescobaldi, assumed prominence as bankers in Venice and as members of the *scuola*.[187] The number of Florentines and of Medici affiliates in Venice was increased in early 1522 by the arrival of former residents of Leo X's court who had abandoned Rome at the election of Adrian, including the Venetian *cittadino* Zuan (Giovanni) Manenti (see Chapters 3 and 4). Their presence had cultural correlates, including the staging of Machiavelli's *Mandragola* by the Lucchese actor Cherea, a favorite of Leo's, during the 1522 Carnival, in which Manenti too was probably involved.[188]

The activities of Leo's former courtiers, the Florentine bankers, and their affiliates intertwined in interesting and as yet only partially known ways with those of Venice's governing councils and of Ruzante and his affiliates. In early 1522 Hironimo Bambarara, a ragpicker, organized a lottery to turn a small stake into a great deal of money. As Sanudo noted, Ludovico Afaitadi, a member of the wealthy Cremonese Afaitadi family that had many financial dealings with the Venetian state and leading patricians, wanted to put up a pool of 4,000 ducats for Bambarara's lottery. Perhaps not coincidentally, this was three days before the Senate entrusted Afaitadi with 4,000 ducats to send to Venice's French allies in Lombardy to pay the troops that they hoped would retake Milan, seized by imperial forces several months before.

In February, a few days after the staging of the Florentine play, the Venetian government, inspired by the success of the private initiative (or perhaps even covertly involved in it through Afaitadi), settled upon a state lottery as a new source of financing for the expensive Lombard war. The Provveditori di Comun named Manenti, whose service as a broker to patricians including Marco Grimani

---

184   See note 64 above.

185   Parronchi, pp. 96–7.

186   ASPd, *AO, ASC*, busta 231, fols 45–6.

187   Mueller, p. 240; de Roover, p. 337; Sanuto, 1: 725 and cf. 873–4.

188   Sanuto, 32: 458, 487; cf. 434, 445; for overview of Manenti, Dante Pattini, "Manenti, Giovanni," *DBI*, 68 (2007).

confirmed the level of trust that he enjoyed, to run it. He pledged the 4,000 ducats required, then turned to financiers to put up the funds: one half was provided by Piero Ram or Rames, the *consolo* (representative) of the Catalan merchants in Venice, one quarter by Gaspare Besalù, and an eighth by Ferigo dei Nerli. Given Charles's increasing pressure on Venice to join him in the Lombard war and the recent election as Pope Adrian VI of his former tutor, it is reasonable to hypothesize that the Venetian leadership saw an opportunity to turn the eagerness of Spaniards and other foreigners to influence Venice into a means of making them pay for Venice's pro-French campaign in Lombardy by underwriting the lottery. This would return the favor to Charles V, whose grandfather Maximilian, as the banker Alvise Pisani who underwrote the sum complained, had extracted war reparations from Venice in 1518 as a way of funding his ongoing efforts to take Venice's mainland state.[189]

However, by March 1 the financing had apparently been transferred to locals: Piero di Francesco Dall'Oro with a counter guarantee by Donado Malipiero qu. Pasquale. Certain details, though, hint that the cash was provided by the Afaitadi, possibly from government funds. The original investors underwrote instead a second lottery, run by the Bolognese Ludovico di Orazio, whose grand prize of 1,000 ducats was won by the Triumphanti. They, as well as Ferigo dei Nerli, Gaspare Besalù, and Lunardo Afaitadi all won prizes in Manenti's lottery, which was drawn in the Frari (probably the refectory of the monastery, currently the Sala di Studio of the Archivio di Stato). The dynamic would be repeated in the autumn of 1524 (see Chapter 3).[190]

Gaspare Besalù, the son and nephew of those buried in the Frari, was a member of the Ortolani. The *compagnia* hosted a festivity lasting more than eight hours for his wedding in 1518. In April 1519, despite his foreign origins, he was made a *cittadino*.[191] Shortly thereafter the Senate charged Cardinal Corner to work to resolve the payment of Venice's debt to the pope's banker Chigi, whose agents in Venice were the Besalù and later their relatives the Beltrame.[192] The Beltrame invested in Mafio Bernardo's re-founded bank in 1521.[193] Another Besalù helped finance a later state lottery, also together with the Beltrame and a Nerli, one not run by Manenti.[194] Despite their wealth, the family went bankrupt in 1530 with 80,000 ducats' worth of debt and sought shelter not in the monastery of the Frari but in that of San Zanipolo.[195]

---

189   ASVe, Provveditori di Comun, *Atti*, busta 9, fols 81ᵛ–3ᵛ, 85ʳ, 86ʳ; for Rames: Sanuto, 32: 107, 110–11, 163, 503; Tanai Nerli living Sant'Aponal: ASVe, *AGRM*, busta 357, unnumbered pergamena, date of July 24, 1523; another member of the Dall'Oro: Sanuto, 33: 423, 439, 447–8. See also Chapter 3 for further information. For 1518, Sanuto, 25: 581–2, 592, 596, 598.
190   Sanuto, 32: 502–3; Chapter 3.
191   Sanuto, 27: 187.
192   Sanuto, 25: 248, 668; 28: 618; 30: 31, 134, 290, 291, 469; ASVe, Senato, *Secreta*, reg. 48, fols 53ᵛ–4ʳ, 59ᵛ–60ʳ, 61ʳ⁻ᵛ, 77ʳ–80ʳ, 98ᵛ–9ᵛ.
193   Sanuto, 31: 182.
194   Sanuto, 37: 146; see Chapter 3.
195   Sanuto, 41: 22; 52: 598–9.

Alvise Pasqualigo, the imperial count, was an investor in the 1480s voyage; the family owned millwheels in Padua near the Beolco home and were adding to their mainland holdings during the period in which Angelo was performing in Venice.[196] A cousin of the prominent Pasqualigo brothers, Pietro qu. Marco, was a member of the Immortali. A resident of the Savonarola quarter of Padua located beyond the Santo, Pietro and his brother also had a house in Alvaroto's parish of Santa Sofia. Like Alvise Cornaro, the Pasqualigo owned agricultural property in Codevigo near Piove di Sacco, where Alvise Pasqualigo's sister ran her own large farm (as the peasant women characters of the *Betia* do). Pietro was chosen in 1523 by Cornaro to serve as the arbiter of a dispute. Pietro also had his own troubles; he lost the lucrative delegate to collect some of the bishop's tithes after failing to turn them over and was the subject of scandal when the former nun with whom he lived died unshriven.[197] In light of the unusually strong role of working class characters and women in Ruzante's plays, it is interesting to note that one of the Pasqualigo brothers' properties in Venice housed a school where a 'maestra' taught little girls as well as little boys to read.[198] That Sanudo does not take any special note of little girls being included in the school or of the teacher's being a woman may hint that the situation was more common than currently thought.

The last of the Frari patrons, Pietro Bernardo qu. Hironimo, had numerous, though indirect, links to Angelo Beolco and his circle. His uncle Antonio was a lecturer in law at the University of Padua, where the Alvaroto were prominent in that field. He had a house at *livello* in Padua in a cluster belonging to the bishopric, one of which was Marc'Aurelio's home. His large holdings in the *padovano*[199] included the Bastia of Strà, possibly echoed in the name of Donna Menega Bastia of the *Betia*. Pietro's brother Sebastian also had at *livello* a house from the Paduan bishopric in Santa Sofia and various other properties in and around Padua.[200] Sebastian helped lead the forces that retook Padua in 1509.[201] However, his participation straying into sacking and the desecration of female monasteries, he was called before the Council of Ten and deprived of candidacy for office for a year. Shortly thereafter, his offer of a large loan to the state resulted in his admission to the Senate on special conditions, although he was later accused of cheating to obtain it.[202] Both Sebastiano and Piero were involved in the Guidotti bribing scandal.

196 VBMC, mss. Provenienze Diverse c, 833 / XIII; ASPd, *Estimo 1518*, busta 352, fol. 80ᵛ; ASVe, *Ufficiali alle Rason Vecchie*, reg. 48, fols 34ᵛ–5ʳ, 42ᵛ–5ᵛ.

197 ASPd, *Estimo 1518*, busta 358, fol. 43ʳ; busta 352, fol. 132ᵛ; ASPd, *Notarile*, busta 1116, fol. 433ʳ⁻ᵛ; busta 1315, fol. 260ᵛ; busta 2734, fols 56ʳ–7ʳ; da Corte, fol. 204ᵛ.

198 Sanuto, 26: 131.

199 Barbaro, 2: 17; PACV, *Acta capitularia*, vol. 15, fol. 229ʳ⁻ᵛ; ASPd, *Estimo 1518*, busta 352, fols 137ʳ, 253ᵛ.

200 PACV, *Acta capitularia*, vol. 15, fol. 229ʳ⁻ᵛ; ASPd, *Estimo 1518*, busta 352, fols 252ᵛ–3ʳ; busta 354, fol. 116ʳ; busta 358, fols 57ᵛ–8ᵛ.

201 Sanuto, 8: 522–4.

202 Sanuto, 8: 528–9, 534, 550; 9: 66, 71, 169–70; 10: 248, 261–2; 12: 167.

Hironimo di Nicolò, Pietro's second cousin once removed, was a Triumphante; he won a prize in Manenti's first lottery. His father Nicolò—great-grandson of Doge Francesco Foscari, nephew of Marin Venier, former *podestà* of Padua, and member of governing councils during the Cambrai wars active in efforts to regain the mainland state—attended the 1525 performance.[203]

Tentative Conclusions

The consistent pattern evidenced in the above data allows some tentative conclusions.

The first involves the intricate interrelationships among the devotional themes of the works of art commissioned for the Frari, prominent theological issues, and the life activities of the patrons. Goffen connects the Marian theme in the Pesaro Frari canvases with the Franciscan emphasis on Mary as merciful intercessor with Christ on behalf of sinners.[204] Frari patrons would have been well aware of the greatest image of Mary's intercession in their dominions, Giotto's *Final Judgment* depicting a Scrovegni ancestor of the Corner offering to Mary the chapel he had commissioned to encourage her intercession to save him from eternal damnation for the sin of usury. The frescoes adorned Padua's Arena Chapel, in this period purchased by the Foscari. While the chapel was in a private home, Giotto was an artist particularly identified with the Franciscans, as was Padua through St. Anthony. It would seem that Mary's intercession was of particular interest to those engaged in commercial and financial endeavors that could or did verge into practices condemned by the Church. The number of merchants who by family or by *scuola* associated themselves with the Frari would seem to indicate that it became particularly the church of merchants.

The second tentative conclusion involves the number of works commissioned of artists from Venice's mainland dominion, especially Padua, which would seem to indicate that through such commissions, as through involvement in other of the creative and performing arts as detailed in Chapters 2 and 3, patricians sought to foster connectedness between themselves and the mainlanders whom they governed. The successful rejection of Venetian rule by many mainland cities after the defeat of Agnadello signaled how much resentment could fester there and it was to Venice's advantage to neutralize it by offering to certain mainlanders an affirmative or profitable connection to the capital and influential patricians.

The third tentative conclusion involves patricians' use of selected non-patricians as unofficial conduits to outside governments or individuals as sources of information, conveyors of messages, and generally instruments for advancing Venetian interests, but also the potential for such individuals to extract as many advantages for themselves as possible from their favored situation. The enormous increase in power achieved by Charles in his election to the imperial throne made him the most important external power to be dealt with. Months

203   Sanuto, 32: 503; 37: 559; Barbaro, 2: 14.
204   Goffen, *Piety*, p. 98.

after he was elected emperor, Angelo Beolco, whose paternal family belonged to the Milanese imperial faction and were financiers to the Sforza, performed in public in Venice for the first time in a festivity for Federico II Gonzaga that featured a Trojan theme favored by the Habsburgs. During the years of his Venetian performances, the Republic moved closer to the empire, joining a formal alliance that included Milan in 1523. Beolco's final, scandal-associated performance as Ruzante in Venice in 1526 occurred weeks before the Serenissima publicly reverted to its preferred alliance with France. The exact correspondence between the temporal arc of his visits and the period in which Venice attempted to find a *modus vivendi* with Charles does not seem coincidental. Neither does the revival during that period of the business relationship between Ruzante's father and his Milanese cousin at precisely the time in which Charles pressured Venice into alliance with him and Milan and in which Venetian merchants began to consider land commerce as a means of saving northern trade from interference with maritime routes.

The known crucial assistance that the Beolco family provided Venetian merchants in the 1480s and the prospect of their assistance in the 1520s along with potential useful connections to adherents of the empire go a long way to explaining Ruzante's audacious 'telling of truth to power' to his Venetian hosts.[205] For a brief period of time, their need of his family and other members of his circle made them tolerant of his candor, even at the expense of having to hear some difficult truths about themselves and some advice uttered through Beolco's transparent mask of Ruzante. Perhaps their tolerance was increased by the fact that some of their own had been telling the same difficult truths and giving them the same advice since the defeat of Agnadello. However, Venice's official alliance with France in 1526 immediately put a full stop to that period. It seems that Beolco immediately went into army service to fight for a side whose values he rejected, as he makes clear in the *Reduce* of that period, perhaps because of the dependence on patronage caused by his exclusion from inheritance, perhaps out of a sense of loyalty to those who had supported him, or perhaps simply to satisfy his craving to be where the action was. The service, however, clearly generated the deep and corrosive inner conflict giving rise to the apparent madness of his character in the *Reduce* and the alternation between servility and bombastic but ultimately empty rebellion of the *Moscheta*.

---

205 See Carroll, "Ruzante Speaks Truth to Venetian Power: Some Hows, Whys, Whens, and Wherefores," in *Speaking Truth to Power*, ed. Jo Ann Cavallo, forthcoming.

2   Bodleian Library Canonician Ital. 36

Stefano Magno and the Move from Commerce to Culture

Introduction

Owned by Venetian patrician Jacopo Soranzo and subsequently by the Venetian Jesuit Matteo Luigi Canonici, the anonymous manuscript currently denominated Canonician Ital. 36 entered Oxford's Bodleian Library with the purchase of the latter's collection. Because the manuscript and its contents, some of which are unique and of great interest, have not been the subject of special study, the approach here will be to identify the copyist and provide information about his life and interests, identify and elucidate the contents of the manuscript, and indicate how they reflect the tastes and goals of the copyist and of some important Venetian and mainland cultural figures of the time.

The manuscript illustrates and embodies the move of many young patricians away from their families' former involvement in commerce and in governance and toward written endeavors including the compiling of historical records and literary texts. It and other manuscripts compiled by the same copyist indicate, moreover, that the interest of these Venetians in literary and theatrical activities particularly encompassed works linking the capital city with its mainland dominion and the courtly traditions of the mainland's (former) ruling classes. The forging of such linkages in the decades just before and just after 1500 resulted from and furthered the Venetian patrician turn to the mainland as an alternative source of goods such as income, foodstuffs, and primary materials for manufacturing, as well as for power and pleasure. The development was necessitated by the perfect storm of Portuguese competition, Turkish aggression, and European warfare that made Venice's traditional far-flung maritime commerce unreliable and dangerous at best and impossible at worst. A second, related development was Venetian cultivation of the benefices and offices of the Catholic Church, whose wealth and international scope compensated for the restriction of their civic and commercial endeavors. Extensive material from previously-unutilized manuscript sources will be presented below in the service of penetrating the mythologized collectivity of the Venetian patriciate by identifying specific patricians and families who organized such linkages and describing the means by which they did so. A wealth of detail is given to provide a map of such sources to other scholars.

Canonician 36 measures 8 3/4 inches or 22 centimeters in height including the binding (the paper 8½ inches or 21.5 centimeters) and 6½ inches or 16.5 centimeters in width including the binding (the paper about 6 inches, or about 15.5 centimeters).[1] Containing a miscellany of literary works in Italian and Latin, chiefly poetry, the manuscript bears the rubric "Jesus 1520 Vene[tiis]" at the top of the recto and the verso of most folios. The hand is consistent throughout, in a cursive style used widely by notaries and also by Venetian merchants, chiefly in a slightly earlier period but maintained by important merchant families into the early sixteenth century.[2] As Carlo Dionisotti recognized, Canonician 36 was compiled by the Venetian patrician Stefano Magno qu. Andrea, a prolific copyist of poetic and dramatic works as well as the author of chronicles and sourcebooks. Appearing only in footnotes of others, Dionisotti's identification has not been further developed.[3]

Stefano Magno initiated the collection of literary works when he was about twenty, apparently with Canonician 36.[4] It embodies the ethos of manuscript circulation in the early age of print which, as Brian Richardson observed, "created and fostered a sense of close communication and solidarity among those with similar interests and tastes."[5] It appears to have functioned as a kind of first-stage repository of items of interest, the extreme heterogeneity of its contents somewhat reminiscent

---

1 The manuscript hereafter will be referred to as Canonician 36. Partial information is provided by Alessandro de Mortara, *Catalogo dei manoscritti italiani che sotto la denominazione di codici canoniciani italici si conservano nella Biblioteca Bodleiana a Oxford* (Oxonii, 1864), cols 42–6; M.A.F. Madan, *A Summary Catalogue of Western Manuscripts in the Bodleian Library at Oxford*, 7 vols (Oxford, 1897), 4: 412; Massimo Castoldi, *Per il testo critico delle rime di Girolamo Verità* (Verona, 2000), p. 85; Valerio Marucci, Antonio Marzo e Angelo Romano, eds, *Pasquinate romane del Cinquecento*, 2 vols (Rome, 1983), 1: nos 202, 170, 180, 184, 178, 191, 204, 101, 102 [citations are to the number of the poem rather than page number]; while the *Indice dei capoversi* (2: 1118) lists Canonician as the source for no. 205, it is not, although no. 205 is a variant of no. 202.

2 For examples see ASPd, *Estimo 1518*, busta 352, fols 237ᵛ–40ᵛ; PACV, *Acta capitularia*, vol. 11, unnumbered sheet inserted between fols 44 and 45; ASVe, *Archivio Grimani Santa Maria Formosa*, busta 2, unnumbered fascicle, fol. dated 1521; *AGB*, busta 8, unnumbered doc. dated 1519, hand of Hironimo Grimani di Marin, a member of the *compagnia della calza* Triumphanti and the uncle of the future wife of Stefano Magno, for whom see below.

3 Giorgio Padoan, *La commedia rinascimentale veneta* (Vicenza, 1982), p. 251; the identification also appears (though not attributed to Carlo Dionisotti) in Bianca Maria Da Rif, "Introduzione," *La letteratura 'alla bulesca'. Testi rinascimentali veneti* (Padua, 1984), ed. Bianca Maria Da Rif, pp. 3–47, p. 43 note 11. Curiously, in the copy of Girolamo Verità, *Girolamo Verità. Filosofo e poeta veronese*, ed. Lamberto Carlini (Verona, 1905) of the library of Harvard University, where Prof. Dionisotti gave a seminar in literature in the early 1970s that I was privileged as a graduate student to attend, there is a slip of paper marking a work of Verità's included in Canonician 36. For the miscellany's hand as identical to that used by Magno in other manuscripts see *e.g.* VBMC, ms. Cicogna 3533.

4 ASVe, Marco Barbaro, *Arbori dei patritii veneti*, copied by Tommaso Corner and Antonio Maria Tasca (1743); ASVe, *Misc. Codici I, Storia Veneta* 17 (hereafter Barbaro), 4: 376; Emmanuele Antonio Cicogna, *Delle iscrizioni veneziane raccolte ed illustrate*, 6 vols (Venice, 1827), 5: 225–31.

5 Brian Richardson, *Manuscript Culture in Renaissance Italy* (Cambridge, 2009), pp. 1–2.

of the Venetian merchant handbook known as the *zibaldone*.[6] In terms of literary traditions, its formation corresponds to the explication that William Prizer has given to the Mantuan manuscript MAc A.I.4: "a continuing repository for *poesie*."[7] Or, as Rodolfo Renier observed of a manuscript of the works of Il Pistoia: "Il cod. Trivulziano è una specie di gazzettino, così personale come pubblico. Sembra proprio che tutte le impressioni, i desideri, i bisogni del poeta gli si venissero concretando nella forma del sonetto" (The Trivulzian manuscript is a species of gazette, both private and public. It truly seems that all the impressions, the desires, and the needs of the poet take material shape there in the form of sonnets).[8]

While the subject matter of works was eclectic, Magno's arrangement of them was strictly by genre, with each section labeled. He included over one hundred sonnets (nine of which involve the election of Adrian VI), a pasquinade, two collections of inscriptions on medals, ballots and commentary on the election of Adrian VI, 16 *capitoli*, 17 *canzoni*, two eclogues, 12 madrigals, four *frottole*, a prose *novella*, a poem to be recited by five, another *capitolo*, an *ottava*, two love letters, and 15 epitaphs. Some of the works are serious, some comic, and some scandalous. Although he omitted the names of many of the authors, Alessandro de Mortara identified the sonnets as largely by Pietro Bembo, Giovanni Antonio Brocardo and Bernardino Daniello of Lucca; some of the *capitoli* as by Bembo, Ludovico Ariosto, Andrea Navagero, Bernardino Daniello, and Onofrio Veronese; most of the *canzoni* as by Ariosto, Bembo, Brocardo, Girolamo Verità, Francesco Maria Molza, and Daniello; and eleven of the madrigals as works of Daniello and one of Onofrio Veronese. As will be detailed below, the authors of some additional works have been identified, while others remain anonymous. Dating of the works in the absence of external evidence is complicated by the fact that the date inscribed at the top of the folios is the one on which the manuscript was inaugurated (not the one on which a given folio had work entered onto it) and by the division into genre sections, to which works were apparently added separately on various dates.

Biographical Background

The Magno family's history and activities in this period exemplify the Venetian turn from maritime mercantile endeavors to mainland and cultural interests. As Canonician 36's compiler twice observes, his father served as *capitanio* of

6   See, *e.g.* Anon., *Merchant Culture in Fourteenth Century Venice. The Zibaldone da Canal*, translated with an introduction and notes by John E. Dotson (Binghamton, NY, 1994); Pamela O. Long, David McGee, and Alan M. Stahl, eds, *The Book of Michael of Rhodes. A Fifteenth-Century Maritime Manuscript*, 3 vols (Cambridge, MA and London, 2009).

7   William Prizer, *Courtly Pastimes. The Frottole of Marchetto Cara* (Ann Arbor, 1974), p. 31. Despite the association with music of many of the poetic genres that Canonician 36 includes, the musical element is absent.

8   Rodolfo Renier, "Prefazione," in Antonio Cammelli, Il Pistoia, *I sonetti del Pistoia giustal'apografo trivulziano*, ed. Rodolfo Renier, Biblioteca di Testo Inediti o Rari 2 (Turin, 1888), pp. vii–xlviii, p. xxx.

Padua. In 1518, to that office's duties was added the preservation of real estate tax records (Estimo) then undergoing renewal for the purpose of defense financing. Given Padua's critical role as the bastion of Venice's mainland defense and its large revenue, its *capitaniato* was held by trusted patricians who, over a long public career, had proved worthy of the responsibility. Such was the copyist's father, Andrea Magno qu. Stefano, who in 1520 at the age of 67 was elected both a member of the Council of Ten and *capitanio* of Padua.[9] He had only recently returned from another important governorship, the *podestaria* of Verona. Also important and wealthy, Verona was the last mainland town regained by Venice from the peninsular and continental powers arrayed against it in the wars of the League of Cambrai (1509–17). During Magno's *podestaria*, Verona hosted the successful treaty negotiations between the Republic and Maximilian I that concluded the wars.

Andrea's 1520 electoral victories reflected his able conduct of the numerous important offices he had held, recorded by his son Stefano and by diarist Marin Sanudo.[10] Andrea's public life had begun early, with his father Stefano sponsoring him for the Barbarella, a lottery that allowed a small number of patricians to enter the Maggior Consiglio, or basic legislative body, at the age of 18 instead of 25.[11] The elder Magno's eagerness may have stemmed from his own failings: in the early 1430s his participation in a plot hatched by his older brother and a group of patricians to rig elections in their favor had resulted in his banishment from Venice for a year.[12] He rehabilitated himself on his return, obtaining the low-ranking but not unimportant state job of guardian of Padua's Saracinesca Gate. He married in 1442, to non-patrician Isabetta de Lunardi. His son Andrea, who seems to have been determined to cleanse the family name through absolute probity, fared much better. After an initial election, Andrea's *curriculum* displays the typical patrician hiatus of two decades, during which he was engaged in commerce in Damascus. Respect for his mercantile acumen was demonstrated in his election as *consolo dei mercanti* (representative of the merchant community) in Alexandria,

---

9   Marino Sanuto, *I diarii*, ed. Rinaldo Fulin et al., 58 vols (Venice, 1879–1902), 29: 146; the error in this passage that he had been elected *podestà* had created some confusion among earlier scholars, but the consistency of all other entries (*e.g.* 29: 566, 642; 30: 492; 31: 131, 234, 337, 340; 33: 384) and of other documents (*e.g.* PSVBA, ms. 555, Antonio Monterosso, *Reggimenti di Padova dal 1459 sino al 1533 Reggimenti*, vol. 4, fasc. X, fols 34ʳ–5ʳ) in their identification of the office as *capitanio* leaves no doubt. Cf. Giorgio Padoan, "La *Veniexiana*: 'Non fabula non comedia ma vera historia'," in *Momenti del Rinascimento veneto* (Padua, 1978), pp. 284–346, 285–6.

10 Sanuto, 3–28 *s.v.*; VBM, Ital. VII, 513–18 [=7879–84], Stefano Magno, *Cronaca Magno*; VII, 515 [=7881], fols 169ʳ–77ʳ. Vol. VII, 515 is of greatest interest to the present analysis; further references will be to it unless otherwise specified.

11 Barbaro, 4: 376; on the Barbarella, Stanley Chojnacki, "Kinship Ties and Young Patricians," *Women and Men in Renaissance Venice. Twelve Essays on Patrician Society* (Baltimore and London, 2000), pp. 206–26.

12 PSVBA, ms. 609, fols 130ᵛ–31ʳ; Donald E. Queller, *The Venetian Patriciate. Reality versus Myth* (Urbana, 1986), pp. 79–80.

the important north African entrepôt where the Magno, like many Venetian patrician families, were involved in commerce.[13]

In the last years of the fifteenth century, Andrea returned to Venice and undertook his public career, in 1498 being elected *proveditore di comun*. In 1499 he married Isabetta Giustinian di Onfrè, a member of a large and prosperous clan well connected to many other important ones of the day. He achieved increasingly prestigious offices including Senator; membership in one of the committees electing the doge (Leonardo Loredan); governorships of militarily important locales such as the border town of Crema; offices with fiscal and decision-making responsibilities including the salt commission, the tax commission, the revenue commission; and numerous terms on the Council of Ten, as one of its monthly Heads, and as its treasurer. He was among those patriotic Venetians offering to personally send men to defend Padua and Treviso in one of the darkest moments of the wars of the League of Cambrai.[14]

As demonstrated by his declaration for the 1518 Estimo, Andrea invested his rather meagre capital in a carefully chosen series of agricultural properties in the *padovano* beginning in 1498. His decision represented a first move away from his family's mercantile history, and occurred after severe and continuing disruptions to trade had begun. He pursued real estate acquisitions even through the early years of the Cambrai war, when property was unusually cheap because of the destruction that the fighting wrought on the region. The pieces were located chiefly in the area north of Padua, perhaps not coincidentally that upon which the Porta Saracinesca looks, especially near Limena and Cittadella, close together and mainly suited to grain-growing. The demanial house and workers' *cortivo* near Limena were burned during the war; Andrea prudently first rebuilt the *cortivo*, which provided work space as well as worker dwellings, and then reconstructed the house.[15]

Although it has been assumed that Stefano was born shortly after Andrea and Isabetta's marriage, the circumstances surrounding the younger Magno's entrance into the Maggior Consiglio may hint otherwise. In January of 1515, in an expansion of the Barbarella, the Council of Ten decided to permit entrance at the age of 18 in exchange for a loan to the state of 100 ducats. In December of 1516, just weeks after his father had completed a term on the prestigious Ducal Council that presided over the Ten, Stefano approached the latter body and offered to lend an additional 50 ducats to be allowed to enter the Maggior Consiglio even before 18. It should be noted that here, as elsewhere, Stefano in his record leaves a blank for the day of the month on which this occurred; Sanudo records the action at December 23, where he observes that "li manca certo tempo" (he falls short by some time).[16] Whether or not 'certo' carries the disdainful overtones here that it

13   VBM, *Cronaca Magno*, fol. 170ᵛ; Sanuto, 39: 335.
14   See Sanuto, *s.v.*, esp. 6: 392; 9: 519; 15: 136; 17: 254, 431, 438; 26: 252.
15   For Andrea's holdings, see ASPd, *Estimo 1518*, busta 352, fols 323ᵛ–4ʳ.
16   Sanuto, 23: 261, 360.

often does in Sanudo's prose, the date raises a delicate question. Even if Andrea had married very early in 1499, Stefano, if legitimately conceived, could not have been born before the end of that year; moreover, if the marriage occurred early in the year recorded as 1499 in the Venetian practice (*more veneto*), in which the year was not changed until March, it would correspond to 1500 in the common system. At the very earliest, then, Stefano would have turned 18 at the end of 1517 and could have done so as much as two years later. An early conception or birth may explain the marriage between a daughter of one of Venice's most successful families and the son of a scapegrace and a commoner. Casualness in such matters was then drawing the opprobrium of the Venetian government, which shortly thereafter began to institute new requirements for maintaining the patrician status of offspring: in 1506 the registration of births within a week of their occurrence and in 1526 the registration of marriages and verification of the bride's patrician status, similarly time-restricted.[17]

Stefano made permanent his father's disengagement from commerce, whose declining profits and increasing dangers were reified in the 1517 shipwreck that cost his kinsman Vicenzo his fortune and his life (see Chapter 3).[18] Nor, at first, did Stefano make much effort to seek public office. His first nomination came in 1523, and it was by his father and without success. The most important factor in the paucity of nominations, beyond his extreme youth, was probably his family's relative poverty and his father's choice to invest his slim capital in land. Such poverty was a severe handicap at the time, when the emptying of state coffers by war expenses and lack of revenue had resulted in the practice of a substantial loan as a prerequisite to candidacy to state office. It was not until Stefano's own marriage provided him with a significant dowry that he again was nominated, this time for the prestigious *Ufficio ale raxon vecchie*, whose duties included the sale of state-held lands to private parties. Sanudo records that his candidacy was accompanied by a 400-ducat loan.[19]

During his youthful fallow period Stefano accompanied his father to his mainland posts, participating in some of the duties. He distinguished himself while his father was *podestà* of Verona, escorting Count Cristoforo Frangipani, a captured imperialist enemy sent there for a prisoner exchange.[20] While on the mainland Stefano came into contact with local cultural circles, whose predilections included highly-developed traditions of courtly love lyric and of theater, in whose importation to a Venice increasingly fascinated with courtliness and the stage he became a leader.[21] Among the authors for whose works he developed

17 Victor Crescenzi, *"Esse de Maiori Consilio": legittimità civile e legittimazione politica nella Repubblica di Venezia (secc. XIII–XVI)* (Rome, 1996).

18 Sanuto, 24: 11–12, 18, 22–31, 211 (Vicenzo misidentified as Stefano).

19 VBM, *Cronaca Magno*, fol. 178r–v; Sanuto, 37: 440; 43: 734.

20 Sanuto, 26: 199, 211, 383.

21 James S. Grubb, *Firstborn of Venice. Vicenza in the Early Renaissance State* (Baltimore, 1988), pp. 171–2 for Venetian turn to fascination with courts.

a taste was the Veronese Girolamo Verità.[22] It apparently was in Verona, too, that he became acquainted with the custom of compiling repositories of literary works. Some of the paper that he used for his literary manuscripts bears water-marks characteristic of Verona in this period.[23] He undertook the Canonician manuscript on his return to Venice in 1520, as he faithfully recorded on its folios. He opened its contents with a striking address to the reader: "Si sapis excipie[n]s auru[m] de stercore lector / Emus iste tibj tu maro lector eris" (Reader, if you know how to extract gold from dung, you will acquire this and you will be a Virgil).[24] The combination of high and low culture embodied by the address and by the rest of the manuscript's contents makes clear that Magno's intended readers were intimates, fellow youthful patricians or their adherents, with broad cultural interests.[25]

A brief excursus into some of Magno's other manuscript endeavors will pro-vide background for a more thorough examination of Canonician 36. The (later) author of a chronicle of Venice, a four-volume set of *annali* of Venice, and a volume on the origin of Venetian patrician families,[26] Magno in this early period in addition to Canonician 36 produced at least two other manuscripts preserving key contributions to Venice's literary riches. Camillo Soranzo, a librarian of Venice's Biblioteca Marciana, first identified him as the anonymous copyist-collector of a manuscript miscellany of plays in the library's collection containing Angelo Beolco's *Pastoral* (VBM, ital. cl. IX, 288 [=6072]). Noting that the copyist prefixed the date '1521' to the manuscript folios and concluded the transcription with a statement that he came into possession of the play when his father was *capitanio* of Padua, Soranzo demonstrated that the *capitanio* in question was Andrea Magno, that his son Stefano was the author of the *Cronaca Magno* also in the library's collection, and that Stefano was the copyist of the *Pastoral*.[27] Giorgio Padoan advanced understanding of the manuscript signifi-cantly through an analysis showing that the *Pastoral* was originally part of a

22   A curious detail: as *podestà*, Andrea Magno dispensed justice in the case of a Girolamo Verità, victim of an attack, although it was likely a homonymous kinsman rather than the poet: Sanuto, 27: 66; Gioacchino Brognoligo, "Rime inedite di Girolamo Verità," *Studi di letteratura italiana* 7 (1906): 98–129, 101–3.

23   Emilio Lovarini, "La *Pastoral*," in *Studi sul Ruzzante e sulla letteratura pavana*, ed. Gianfranco Folena (Padua: 1965), pp. 271–92, esp. 273–4; Giorgio Padoan, "Introduzione" and "Nota ai testi," in Beolco, *La Pastoral*, ed. and trans. G. Padoan, pp. 1–57, esp. 29–30. The presence of such watermarks on folii 1–5 invalidates Da Rif's statement (p. 40) that these sheets were added in an eighteenth-century restoration.

24   Fol. iiʳ. I am grateful to Dr. Roberto Nicosia for assistance with the translation.

25   Cf. Richardson, *Manuscript Culture*, pp. 259–68.

26   VBM, It. cl. VII, 513–18 [=7879–84], Stefano Magno, *Cronaca Magno*; VBMC, mss Cicogna 3529–33, Stefano Magno, *Annali Veneti*, of which the first volume, ms. Cicogna 3529, is the *Origine delle case patrizie*.

27   Ruzzante, *La Pastorale*, ed. Emilio Lovarini, Filologia Italiana e Romanza. Biblioteca di Studi Superiori, 14 (Florence, 1951); Ruzante, *La Pastoral* in *RT*; Angelo Beolco Il Ruzante, *La Pas-toral, la Prima Orazione, Una lettera giocosa*, ed. and trans. Giorgio Padoan, Medioevo e Uman-esimo, 32 (Padua, 1978).

different manuscript, the remainder of which is VBM ital. cl. IX, 71 [=5938].[28] Both will be described below.

Stefano Magno's connections through his mother's numerous siblings to other patricians with literary interests and endeavors were also documented by Padoan. Further research establishes additional family connections and support of the literary and performative worlds. Stefano's maternal aunt Lucietta, the wife of Pietro Dolfin, became the mother not only of Lorenzo Dolfin (who, as Magno records in IX, 71, provided the manuscript of its initial work) but of Nicolò and Dolfin Dolfin. Nicolò, a prominent figure in the development of vernacular literary culture in the early sixteenth century, published an edition of Boccaccio's *Decameron*.[29] Dolfin was a member of the Ortolani, the *compagnia della calza* most closely associated with Beolco and to which the Giustinian family contributed three of the 43 members. He was also the dedicatee of poems in a collection likely to have also contained poems by the Veronese Lodovico Corfino, whose *Philetus* is contained in a Veronese manuscript bound with one containing several of Beolco's works.[30]

The Manuscript

Canonician 36, the first known literary manuscript transcribed or compiled by Magno, provides some valuable clues concerning his practices. He inscribed the date (often missing the day) and place of its inauguration at the head of each folio, as he did with the manuscript of the *Pastoral*. That the manuscript was only begun in 1520 and not completely transcribed in that year becomes clear through details including Stefano's reference to his late father, whose date of death was 1525.[31] Precise conclusions about the dates of the works included in the manuscript and of their copying thus become difficult if not impossible in the absence of external

---

28 Padoan, "Introduzione" and "Nota ai testi," 1–38; Giorgio Padoan, "Sulla fortuna della *Pastoral*, della *Veniexiana* e di altri testi," in *Momenti*, pp. 193–207.

29 Brian Richardson, *Print Culture in Renaissance Italy: The Editor and the Vernacular Text 1470–1600* (Cambridge, 1994), p. 60; Simona Foà, "Dolfin, Niccolò," *DBI*, 40 (1991), however the statement there that he was "Figlio di Pietro di Fantino di una figlia di Dolfin di Onfrè di Pangrati Giustinian" erroneously blends Nicolò's paternal and maternal lines; he was, instead, the son of Pietro di Fantin Dolfin and of a daughter (Lucietta) of Onfrè di Pangrati Giustinian: Barbaro, 3: 289.

30 For *compagnie della calza* in general, see Matteo Casini, "The 'Company of the Hose': Youth and Courtly Culture in Europe, Italy, and Venice," *Studi Veneziani* 63 (2011): 1217–37; for the Ortolani, see Linda L. Carroll, "Venetian Attitudes toward the Young Charles: Carnival, Commerce, and *Compagnie della Calza*," in Alain Saint-Saëns, ed., *Young Charles V, 1500–1529* (New Orleans, 2000), pp. 13–52 and bibliography cited therein; for Dolfin Dolfin, Linda L. Carroll, "Introduction," in Angelo Beolco (Il Ruzante), *La prima oratione*, ed. and trans. Linda L. Carroll, MHRA Critical Texts vol. 16 (London, 2009), pp. 5–74, esp. pp. 14, 29, 30–32, 36, 46, 70, and with the family relationship here corrected to cousin; for Corfino, see Giuseppe Biadego, "Notizie," in Ludovico Corfino, *Istoria di Phileto veronese*, ed. Giuseppe Biadego (Livorno, 1899), pp. ix–xxvii, xviii–xx.

31 Canonician 36, fols 82ʳ–3ᵛ; Sanuto, 39: 335.

evidence. One sure observation about the manuscript, on the other hand, is the strict division of the works by genre, similar to the rubric 'Libro de comedie de piu hautori' (Book of comedies by various authors) that Magno prefixed to the miscellany to which he transferred the *Pastoral*. The divisions are underlined by his marking of each section's conclusion with the (incorrect) Greek word τελωσ (*recte* τελωσ); that Magno intended to add works to several sections is evident from the rubricated blank folios and lack of the concluding τελωσ.

The arrangement is as follows: sonnets (1ʳ–40ᵛ), *capitoli* (41ʳ–61ᵛ), *canzoni* (67ʳ–90ʳ, but 62–6 are blank and the folio now numbered 67 originally bore the number 73, indicating that sheets were removed as from VBM Ital. Cl. IX, 288), 90ᵛ–98ᵛ blank but with rubric 'canzon' and no τελωσ, 99ʳ [but renumbered, originally 100]–120ᵛ eclogues, 121ʳ–3ᵛ madrigals but missing τελωσ, 124ʳ–30ᵛ blank but with madrigal rubrication, 131ʳ–8ᵛ *frottole*, 139ʳ–46ᵛ blank but with *frottola* rubrication; 147ʳ–56ʳ a novella; 156ᵛ–7ᵛ a *stanza*; 158ʳ–60ᵛ love letters; 161ʳ–2ᵛ epitaphs; 163ʳ–9ᵛ blank. The heavy paper used evidences no watermark. The method for analyzing the material here will be to first list the contents of a given section and then provide elucidation.

Opening the manuscript is the section devoted to sonnets, beginning with one whose author's initials P.B. are easily decoded as 'Pietro Bembo' (fol. 1ʳ). It is a youthful version of *Sì come suol, poi che 'verno aspro e rio* (As is the custom, given the bitter and awful winter) found also in a manuscript of the Biblioteca Ambrosiana, which Carlo Dionisotti dated to no later than 1503.[32] The section continues with works labeled simply 'Soneto' until fol. 10ʳ, where Magno enters 'Soneto d[e]l brocardo' (Sonnet by Brocardo) and transcribes *Donque fia 'l ver ch'el caro ben pur lasj* (Thus could it be true that you even leave your beloved). He next transcribes two unattributed sonnets; then three further sonnets by Brocardo; six anonymous ones; one labeled as by S.N., Jacopo Sannazaro's *Sonanti liti e voi rigidi scogli* (Echoing beaches, and you, rigid boulders; *Rime disperse* VII)[33]; a sonnet by Brocardo; and one addressing Brocardo. Following these is a series of topical or occasional sonnets that begins with three dedicated to Paduan women. Next is a curious group of works, largely but not entirely sonnets, commenting in frequently scabrous terms on the election of the successor to Leo X and on matters in the Roman Curia in general. These are followed by a group of sonnets by Bernardino da Lucca (Bernardino Daniello), interrupted by one by Unico Aretino (Bernardo Accolti). The section concludes with a group of anonymous sonnets and is sealed with Magno's τελωσ (fol. 40ᵛ).

The Sonnets

The above overview indicates that genre sections were further organized by sub-sections according to topic or affiliation. The first group of sonnets is by Pietro Bembo and authors associated with him. In 1519, Bembo returned to Venice from

32 Pietro Bembo, *Prose e Rime di Pietro Bembo*, ed. Carlo Dionisotti, 2nd ed. (Turin, 1966), p. 508.
33 Jacopo Sannazaro, *Opere volgari*, ed. Alfredo Mauro (Bari, 1961), pp. 228–9.

Rome for a year,[34] possibly the inspiration for the collection and the subgroup. The Petrarchan themes and vocabulary of the sonnets by Brocardo, a Venetian born around 1500 who joined the circles of Trifon Gabriele and Pietro Bembo subsequent to philosophical studies in Bologna and Padua, indicate that they, like the others, were of this early period.[35] Sannazaro, who had warm relations with Bembo, was a favored literary figure in Venice, where his *Arcadia* was frequently printed and copied and where the maritime theme of the sonnet chosen by Magno may have held particular appeal.[36] The overall impression given by the works in this section, thus, is that a very youthful Magno collected them in Venice, transcribing them at the manuscript's inauguration in 1520.

Initiating the following group of sonnets is one dedicated to Paduan women (fol. 21ʳ "Soneto d[e] le done padoane"). While identification of individual women is rendered uncertain by the indirectness and incompleteness of details, some reasonable hypotheses may be offered about some of them. Leading the series is an "excelsa cavaliera . . . tanto urbina al suo marito e chara" (highest consort of a knight, so urbane to her husband and dear). The title 'cavaliera' and attribute 'urbina' might hint that she was Eleonora, the wife of Francesco Maria della Rovere Duke of Urbino and the daughter of Gian Francesco Gonzaga Marquis of Mantua and Isabella d'Este Gonzaga. In 1520, shortly after her marriage, Eleonora accompanied her brother, Federico II Gonzaga, to Venice for the feast of the Sensa and a festivity in his honor sponsored by the Immortali, which had inducted him during Carnival with the festivity including the Ruzante play usually identified as the *Pastoral*.[37] Her husband, then in exile from his duchy after Leo X had seized it, became involved in the growing conflict in Lombardy as a *condottiero*. In early 1522, after Leo's death, he regained his state and the following year was hired as the *capitano generale* of the Venetian army.[38] He brought his wife to Padua, where the army was headquartered, in early 1525. Shortly thereafter, as the war in Lombardy between Charles and Francis escalated, he set up his command in Verona, where she soon followed him.[39] The limitation of her time as a 'Paduan woman' to early 1525 could indicate that as the date at which Magno began to enter this group of sonnets into the manuscript.

---

34 Carlo Dionisotti, "Nota biografica," in *Prose e rime*, pp. 57–60, p. 58.

35 Brocardo in later works indulged a less aulic side, moving with a shift in popular taste away from the dignified expression of longing for a remote woman to experimentation with criminal jargon (*furbesco*) and popular poetic styles and to a courtesan beloved: Cesare Mutini, "Brocardo, Antonio," *DBI*, 14 (1972).

36 Sannazaro, *Opere volgari*, pp. 421, 427, 428, 445, 446, 447, 475; Letters from Sannazaro pp. 310, 318–19, 324–8, 338, 360, 376, 388–9, 389–91; Letters to Sannazaro pp. 404–5, 409–10, 410–11; Pietro Bembo, *Lettere*, edizione critica a cura di Ernesto Travi, 4 vols (Bologna, 1987–93), 1: 192; 2: 129–30, 152, 354, 384; for a synthesis see Linda L. Carroll, "The Shepherd Meets the Cowherd: Ruzante's *Pastoral*, the Empire and Venice," *Annuario dell'Istituto Romeno di Cultura e Ricerca Umanistica* 4 (2002): 288–97.

37 Sanuto, 28: 513, 516, 533; Carroll, "Venetian Attitudes, " pp. 35–6.

38 Sanuto, 29: 603–4; 30: 457; 32: 492; 34: 454–4.

39 Sanuto, 37: 639–40; 38: 55, 73, 138, 347, 358, 364; 39: 47, 112, 157–8, 183, 187–8, 216; 40: 449.

The sonnet next praises "Zabarella . . . [cara] a tuti e tanto grata" (Zabarella . . . [dear] to all and so welcome). The Zabarella were a prominent Paduan noble family.[40] In the previous century Cardinal Francesco Zabarella, talented in reconciling the roles of various parties into a unified system, had played a prominent part in public life. He officiated at the formal ceding of Padua to Venetian control in 1406 and figured importantly at the Council of Constance's resolution of the issues behind the papal crisis with his proposal that a new pope be elected by the College of Cardinals.[41] Even the irreverent Ruzante praised him in the Paduan prologue of the *Betia* as "quel grande Cardinale Zabarella savio sincio iusto e dogni raxon bon che ha lago la rason chaluoricha in pe" (that great Cardinal Zabarella, wise, learned, just, and observant of every law who left canon law standing).[42] The family's prominence continued in the early sixteenth century, with Paolo Zabarella serving as the suffragan Bishop of Padua, including during the years of Andrea Magno's *capitaniato*, and holding other important benefices.[43] When the city council of Padua was reinstated in 1517, it was headed by Giacomo Zabarella.[44]

What had been an encomiastic work may show its first sign of turning critical in the next descriptions: "Ne si di graso e cypriana armata / ne i[n] tanto degno honor ursina i[n] chiara" (Nor is Cypriana so well armed with fat [or: with Grasso]/nor does Ursina's worthy honor shine so brightly [or: Nor does Ursina have much honor in Chiara]). (The value of *graso* and *chiara* as both common adjectives and proper names creates ambiguity.) The conjugated surname 'Ursina' would likely indicate a relative of one of the two Orsini *condottieri* who served the Venetian Republic in Padua. Brigida, the daughter of the late Niccolò Orsini Count of Pitigliano and *capitano generale* of the Venetian army, was involved in a land transaction during Andrea Magno's *capitaniato* that was witnessed by the *vicario* of the *podestà*. In May, 1521, the Venetian Senate arranged for Orsini's widow to pay the *livello* (lease) that she owed on a farm that the Republic had granted her, a matter in which Andrea Magno as *capitanio*

---

40 G.B. di Crollalanza, *Dizionario storico blasonico delle famiglie nobili e notabili italiane estinte e fiorenti*, 3 vols (1886; Bologna, 1965), 3: 113; PBC, B.P. 137 Benetto Bertoldi, *Historia cronologica di Padova*, fols 48ʳ⁻ᵛ, 53ᵛ, 68ᵛ–9ʳ.

41 Anne Hallmark, "*Protector, imo verus pater*: Francesco Zabarella's Patronage of Johannes Ciconia," in *Music in Renaissance Cities and Courts. Studies in Honor of Lewis Lockwood*, ed. Jessie Ann Owens and Anthony Cummings (Warren, MI, 1997), pp. 153–68; for his speech, see PBC, B.P. 802, fasc. xvii, fols 199–222; Francesco Scipione Dondi Dall'Orologio, *Dissertazioni sopra l'istoria ecclesiastica padovana*, 9 vols (Padua, 1802–17), 8: 282; Brian Tierney, *Foundations of the Conciliar Theory* (Cambridge, 1955), pp. 220–37; Thomas E. Morrissey, "'More Easily and More Securely': Legal Procedure and Due Process at the Council of Constance," in *Popes, Teachers, and Canon Law in the Middle Ages*, ed. James Ross Sweeney and Stanley Chodorow (Ithaca, 1989), pp. 234–47.

42 Beolco, *Betia*, Prologo per le recite in pavana, par. 5; VBMC, ms. Grimani-Morosini 4, fols 4ᵛ–5ʳ (*RT*, p. 155).

43 PACV, *Acta capitularia*, vols 11, 12, 13; *Actorum civilium*, vols 187, 189, 190, 191.

44 Monterosso, *Reggimenti*, vol. 4, fasc. X, fol. 22ʳ.

would have had a role.[45] The referent may have been a relative of Lorenzo da Cere Orsini, but that is less likely. While he had served with distinction during the wars of Cambrai as *governador zeneral* (commander of infantry) of the Venetian army,[46] during this period he was far from Padua.

The poem's negative turn becomes pronounced with "tanto avara / l'alma fiameta a tutj ama[n]tj i[n]grata" (So miserly / is the noble Fiameta, ungrateful to all who love her), concluding with a crescendo that reveals the poet's own disappointed love: "Ne ta[n]ta po[m]pa fa la vil spagnola / ne chatarina maj fa tanto amore / ne la salleta tantj corj i[n] vola / Ne ta[n]to preggio merta e tanto hanore / la vaga amaj de gratie almo[n]do sola / quant'io p[er] troppo amar troppo ho dolore" (The low Spanish [or: Spagnolo] woman does not act with so much ceremony, / Nor is Catarina ever so loving, / Nor does the Saletta woman steal as many hearts, / Nor does the lovely Amai whose graces are unique in all the world / Merit so much esteem and so much honor / As I have pain for loving too much). No available information permits a hypothesis concerning 'Fiammetta'; many individuals of Spanish origin in Padua including a member of the Sephardic Besalù banking family could qualify as 'Spagnola'[47]; of 'Salleta' one may only observe that there was a village of that name near Padua. However, a young woman named Caterina connected to Zuan Antonio da Corte, a Venetian priest and diarist who lived in Padua, married a servant of Andrea Magno's in October, 1521 "p[er] amore" (for love, *i.e.* indicating that his state was below hers).[48] Her bestowal of her love on someone below her in class may have provoked the resentment of the poet. The Amadi (Amai), a Venetian patrician family, had received citizen status in Padua in 1420.[49]

The following sonnet (fol. 21[r–v]) also praises Paduan women, with even less clear descriptions. A third (21[v]–2[v]) mourns the death of 'la Boromea'. While, again, identification of a specific family member cannot be certain, the most prominent woman in the Paduan branch of this far-flung banking family was Margherita. The referent may have been her or her daughter-in-law Benvegnuda. Margherita, whose father was an eminent Caodelista jurist, was related to two important participants in the Paduan rebellion that followed on Venice's disastrous 1509 defeat at Agnadello. She was the widow of Alessandro and mother of Achille, who had managed to escape and entered imperial service.[50] Considered dangerous enough to require confinement to Venice during the war, Margherita made a will there. The names of two executors, the patrician Marco da Molin and his wife, are indicative of the esteem in which the family was held by the Republic, as well, perhaps, as the government's desire to keep them under surveillance, especially if, as is likely, the Marco Molin involved was the one recently

---

45 *AGRM*, busta 314, *pergamena* of May 13, 1522; Sanuto, 30: 248.
46 PBUC, ms. 874, 3: 11[v]–60[r].
47 Cf. Sanuto, 42: 279.
48 PBC, ms. B.P. 3159, Zuan Antonio da Corte (Cortivo), *Historia di Padova, 1509–1530* (*Diario degli avvenimenti padovani dal 13 giugno 1509 al 12 ottobre 1529*), fol. 149[v].
49 PBC, B.P. 137, fol. 7[v].
50 Roberto Zapperi, "Borromeo, Achille," *DBI*, 13 (1971); Sanuto, 9: 52.

elected to the Zonta of the Council of Ten.[51] The list of witnesses to the will constitutes a veritable Who's Who of the Paduan imperialist élite, including members of the Leon, Frigimelega, Speroni, Caodevaca, and Guarnerio families. In October, 1523, the *Ufficio of the Raxon Vecchie*, along with Margherita's sons' property, sold the land that she had been allowed to keep when her husband's was confiscated. This likely meant that she had died shortly before, as the state generally allowed women in these circumstances small amounts of property to live on. In 1524 her daughter-in-law petitioned for the return of her dowry; her apparent and unusual lack of success may be linked to her husband Achille's being considered a 'gran rebelo' (great rebel).[52] Complicating matters and emblematic of the painful juxtaposition of political affiliations and passages that characterized the period is Pietro Bembo's purchase of Achille Borromeo's confiscated Paduan palazzo in 1527.[53] Another possible referent is the widow of Francesco Borromeo of Padua's S. Agostin parish, whose brother, living with her in violation of his exile, was arrested on order of the Heads of the Council of Ten in May, 1521.[54]

The Election of Leo X

An abrupt change of topic occurs with Canonician 36's next section, composed of works describing the defects of the cardinals vying in the election of the successor to Pope Leo X, which began in December, 1521.[55] The subject was of such great interest in Venice, the home of principal contenders Domenico Grimani and Marco Corner, that the *podestà* of Bergamo referred to the Signoria reports he had heard that Grimani lost because not supported by Corner and the third Venetian cardinal, Francesco Pisani.[56] The initial work, a sonnet that refers to the cardinals either by family name or by a benefice, is worth quoting in full, with the translation following:

> Soneto fato i[n] creatio[n] d[e]l novo po[n]tifice morto el lio[n] X noma[n]do
> i cognomi de tutj i card[en]elj et qual de loro starave meglio pontifice

51 ASPd, *Notarile*, busta 3969, fol. 10ʳ⁻ᵛ; Sanuto, 15: 401; another Marco Molin was unmarried and had been active at the Lombard battlefront shortly before: Sanuto, 14: 262, 333–4, 593; 31: 254.

52 ASVe, *Ufficiali ale Raxon Vecchie*, reg. 48, fols 4ᵛ–5ʳ; Dieci, *Miste*, filza 53, fols 110 and attachments referring to a dower contract of 1497; Sanuto, 36: 329 quotation. If the daughter-in-law is the referent, this would concord with other evidence that works in this section were composed later than 1520.

53 Lionello Puppi, "Il rinnovamento tipologico del Cinquecento," in *Padova Case e Palazzi*, ed. Lionello Puppi and Fulvio Zuliani (Vicenza, 1977), pp. 101–40, 124–5.

54 Sanuto, 30: 245–6.

55 For an overview of Italian cardinals, see Barbara McClung Hallman, *Italian Cardinals, Reform, and the Church as Property* (Berkeley, 1985).

56 See Sanuto, 32: 326–9 for a complete list of cardinals, 374 report, 412–18 for a running account; for the texts see, in the order in which they appear in Canonician 36, Marucci, Marzo and Romano, nos 202, 170, 180, 184, 178, 191, 204, 101, 102; while the *Indice dei capoversi* (2: 1118) lists Canonician 36 as the source for no. 205, it is not, although no. 205 is a variant on no. 202.

A santa croce nuoce esser marrano, / al soderino la patria fa gra[n] damno, / le lite e ostinatio[n] impacio fa[n]no, / al car.le di flisco & agrimano / Farnese e adulator doppio e romano / mo[n]te i[n] gra[n]zo[n] mo[n]ta col mala[n]no // [23r] guercio, bastardo, e medicj e tiran[n]o / grassi p[er]ch'ha la moglie spera i[n] vano. / Falsario e puccj e ladro e larmelino / e so[n] p[er] troppo giova[n] reffutatj / cibo, pisani, triulcij e cesarino. / Li duo senesi sono repputatj / di ragio[n] matj exp[re]ssi et e dapocho ursino / como e p[er] fra[n]cia e ipocritj li fratj. / Ridolfi e salviatj / so[n] fiore[n]tinj, di campegio e cortona / mi par che pocho o nulla si ragiona / Et mal veduto ancona. / E gra[n] capo di parte e il collonese / e barbarj so[n] vico e sedune[n]se. / Ivrea e pur fra[n]cese / Babio[n] el mantova[n] e bardassa ra[n]gonj / cesis villa[n] e infame caveglionj. / ci so[n] mille ragionj / Che esser no[n] pol la valle ne cornaro / ma[n] cho el ponzeta p[er] che e troppo avaro. / Li jacobaccj e chiaro / Che maj no[n] sper[a] al regno pastorale / p[er] che ha quel renzo suo troppo bestiale / Siche p[er] ma[n]cho male // [23v] Di tranj la matre da q[ue]sto co[n]siglio / che seria bene afar papa suo figlio (fols 22v–3v).[57]

Sonnet composed on the creation of the new pope at the death of Leo X, giving the names of all the cardinals and which of them would be best as pope. / Santa Croce is harmed by being Sephardic, / Great damage is done to Soderini by his homeland, / Quarrels and stubbornness have been an obstacle / to Flisco and Grimani. / Farnese is a double sycophant and a Roman, / Monte mounts a male spiny crab to his damnation. / Medici is blind in one eye, a bastard, and a tyrant, / Grassi hopes in vain because of his wife, / Pucci is a counterfeiter and Armellino a thief, / and rejected as too young / are Cibo, Pisani, Triulzi, and Cesarino. / The two Sienese are reputed with reason / barking mad and Orsini is worthless, / Como is for France, and the friars are hypocrites. / Ridolfi and Salviati are Florentines, of Campeggio and Cortona / it seems to me there is little talk. / Poorly viewed is Ancona. / A great leader of a faction is Colonna, / and Vico and Sedunense are barbarians. / Ivrea is French, unfortunately / and the Mantuan is an idiot and Rangon a passive homosexual. / Cesis is a clod and Caveglioni infamous. / There are a thousand reasons / why it will not be La Valle or Cornaro, / Nor Ponzeta because he is such a tightwad. / It is clear that Jacobacci does not hope for the pastoral reign / because he has that Renzo, who is such an animal. / Thus as the least of the evils, / Trani's mother advises that it would be good to make her son pope.

Cardinal Santa Croce was Bernardino de Carvajal. Cardinal Francesco Soderini's home country was Florence, shorthand for its dominant family, the Medici, who were unalterably opposed to him because his bishopric of Vicenza could serve as an independent power base. Medici claims of Soderini's involvement

---

57 The word 'exp[re]ssi' is added in the margin. The transcription here differs on some important points from that given in the Marucci edition, no. 202, not noted in the "Apparato," p. 1003; see also the ballots published in Sanuto, 32: 384–5.

in a 1517 plot against Leo, moreover, had resulted in his exile to Mantua, which only increased their fears by putting him in contact with anti-Medici forces gathered there.[58] Behind the criticism of the personal quarrelsomeness and court cases (*lite*) of the Genoese Cardinal Nicolò Fieschi and the Venetian Cardinal Domenico Grimani may have lain fear of their powerful merchant banking families.[59] Cardinal Alessandro Farnese is vilified for numerous vices found with a certain frequency among the Roman curia. The slip or variation in the description of Cardinal Antonio Ciocchi dal Monte of *granzon* (a spiny male spider crab) for *garzon* (a young male servant) reveals the transcriber's acquaintance with the Venetian language and may have alluded to the cardinal's 1518 visit to Venice. At the conclave he was charged with ejecting those not authorized to participate.[60] The accusation of tyranny levelled against Cardinal Giulio de' Medici had been made against his family by Soderini and other Florentine republicans.[61] Cardinal Achille de Grassis's uxorious disposition was well known, even in Venice.[62] Francesco Armellini's surname may come after Lorenzo Pucci's because of its meaning 'weasel' (more precisely 'ermine', a member of the weasel family and infamous for barnyard theft); months before, he had outbid Leo's nephew Innocenzo Cibo for the office of papal *camerlengo*. The youthful cardinals Innocenzo Cibo,[63] Francesco Pisani,[64] Agostino Trivulzio, and Alessandro Cesarini in addition to lacking in maturity had achieved their status through family intervention or connections, making them especially susceptible to manipulation. The two Sienese cardinals were Raffaele Petrucci and Giovanni Piccolomini. The feckless Orsini was Franciotto, and Como was Scaramuccia Trivulzio, of a Milanese family well known for French partisanship. Hypocrisy is the perceived defect of the friars, Tommaso de Vio, the general of the Dominicans often referred to as Cajetan; Egidio Canisio of the Augustinian friars[65]; and Cristoforo Numai of the Franciscans. Cardinals Niccolò Ridolfi and Giovanni Salviati are dismissed as Florentine with the clear implication that Cardinal Medici would not brook their

---

58 K.J.P. Lowe, *Church and Politics in Renaissance Italy. The Life and Career of Cardinal Francesco Soderini (1453–1524)*, Cambridge Studies in Italian History and Culture (Cambridge and New York, 1993), esp. pp. 106–28; for another similar pasquinade p. 123 note 11; cf. Sanuto, 32: 230.

59 See Carlo Taviani, *Superbia discordia: Guerra, rivolta e pacificazione nella Genova del primo Cinquecento*, I libri di Viella 80 (Rome, 2008); Pio Paschini, *Domenico Grimani Cardinale di S. Marco (+1523)* (Rome, 1943); for fear of stingy banking practices, cf. Marucci et al., no. 170.

60 Giuseppe Boerio, *Dizionario del dialetto veneziano*, 2nd ed. (Venice, 1856), *s.v.*; cf. Marucci *et al*; Sanuto, 25: 438; 26: 135, 136, 137, 143, 144–5, 146, 147–8, 152–4, 155–6, 176, 180–81, 182; 30: 331. He subsequently agreed to help achieve the canonization of Blessed Lorenzo Giustinian.

61 Sanuto, 32: 288.

62 Cf. Sanuto, 32: 414.

63 F. Petrucci, "Cibo, Innocenzo," *DBI*, 25 (1981); see also Carroll, "Introduction," pp. 5–74, esp. 22–4, 56–7, 59, 69, 70–71.

64 Linda L. Carroll, "Dating *The Woman from Ancona*: Venice and Ruzante's Theater after Cambrai," *Sixteenth Century Journal*, 31 (2000): 963–85.

65 For a complex view of Canisio, see Gennaro Savarese, *La cultura a Roma tra Umanesimo ed ermetismo (1480–1540)* (Anzio, 1993), esp. pp. 23, 30, 34–5, 51, 69, 71–90, 104.

election. That no one was mentioning Cardinal Lorenzo Campeggio of Bologna is confirmed in the accounts in Sanudo. Silvio Passerini (Cortona) was excluded because he was a client of the Medici, having been put in charge of Florence by Leo in 1519 after the death of Lorenzo duke of Urbino. Pietro Accolti, born in Florence of an Aretine family and Bishop of Ancona, had been close to Leo; with Giulio de' Medici as a rival rather than a supporter, he had no chance of election.[66] Pompeo Colonna's heading of a large (Roman) faction was well known to his fellow cardinals who, not trusting the Swiss guards, entrusted the conclave's security in equal measure to the Colonna and their rivals the Orsini.[67] Two foreigners, the Spaniard Raimond Vich and the Swiss Matteo Schinner, are defined as barbarians, a common insult for non-Italians considered to be lacking in culture, especially humanistic culture. Perceived political or personal defects excluded the Cardinal of Ivrea Bonifacio Ferrero, the Mantuan Cardinal Sigismondo Gonzaga, the Modenese Ercole Rangone,[68] Paolo Cesi, and Giovanni Battista Pallavicini Bishop of Cavaillon. As Sanudo's accounts show, Andrea della Valle's vote totals at first increased but then declined. Discreetly not mentioned among the 'thousand reasons' for Marco Corner's inability to be elected is the lack of support from the other two Venetian cardinals. Excluded, again for personal vices, are Ferdinando Poncetti and Domenico Jacobacci. Ignoring the eventual winner Cardinal Adrian Flourent, the sonnet's author declares the sole remaining candidate Giovanni Francesco Cupi Archbishop of Trani, mocked for his famous closeness to his mother. Cupi was in fact instrumental in Flourent's victory. After many rounds of voting with no clear frontrunner, Cardinal Medici proposed Flourent as the compromise candidate; although he had been the tutor of Charles V, it was hoped that his ascetic nature would make him acceptable to all factions. With the nomination gathering support, Cupi switched his vote and began the process by which enough others were attracted to produce a majority.[69]

An account of the election with which to compare the sonnet's is given in several anonymous letters transcribed by Sanudo. They are addressed to Venetian patrician Zustignan Contarini and the author cites a source close to Pasquino and a relative in service to Cardinal Rangone and close to Cardinals Campeggio and Cibo. The author, possibly the Francesco Maredini who signs one of them, reports that the pope's favorite cardinals have received medals with "motti bellissimi" (wonderful sayings), though he does not include them because Contarini is not familiar with the cardinals. He gives the bets placed on various candidates and reports the lamentations that arose immediately from

66 B. Ulianich, "Accolti, Pietro," in *DBI*, 1 (1960); and see now Elena Bonora, *Aspettando l'imperatore. Principi italiani tra il papa e Carlo V* (Turin, 2014), pp. 18–30.

67 Sanuto, 32: 291.

68 For *bardassa* as 'passive homosexual', see Michael J. Rocke, *Forbidden Friendships. Homosexuality and Male Culture in Renaissance Florence* (New York and Oxford, 1996), pp. 106–7, a description that was substituted in the version published by Marucci et al. with the bland 'gioven' (young).

69 Sanuto, 32: 414–15.

prelates, their circles, and other officials as they learned that the saintly and thrifty northerner Flourent had been elected. The letter written at the moment of the election includes two sonnets, an epitaph and a complete record of the ballots.[70] In a subsequent missive, the writer states, "Missier Antonio Thebaldeo nostro huomo, come sapete, diligentissimo in notar tute le cose degne di nota, mi ha narato distintamente le pratiche et li progressi dil conclavi [*sic*]" (Sir Antonio Tebaldeo our man, who is, as you know, extremely diligent in noticing all of the things worthy of note, narrated to me in detail the practices and the progress of the Conclave). Tebaldeo, a member of Cardinal Ercole Rangone's household, accompanied him throughout the procedure. Noting that the complete absence of religious sentiment from the choice of pope has cost Tebaldeo his faith, the letter-writer provides an additional account of the cardinals' election manoeuvers, of Medici's decisive backing of Flourent, and of the contrast between Rome and Flourent, who is depicted as a school master caning the bare bottoms of the cardinals.[71] The passage raises two questions: was Tebaldeo the source of the information in other letters and was he the author of some of the anonymous works in Canonician 36?

Following the sonnet (fols 23^v–5^r; cf. Marucci et al., no. 170) is a dialogue between Rome and Pasquino. Rome, lamenting the draining of her purse by the Medici and praising Pasquino's astrological knowledge, asks him who the next pope will be. His predictions include that if Grimani wins he will sing a *miserere* and bring Rialto (*i.e.* merchant banking) to Rome. If it is Corner or Cibo, however, large numbers of dogs and whores will be gathered from all over the world.[72] Five sonnets and a sixth in dialogue reflecting on the election in much the same vein follow, one even enumerating the clientelage of each cardinal (fols 25^r–7^v; cf. Marucci et al., nos. 180, 184, 178, 191, 204, 101, 102). Although one sonnet supports the election of a Medici pope as serving the common good (no. 184), two vehemently condemn Leo (nos. 191, 204). Indeed, one is filled with the despair of a faithful Christian at the sorry state of Italy and the abandonment of the flock of the faithful by a corrupt Church to the point that its author (Tebaldeo?) even blasphemes against Christ for failing to intervene (no. 101). Response is given by the final two sonnets, which admonish the complainer to leave the matter to Christ, who is allowing Italy's descent into war and lamentation to induce repentance for sins.

The author of the first of the two (no. 102) is named as "ber. da lucha," probably Bernardino Daniello da Lucca. If it is his work, he either had direct experience with northern Italian dialects or a speaker of one contributed to the sonnet: the vilification of the complainer in crude anatomical terms reflects some widespread

---

70 Sanuto, 32: 274–5, 287–93 (quotation 288), 302–3, 330–34, 355–8, 378–85. However, while some of this correspondent's accounts offer more information about deal-making for votes, none provides the richness of personal detail contained in the Canonician 36 works.
71 Sanuto, 32: 412–18.
72 See Carroll, "Introduction."

features of that linguistic group. Daniello established himself in Padua at a date estimated to be 1523, and joined the circle around Pietro Bembo.[73] The language of the sonnet may indicate that at the time of the conclave he had contact in Rome with Bembo's household or with the household of a Venetian cardinal, possibly Marco Corner given that Daniello dedicated his 1536 *Poetica* to the cardinal's illegitimate half-brother Bishop Andrea Corner.

Next in the manuscript are two curious works purporting to be descriptions of medallions relating to the cardinals. The first is a collection of personal medallions of various cardinals, with appropriately symbolic images and candidly mocking mottoes, likely those to which Zustignan Contarini's correspondent referred.[74] Several examples may suffice. Cardinal Grimani's had the image of a pair of ox testicles and the inscription "et i[n] magna quantitate" (and in great quantity); Cardinal Grassi's bore the image of a whorehouse and the inscription "domus mea" (my home). Pallavicino's image was a priapus and the motto "sequere me" (follow me). Cibo was represented by the French disease and the motto "dominus dedit dominus abstulit" (the Lord gave and the Lord hath taken away). The second work describes a single, large medallion with two heads on each side. One shows the cardinals who support the emperor versus those who support the King of France. The reverse, with two papal reigns, bears the inscription "omne regnu[m] i[n] se divisu[m] va al bordelo" (every kingdom divided against itself goes to the whorehouse). Following are the ballots (fols 31^r–2^r), which correspond closely with those recorded by Sanudo.[75] Magno concludes this thematic section with a commentary on the election (32^{r-v}) according to which the cardinals settled on Adrian on the eighth ballot because they finally realized that there was no other candidate acceptable to a majority.

As has been observed,[76] the detailed knowledge of the papal election and of the cardinals evident in these works could only have come from a source close to the Roman curia. Those available to Magno, beyond Antonio Tebaldeo and Bernardino Daniello, were almost too numerous to count. In August of 1521, Cardinal Marco Corner had come up from Rome to make his entrance as Padua's bishop, bringing with him a retinue of servants and clients. Magno's father as

---

73   M. Raffaella De Gramatica, "Daniello, Bernardino," *DBI*, 32 (1986); Bernardino Daniello, *Poetica* In Vinegia per Giovan'Antonio di Nicolini da Sabio, l'Anno de nostra salute M D XXXVI (reprint; Munich, 1968). His best-known work is his commentary on Dante: *L'Esposizione di Bernardino Daniello da Lucca sopra la* Comedia *di Dante*, ed. Robert Hollander and Jeffrey Schnapp with Kevin Brownlee and Nancy Vickers (Hanover, NH and London, 1989). As the editors note, it shows deep and wide humanistic learning and had a strong influence on Milton. See also Ezio Raimondi, "Bernardino Daniello e le varianti petrarchesche," *Studi petrarcheschi* 5 (1952): 95–130; Aldo Vallone, "Trifone Gabriele e Bernardino Daniello dinanzi a Dante," *Studi mediolatini e volgari*, 10 (1962): 263–98; Carlo Dionisotti, "Daniello, Bernardino," in *Enciclopedia dantesca* (Rome, 1970), 2: 303–4; Bernard Weinberg, *A History of Literary Criticism in the Italian Renaissance*, 2 vols (Chicago, 1961), 2: 721–4.

74   Sanuto, 32: 288.

75   Sanuto, 32: 384–5 and see 383–4 for several works similar to those here.

76   Richardson, *Manuscript Culture*, pp. 40–41.

capitanio was among those hosting the fêted prelate, as was the *podestà*, Marino Zorzi, who had been Venice's ambassador to the pope from 1515 to 1517.[77] In addition, Andrea Magno's brother-in-law, Hironimo Giustinian, was a canon of the Padua cathedral and apostolic protonotary who had an important role in Corner's 1521 entrance.[78] The cardinal-bishop's sojourn lasted several months, providing innumerable opportunities for establishing relationships through which information could flow after he returned to Rome in late November, five days after Leo X's brother Cardinal Giulio, at the head of the papal-imperial army, caused the French to flee from Milan.[79] Leo would die celebrating the victory on December 1.

Stefano had his own potential sources. One of the Immortali, Zuan Corner, was the brother of Cardinal Marco. Also accompanying the cardinal-bishop was Andrea Vendramin, to whom Cardinal Marco had assigned his Paduan canonry and who was the brother of the Nicolò who in January 1522 staged the tragedy by Jacopo Dal Legname that Magno copied into VBM, ital. IX, 71.[80] Other Venetian patricians were receiving accounts from relatives and acquaintances living in Rome, including Zuan Francesco Valier, the illegitimate son of Venetian patrician Carlo, linked by Padoan to the *ambiente* of *La veniexiana* that Stefano Magno also included in IX, 288.[81] The Valier had deep associations with many in Magno's circle, with Padua, and with literary and theatrical figures including Ruzante. A merchant-banker, Carlo Valier had relations with other governments, particularly the Gonzaga court of Mantua, to which he conveyed money owed by the actor Cherea and apparently even passed Venetian government information.[82] From early in his life he had connections with Stefano Magno's maternal uncle Pangrati Giustinian both personally and through Lorenzo Giustinian qu. Bernardo, Valier's brother-in-law.[83] In 1488, the same year in which Carlo's relative Hironimo Contarini 'da Londra' invested in the Flanders galleys, Carlo had become a member of the wool guild in Padua, a leading center in the production of woolen cloth to which the imported northern wool was probably destined.[84] In his chronicle, Stefano Magno describes the disastrous conditions encountered by that

---

77 Carroll, "Introduction," pp. 29–32; Sanuto, 19–24, *s.v.* Marino Zorzi.

78 PACV, *Acta capitularia*, vol. 13, esp. fols 35ᵛ–43ᵛ.

79 Sanuto, 32: 164, 187, 208.

80 Sanuto, 31: 234; Francesco Scipione Dondi Dall'Orologio, *Serie cronologico-istorica dei canonici di Padova* (Padova, 1805), p. 214; VBM, ital. IX, 71, fol. 77ʳ.

81 Padoan, "Introduzione," in *La Veniexiana*, pp. 17–25, 29–33; Padoan, "La *Veniexiana*," pp. 336–45.

82 Linda L. Carroll, "Dating *La Veniex[ia]na*: The Venetian Patriciate and the Mainland Nobility at the End of the Wars of Cambrai, with a Note on Titian," *Annuario dell'Istituto Romeno di cultura e ricerca umanistica* (Venice) 5 (2003): 511–19; cf. Sanuto, 7: 727 and in general vols 7, 8, 9, 10, 11 (for both father and son) *s.v.*; Padoan, "La *Veniexiana*," p. 336 note 167.

83 Sanuto, 3: 151, 181–2.

84 Sanuto, 27: 118; PBC, B.P. 801 V, Giovanni Lazara, *Memorie di famiglie nobili di Padova descritte nel Collegio dell'arte della lana e di famiglie nobili applicate all'esercizio di banchiere e cambista, raccolte dal c. Giovanni Lazara*, unnumbered folio.

round, the resulting deep losses of which were softened for the Venetian patrician investors by two lines of Ruzante's family.[85] Zuan Beolco of Milan, his great-uncle and a wealthy banker, provided the Venetian merchants with funds and perhaps additional investors. Antonio da Pernumia, brother of Ruzante's grandmother Paola, purchased a large property in Pernumia from investor Antonio Giustinian qu. Nicolò, a common means of generating cash.[86] In addition to being a galley investor, Giustinian was the father-in-law of Francesco Donà, the only Venetian patrician to whom Ruzante referred by name in a work (the *Lettera giocosa*) except the orations, and who succeeded Andrea Magno as *capitanio* of Padua.[87] Magno's awareness of these deep connections may have motivated his inclusion of the honorific 'missier' with Beolco's name in his copy of the *Pastoral*, one of only two instances in which that respectful title is included with the playwright's name in manuscripts.

Zuan Francesco Valier, who as an illegitimate son did not enjoy patrician status and privileges, pursued some of his father's interests. Even more closely tied to the Gonzaga than his father, he was termed their "servitor" (in their service) and "nunzio" (envoy) by the Venetian Senate in 1510.[88] In late 1517 he was in Padua in connection with his efforts to obtain a cathedral canonry.[89] There, at his request, the Venetian priest and diarist Zuan Antonio da Corte organized a festive occasion for four Venetian patricians and their prostitutes.[90] Not receiving the canonry, Zuan Francesco entered the service of Cardinal Bernardo Dovizi da Bibbiena, who fostered the kind of brutal honesty evident in his *Calandria* as well as in the *Veniexiana* and the Canonician 36 poems. In Bibbiena's circle in Rome, Zuan Francesco frequented literary figures including Jacopo Sadoleto and Francesco Berni. He counted among his friends Antonio Tebaldeo, Andrea Navagero, and Ludovico Ariosto.[91] His Paduan connections were no less: he, as well as Antonio Brocardo, would appear among the interlocutors in Sperone Speroni's *Dialogo*

85 See Introduction, notes 6 and 7 and Chapter 1, note 89.
86 ASVe, *AGRM*, busta 250, second *vacchetta*, fols 16^r, 27^r, 62^v, 63^r, 73^r; ASPd, *Notarile*, busta 1760, fols 106^r–7^r; cf. Giuseppe Gullino, *Marco Foscari (1477–1551): l'attività politica e diplomatica tra Venezia, Roma, e Firenze* (Milan, 2000), pp. 18–19.
87 Barbaro, 3: 335; Sanuto, 32: 444–5.
88 ASVe, Senato, *Secreta*, reg. 43, fols 92^r, 106^r–7^r.
89 Sanuto, 23: 236–7, 482–3, 516; 24: 182, 231, 276, 356, 376, 463; ASPd, *Notarile*, busta 1309, fols 194^{r-v}, 198^r, 303^v.
90 Da Corte, fol. 109^v; cf. Ruzante, *Anconitana*.
91 Francesco Berni, *Opere*, ed. Eugenio Camerini, 2nd ed. (Milan, 1874), pp. 280, 283, 287, 289–92, 295–8; Antonio Virgili, *Francesco Berni* (Firenze, 1881), pp. 59, 206; Anne Reynolds, "Francesco Berni (1497?–1535), An Introductory Biography," in Francesco Berni, *Renaissance Humanism at the Court of Clement VII. Francesco Berni's Dialogue Against Poets in Context. Studies, with an edition and translation by Anne Reynolds* (New York and London, Inc., 1997), pp. 35–57, 35–45; Bernardo Dovizi da Bibbiena, *Epistolario di Bernardo Dovizi da Bibbiena*, ed. Giuseppe Lorenzo Moncallero, 2 vols (Florence, 1955–65), 1: 251 letter LXXXV to Isabella d'Este Gonzaga, 1511; Sanuto, 11: 48, 760; 17: 572–3; 18: 132; 19: 320–21; 20: 132; 23: 236–7, 482–3, 516; 24: 479, 494, 512; 25: 233; 26: 117; 29: 447; 40: 164; 46: 500.

della retorica, set in Bologna at the time of Charles V's coronation.[92] Zuan Francesco's political intrigues also apparently went further even than his father's, involving the communication of Venetian state secrets to the King of France that resulted in his execution by the Republic.

Uniting the next sonnets is their authorship by Ber[nardino] da Lucca, again presumably Bernardino Daniello (fols 32ᵛ–6ʳ). Initiating the series are two that evoke erotic encounters in intimate terms including dialogue between the two lovers. Subsequent sonnets, somewhat surprisingly, offer a mixture of similar erotic themes and those in the Petrarchan tradition of chaste, distant love. The final two sonnets are characterized by an unusual and comic use of language somewhat resembling that of Antonio Cammello Il Pistoia. The first of them is addressed to Magno himself:

> Magno mio caro i' mj ritrovo et cetera / e stomj qui come dio vole et basta / la vita fo di sa[n] fra[n]cescho e basta / vestito so[n] qual el batista et cetera / Quel ch'io vorebbj dir mel taccio, et cetera / ch'el tempo ad[e]so nol co[n] sente, e basta / che verra tempo u[n] dj di dirlo, e basta / e ch'i[n]tender mj po mi[n]tendi, et cetera / Quel che mi duole, e ch'io vorej no[n] piu / el mo[n] do e pie[n] d'inganj e dj no[n] altro / beato q[ue]l che sa finger, no[n] piu / Di fortuna mi doglio, horsu no[n] altro / di me stesso, daltruj no[n] dico piu / basta, no[n] piu, et cetera, non altro.

> (My dear Magno, I find myself etc. / and I stay here as God wishes, enough! / I live like St. Francis, enough! / I am dressed like the Baptist, et cetera / What I would say I keep to myself, et cetera / because the times now do not allow it, enough! / the time will come some day to say it, enough! / may he who understands me understand me, et cetera / What troubles me and what I would stop / is a world full of deceit and nothing else / Blessed is he who knows how to fake it, no more! / I complain about fortune, all right, no more! / of myself, of others I say no more! / enough, no more, et cetera, no further).

The final work of the group curses Cupid for the suffering he causes and wants him hanged.

The section closes (fol. 36ᵛ) with a sonnet by Unico Aretino, Bernardo Accolti, brother of Cardinal Pietro Accolti; two by Antonio Brocardo (fol. 37ʳ⁻ᵛ); and a series of unattributed sonnets (fols 37ᵛ–40ᵛ). It is sealed with Magno's τελωσ.

The *Capitoli*, Especially One on Venetian Women, and its Possible Practical Purpose

Gathered in the next section (fols 41ʳ–61ᵛ) are numerous *capitoli*, a genre devoted to playful but sharply-worded criticisms. Although it was particularly cultivated by Tuscan poets, those collected by Magno were composed by Bembo (not named

---

92   Roberto Buranello, "(Non) Plus Ultra: Charles V and Sperone Speroni's Bolognese Trilogy," in Saint-Saëns, ed., pp. 113–61.

in the manuscript, with one *capitolo* in a version that differs from the printed one), Ariosto (not named in the manuscript), Navagero (or Sannazaro), Bernardino da Lucca, Onofrio Veronese, Bellisario Laura, and additional anonymous poets. Prominent among the targets of the *capitoli* is the suffering inflicted by love, also personified as Cupid.

The anonymous eighth *capitolo* (fols 49ʳ–53ʳ) is the most curious, "Capitolo de alcune done famose di venet[i]a" (Capitolo about some famous Venetian women). The situation that it describes resembles a beauty contest of patrician women held for Paolo Giovio when he visited Venice in 1522–23, hinting that such a contest was a tradition accompanying the competition among patricians for the inclusion of the largest number of beautiful women at their festivities.[93] Its opening stanza "Nela stagio[n] chel ciel dal tauro unit[o] / mostra la sua virtu cu[m] vario modo / sopra il terre[n]o dj color mille tinto / Amor streto mhavea cu[m] tal nodo / ch'el pianto sol e il sospirar fochoso erano[94] / al viver mio tra[n]quilo modo" (In the season in which heaven, joined by the bull, shows its capabilities in various ways / over the earth tinged in a thousand shades, / Love bound me with such a knot / that lonely weeping and fiery sighs were / calm in comparison to my life) weaves together elements of two poems of Petrarch's *Rerum vulgarium fragmenta*: IX, which would be quoted by Daniello in his *Poetica*,[95] and L. The poet recounts a dream in which he observed coming ashore in little boats "una gra[n] turba d[e] n[ost]re matrone" (a great swarm of our matrons) wearing triumphal crowns on their heads as had the emperors of old. He names each and describes most. Exact identification is rarely possible because of the paucity, fragmentation, and dispersion of women's names in historical records. (Marin Sanudo, for example, rarely provides women's given names, instead calling them 'the wife of' or 'the daughter of', as does the Barbaro genealogy.) However, some keys may be provided by the sure identification of two of them—Maria Caravello, member of a tiny patrician clan and the protagonist of a scandalous episode involving some of the other patrician women named, and Marietta Bibbiena—and by the likely identities of several others. The information in the *capitolo* will first be summarized and then background information on individual figures provided.

Leading the group is Isabeta Diedo, whose crown is a globe topped by an angel that seems to say that her beauty flies through the world in verse and in rhyme. Next is Paola Venier, whose cheerful spirit lifts that of the poet and whose insignia is impartial justice. In beauty comes Isabeta Barbarigo, with an angel signifying her goodness. Following her is Cecilia Dandolo, whose insignia, the sun, indicates that the fame of her beauty has spread through the western world. Andriana Pesaro comes after the women of the first rank, her symbol, the moon, demonstrating her modesty and the friendship linking coldness with chastity. Lucretia Venier is wise

93 See Kenneth Gouwens, "Female Virtue and the Embodiment of Beauty: Vittoria Colonna in Paolo Giovio's *Notable Men and Women*," *Renaissance Quarterly* 68 (2015): 33–97, esp. pp. 46–7.

94 Ms. 'erane'.

95 Daniello, *Poetica*, p. 95.

and is guided by her star along the path of virtue. The agile Elena Zane exhibits an inner spark that will kindle conjugal love. Next comes Maria Caravello, who bears the devil and his signs [on her crown], as if to say 'I am the one who is the enemy of the virtuous'. Always opposed to pointless loves is the little Querini girl, who comes next and whose insignia is death with the meaning that she is death to amorous leanings. Similarly hardened against frivolous love is Marieta Capello, followed by Lucieta Soranzo, who shows that time ruins beauty, a woman of the Barozzi family, and Marina Emo. Bianca Grimani, the enemy of vice, was waged war on by love with an arrow that caught her in the lap. Laureta Foscari bends all of her thoughts to being human and has stolen a great deal of beauty from the others, but she is inhuman in love. Maria Lion is neither merciful nor cruel, while Maria da Leze is so devout that she is with the pope. Isabeta Venier is so ardent and willing in love that she almost keeps up with her partner, and her faith is such that she saves others. Marieta Bibbiena, because of her *papessa* (female pope), believes herself to be to the others as the sea is to a river. Hieronima Venier has eternal honor and the title of empress. Helena Zen, with her burning eyes, inspires men who are followers of love, while Laura Cocco fears no word of infamy. The flotilla of women slowly surrounds the dreaming poet and then, one by one, with haughty countenance, they depart, until he is alone. Awaking from his sleep, he decides that Isabetta Diedo was the most beautiful

The scandalous episode that may provide the key to the *capitolo* is the subject of numerous entries in Sanudo's *Diarii* and also has a link to the election of Leo's successor. On the morning of March 4, 1522, 'Marti di carlevar' (Mardi Gras, the concluding day of Carnival), Venetians awoke to learn that during the night the home of Sanudo's relative Marc'Antonio Venier had been smeared with pitch on the land side. This was in addition to what had happened the day before: the tarring of the canal side and main door and its adornment with a pair of horns denoting wifely infidelity. The Venier were not the only victims: also tarred were the homes of the banker Antonio Capello qu. Batista, the Spanish papal financiers Besalù-Beltrame, the banker Alvise Pisani, and Andrea Diedo. As Sanudo notes, such a public accusation of adultery against a (patrician) woman was considered a grave offense, citing the refusal of former Doge Antonio Venier (reigned 1382–1400) to commute the sentence of his son for a similar offense.[96] Marc'Antonio and his brothers-in-law went to the doge to petition the remanding of the case to the Heads of the Council of Ten; the petition was granted immediately and a reward offered for information. Gossip began swirling, with Fantin Corner di la Piscopia (the future father-in-law of Ruzante's patron Alvise Cornaro) being accused of having been put up to it by Maria Caravello, his lover. Another rumor had it that Marc'Antonio Venier had had the other houses

---

96 Sanuto, 33: 11–12, 14, 16, 28–9, 51, 56, 65–6, 101, 141, 142, 155, 368. The text does not give a patronym for Diedo and the indexers identify him with Andrea di Hironimo but Andrea di Hironimo was only 18 at the time (32: 129, 318) and Andrea qu. Antonio had connections with the Priuli bank and a wife celebrated for her beauty, making him the more likely target.

tarred. Sanudo declared both untrue. Written instructions in Maria Caravello's hand were discovered, and it was reiterated that Fantin Corner was mixed up ("impazato") in it. Then Caravello's boatman confessed.

It emerged that Caravello's motive was linked to a party thrown in the Ducal Palace during Carnival by Marco Grimani, grandson of the doge. Grimani wished the presence of the most beautiful women in the city to impress his guest of honor, who was the Bishop of Ivrea and the nephew of Cardinal Bonifacio Ferrero, then studying in Padua. To assist him, Maria Caravello had invited a woman of the Diedo family and one of the Venier family. They declined and she exacted her revenge. When called to account for her actions by the Council of Ten, Caravello sought refuge on the island of Murano in a convent where her sister was a nun. She proposed house arrest as an alternative to prison, but, as Sanudo dryly noted, that was not customary. The Ten declared her guilty, a verdict seen as saving the honor of the Venier and the Diedo families. They banished her for ten years to a distance of at least 15 miles from the city, with a bounty of 1500 lire and a year in prison for violation of the sentence, and sentenced several male accomplices. Caravello decided to repair to her holding in Cervia, on the Romagnol coast south of Venice, where her husband also had a holding and her grandfather had been Venetian governor before the war.[97] Because of the rich salt pans, this region, which also included Ravenna, was continuously contended by the pope and Venice in these years. Eventually she was offered amnesty for a loan to the state of 300 ducats or a gift of 100 ducats; Sanudo does not report whether she accepted.

A review of the women described in the *capitolo* shows them to have been the wives of leading patricians of Magno's day, with many of whom he had personal connections including through *compagnie della calza*, and many of whom had demonstrable or possible connections with the Caravello incident. Their occurrence in the sonnet follows a bell curve that consists of tarring victims and their associates up to Maria Caravello's name and then tapers off with the names of women whose connections with Marco Grimani imply that they would have attended the party. In other words, the women named in the first half of the list are likely those who refused an invitation to Grimani's soirée and their associates, while those in the second half are ones who likely accepted it.

The Isabeta Diedo of the *capitolo* was probably the wife of Andrea Diedo qu. Antonio, as he was married to a very beautiful woman named Isabeta, the daughter of Alvise Priuli qu. Piero procurator of the banking family. In 1521, her beauty had drawn the attention of the Prince of Bisignano, Pier Antonio di Sanseverino, who was visiting Venice on his way from the imperial court to his feudal holding in Spanish-held southern Italy. Isabeta had danced at length with the prince, and with him alone, at a soirée fêting him enlived by Ruzante and Menato with a comedy that Sanudo described as "bella et nova" (lovely and new). It is intriguing to wonder if it was the same "bella comedia" put on in a Diedo home in Padua's

---

97   Sanuto, 5: 502, 945.

(and the Beolcos') parish of S. Daniele during that year's Carnival as well. Andrea Diedo was a member of the Immortali, for whom Beolco and Alvaroto had played in 1520, and owned a home in Padua near Alvaroto's.[98] Paola Venier too was a relative of an insulted wife (for whose identity see below) and was possibly the wife of Piero Venier, who held properties in the territory of Treviso.[99] It is not clear if he was Piero Venier qu. Domenego, who supervised the work on Padua's walls during the latter part of the war.[100] An Isabeta or Elisabetta Barbarigo, daughter of Daniele, was the granddaughter on her mother's side of Francesco Foscari, who had bequeathed her a share in Padua's Arena Chapel.[101] The Barbarigo had connections with both the Venier, including through marriage, and the Cappello.[102] In 1511, Cecilia Foscarini became the wife of the Immortale Andrea Dandolo qu. Alvise.[103] Marco Antonio Venier, a branch of the Dandolo, and the Triumphanti Contarini were related by marriage, as indicated by their 1517 *divisio* of family properties.[104] To date no Andriana Pesaro has been identified, although it is possible that the wife of Piero Pesaro qu. Bernardo had the same name as her mother, Andriana Barbarigo, or that the name was given to a daughter.[105] The chief victim of the tarring episode, the very beautiful Lucrezia Zorzi qu. Marco, married Marc'Antonio Venier, Sanudo's relative, in May of 1518. She thereby became Lucrezia Venier, almost certainly the woman of the *capitolo*. Tragically, she was later murdered, her husband the chief suspect.[106] An Elena Zane was the wife of Zuan Pisani qu. Francesco 'dal Banco', the first cousin of the banker whose house was tarred (see below).[107]

Following Caravello's name are those of women whose connections to Marco Grimani would likely have inclined them to attend his party. Many had associations with the Foscari, principals in the shared commercial ventures of the western galleys from whose records much of the present information is drawn. 'La Querineta' could be Marco's sister Paola, also known by the diminutive 'Paolina', who married Stefano Querini dalle Papozze in 1519.[108] Marietta Capello may be the Marietta Albertini who married Vicenzo Capello in about 1512.[109] The Capello

---

98   Sanuto, 29: 536–7; da Corte, fol. 141ʳ; ASPd, *Estimo 1518*, busta 352, fol. 304ʳ⁻ᵛ.
99   ASVe, *AGB*, busta 24, unnumbered folio.
100 Sanuto, 17–24, *s.v.*
101 VBMC, mss. c 1297 / IV, Provenienze Diverse c, 1297 / IV, busta 1297, doc. 4, fols 45ʳ⁻9ᵛ; ASVe, *AGRM*, busta 3 bis, unnumbered folio dated April 4, 1523.
102 Sanuto, 24: 250–51; 36: 497; VBMC, ms. *Malvezzi*, 144, fols 235ʳ⁻43ᵛ.
103 Barbaro, 3: 187.
104 ASVe, *AGRM*, busta 223, unnumbered printed fascicle.
105 ASPd, *Estimo 1518*, busta 352, fol. 141ᵛ.
106 Sanuto, 25: 436, 448–9, 492–3; cf. 36: 450; 55: 128–9, 134, 135, 190, 196, 210, 248, 282–3. While Sanudo terms Venier his 'nephew', he was actually his first cousin once removed: Barbaro, 6: 650; 7: 239–40.
107 Crescenzi p. 32; Carolyn Kolb, "New Evidence for Villa Pisani at Montagnana," in *Interpretazioni veneziane. Studi di storia dell'arte in onore di Michelangelo Muraro*, David Rosand ed. (Venice, 1984), pp. 227–37, p. 227.
108 Barbaro, 6: 306; ASVe, *AGRM*, busta 51, fasc. 15, document of January 21, 1536.
109 Crescenzi, pp. 426–30.

had a deep history of shared commercial investment with the Grimani involving the western galleys.[110] Lucietta Soranzo is likely to be the then-aging wife of Alvise Soranzo and sister of Filippo Capello, one of several women accused in 1507 of ruining the city through extravagant spending on fashion.[111] Not only her paternal but her marital family had joined the Grimani in northern commerce.[112] Doge Grimani's son Vicenzo had married Isabetta Soranzo.[113] Lucietta's grand-niece, a daughter of Marco Foscari, married Piero Grimani di Francesco in 1519.[114] Also accused in 1507 was Marina Emo, daughter of Lorenzo Capello and wife of Zuan Emo, whose luxurious dress in 1515 at a famous performance by the Immortali in the Pesaro home violated both mourning protocols and sumptuary legislation. Her cousin was the wife of Marco Foscari.[115] Bianca Grimani is likely to be the wife of Marco Grimani; the daughter of Francesco Foscari, she was the maternal aunt of Isabeta Barbarigo and of Lucietta Soranzo's grand-niece.[116] Cupid's catching her in the lap with an arrow is consistent with the impetuous and domineering nature of her husband. Laureta Foscari is likely to be the sister of Zuan Foscari qu. Agostin, who calls her 'Laureta' in three wills; they were the second cousins of Bianca Foscari Grimani. While Zuan's wife was also named Laura, a diminutive is unlikely to have been attached to her name. Strong-willed and beautiful, wealthy in her own right, Laura Sanudo Foscari was among the few married women making her *Estimo* declaration in Padua independently of her husband (who, however, came later and gave it again himself). In 1525 she famously scandalized her relative Marin and other patricians by wearing pierced earrings in the style of *more* (Muslim or black women).[117] Maria Lion has not yet been identified. Maria da Leze would seem to be the wife of Immortale Zuan da Leze, who in 1518 stated that he was married to Marieta Badoer, the daughter of Benedetto.[118] His mother was another of the daughters of Francesco Foscari.[119] Isabetta Gusoni Venier, wife of Lunardo Venier, was another married woman who made an independent Padua *Estimo* declaration, indicating that she was ardent and willing at least in business matters.[120] Her paternal family had married into the Foscari line in question.[121] Marieta Bibbiena was most likely a daughter

110 ASVe, *AGRM*, busta 250, second *vacchetta*, fols 42ᵛ, 44ʳ, 47ᵛ, 55ʳ, 57ʳ, 60ʳ, 60ᵛ, 66ᵛ, 80ʳ, 84ᵛ, 86ᵛ.
111 Sanuto, 7: 158–9.
112 ASVe, *AGRM*, busta 250, second *vacchetta*, fols 2ʳ, 2ᵛ, 8ᵛ, 9ʳ, 15ʳ, 17ʳ, 17ᵛ, 19ʳ, 25ᵛ, 26ʳ, 41ᵛ, 42ᵛ, 43ᵛ, 52ᵛ, 67ʳ, 69ʳ, 80ᵛ.
113 ASVe, *Archivio Grimani Santa Maria Formosa*, busta 3, document dated 1488.
114 Sanuto, 27: 671.
115 Sanuto, 29: 443; Gullino, *Marco Foscari*, p. 30.
116 VBMC, Provenienze Diverse c, 1297 / IV, busta 1297, fols 45ʳ–9ᵛ; ASVe, *AGRM*, busta 269, unnumbered documents of 1520, 1521.
117 Barbaro, 3: 513; ASPd, *Estimo 1518*, busta 352, fol. 95ʳ⁻ᵛ; busta 126, fol. 119ʳ⁻ᵛ; Sanuto, 14: 31; 40: 425; ASVe, *AGRM*, busta 39, fasc. 14 naming wife Laura and sister Laureta; busta 87, second document; busta 251, unnumbered document dated August 16, 1528.
118 ASPd, *Estimo 1518*, busta 352, fol. 112ʳ; cf. Crescenzi, 231.
119 ASVe, *AGRM*, busta 189, unnumbered document of 1531.
120 ASPd, *Estimo 1518*, busta 352, fols 85ᵛ, 238ʳ, 346ᵛ; ASPd, *Notarile*, busta 1532, fol. 133ᵛ.
121 Barbaro, 4: 205.

of Pietro Bibbiena, resident in Venice for many years as the orator at times of the pope and at times of Florence. After his death in 1514, the Venetian state assigned a pension to his impoverished widow and daughters in gratitude for his service. This pleased his brother Cardinal Bernardo, one of the principal functionaries at the court of Leo X. Two of Pietro's daughters remained in Venice as nuns, while two went to Rome. One of the latter was married to a papal functionary, thus potentially the *papessa*, and one to a wealthy Roman. When Cardinal Bernardo died, Zuan Francesco Valier was sent to France to make a settlement with the king on behalf of Pietro's sons about his bishopric there.[122] No Hieronima Venier has emerged as yet; however, Nicolò Venier, who served as *savio dil conseio* with Andrea Magno in 1523 and whose wife was the daughter of Agustin Foscari, had a beloved daughter who was married in Padua in 1524 when he was *capitanio*.[123] The Zen family, connected to the Foscari through the assignment of some of the diocese's feudal properties by Bishop of Padua Jacopo Zen to the Foscari line in question,[124] has not yet yielded the first name Helena. However, she may be the daughter of Piero Zen whom Stefano's homonymous kinsman Stefano Magno qu. Pietro married in 1527.[125] Lastly, while a Laura Cocco has not yet been identified, one of Stefano Magno's maternal aunts had married Antonio Cocco and thus Laura was his relative.

The carnivalesque surface of the tarring episode seems to mask larger underlying issues and a potential practical purpose that may be discerned with the aid of information about the historical context and the economic and political endeavors and strategies of the families involved. Only days before Marco Grimani's party, his uncle Cardinal Domenico had seen the defeat of his candidacy for the papacy, a defeat that many attributed to words spoken by his fellow Venetian Cardinal Marco Corner against him. Those many included Domenico's father, Doge Antonio Grimani, who charged Cardinal Marco with ruining the Venetian state first by helping elect Leo and then by failing to elect Domenico.[126]

That the two families belonged to distinct groupings within the patriciate that were rivals and at times even enemies in financial and political endeavors and that espoused contrasting alliances to achieve them is supported by an array of evidence. All of the families involved in the party, the tarring episode, and the *capitolo* had built their fortunes with the typical Venetian strategy of accumulating capital through trade and then employing it in banking; all responded to the growing contemporary threats to trade by seeking land investments and ecclesiastical

122 Sanuto, 17: 548–9; 18: 149, 182, 185; 24: 12; 29: 113, 401, 405; see also Hallman, pp. 83–4.
123 Sanuto, 34: 103, 363; 36: 403–4; Linda L. Carroll, "'I have a good set of tools': The Shared Interests of Peasants and Patricians in Beolco's *Lettera giocosa*," *Theatre, Opera and Performance in Italy from the Fifteenth Century to the Present. Essays in Honour of Richard Andrews*, ed. Brian Richardson, Simon Gilson, and Catherine Keen, Occasional Papers 6 (Egham, UK, 2004), pp. 83–98.
124 ASVe, *AGRM*, busta 1bis, fasc. 9.
125 Sanuto, 46: 276.
126 Sanuto, 32: 433.

benefices. All were aware of the need to cope with the ambitions of France, Spain, and the empire for control of the Italian peninsula and of the increasingly aggressive westward movement of the Turkish Porte.[127] Beyond this point, their strategies diverged: one group favored the cultivation of France as the best means of maintaining international commerce and influence and one favored the cultivation of Spain and the empire.

This branch of the Grimani had traditionally associated with the latter for two important reasons: on the one hand, Spain and the empire's control of many states along the coastal trade route to northern Europe and of cities that were major trade partners and, on the other, the empire's continuing formal feudal rights over much of Venice's mainland dominion and the attempted actualization of them through recent wars. This strategy was valued all the more after the 1519 election of Charles of Spain provided him with vast amounts of wealth to finance military action and united in him control of most of the litoral and the ports of the western galleys' journeys. Charles shrewdly augmented his leverage through his cultivation of Henry VIII, who controlled the galleys' important destination of London. Even more reasons were added in late 1521 by imperial forces' capture of Milan, crucial to land trade routes and banking, and by Charles's drawing of Henry into a formal alliance against France.[128] Complementing the preference for the empire, perceived as Europe's bulwark against the Turkish onslaught, was a defensive attitude toward the Turks.

The other group instead favored alliance with the French and relatively friendly relations with the Turks, in line with their trade in goods from the eastern Mediterranean (by then entirely controlled by the Turks) principally to France and their efforts to move the maritime route of commerce with northern Europe to French land routes. This was the group with which the Corner and the Foscari were chiefly associated. Its members also looked to France to retake Milan and to elect a French-leaning pope in the near future, an obvious candidate being Cardinal Marco, as then-ambassador to Rome Marco Foscari remarked approvingly in his later *relazione* (official ambassadorial report).[129] The uncle of the Bishop of Ivrea, Bonifacio Ferrero, was an important cardinal who, while on his way to participate in the recent conclave, had been imprisoned by the Spanish in Pavia because of his pro-French sentiments. The conclave had been delayed until he could arrive and he exercised decisive influence over it. As noted above, when Cardinal Giulio de' Medici accepted that he could not be elected, he proposed the saintly Flourent as the candidate who would least interfere with Medici interests, as well as the one acceptable to the largest number of cardinals. After he had persuaded several cardinals to this point of view, Ferrero joined them and turned the

---

127   A comprehensive overview is available in Kenneth M. Setton, *The Sixteenth Century to the Reign of Julius III*, Memoirs of the American Philosophical Society vol. 161 (Philadelphia, 1984), pp. 1–311.

128   Peter Gwyn, *The King's Cardinal. The Rise and Fall of Thomas Wolsey* (London, 1990), pp. 147–57.

129   Sanuto, 41: 288.

tide.[130] For those planning to bide their time and elect a French pope at the next conclave, Ferrero would be a key figure.

It would seem from the details of the party that Marco Grimani, a member of the rising generation having to consider whether Francis I would fulfill his vow to best his imperial rival in the contest to control the Italian peninsula and the next papal election, was positioning himself closer to the pro-French Corner-Foscari group. This was the group to which not only his numerous brothers-in-law belonged but also a large segment of the Venetian patriciate, a preference reinforced by the defeat of Grimani papal ambitions and the approaching demise of the elderly and frail Grimani doge. In short, it would appear that Marco Grimani had decided that the French and their Venetian patrician supporters had a greater chance of emerging the winners in various important contests and was willing to align himself personally with them even if it meant distancing himself from his paternal line's traditional pro-imperial strategy.

Details about the families of the women whose names precede Maria Caravello's support this hypothesis in their stronger affiliations with the older Grimani and the empire or their reasons for cultivating the new Pope Adrian VI, Charles V's former tutor.

The Diedo and the Priuli, who had been intermarrying and co-investing in banks and property since the early fifteenth century,[131] also had strong ties to the Grimani. One of the committees electing Doge Antonio included Andrea Diedo, whose name also appears on the list of relatives attending Grimani's ducal installation ceremony, followed by members of the Priuli family, to which his wife belonged.[132] At the end of the Cambrai wars, the Diedo (specifically Alvise) sought the formal return of their property in Cervia over which the pope had claimed dominion. The effort might more easily meet success if the Diedo were seen to side with the empire, a strategy that the family appears to have cultivated and one that would have become even more appealing with the election of Charles's former tutor as pope.[133] At the 1521 party, Andrea Diedo's wife danced only with the Prince of Bisignano, a favorite of the new emperor. The prince was also fêted with a sumptuous supper by Marc'Antonio Venier on behalf of his *compagnia della calza* Ortolani, strongly associated with the ducal Grimani, in the same home that would be tarred the following year. The Venier too had good reason to cultivate the favor of the emperor. They were leading investors in mainland property, including the feud of Sanguineto of which Marc'Antonio owned a portion, and land purchased from the Paduan noble Forzaté held in common with

130 Sanuto, 32: 260, 263, 272, 273, 274, 284, 288, 290, 301, 302, 328, 329, 384, 385, 415 (Giulio's proposal).
131 Reinhold C. Mueller, *The Venetian Money Market. Banks, Panics, and the Public Debt, 1200–1500*, Vol. 2 of *Money and Banking in Medieval and Renaissance Venice* (Baltimore, 1997), pp. 183–4; ASPd, *Estimo 1518*, busta 352, fol. 220ʳ.
132 Sanuto, 30: 439, 488.
133 Sanuto, 25: 194.

the Dandolo and Contarini.[134] They married into mainland feudal noble families including the Conti di Collalto and the Martinengo, *condottieri* who also owned a portion of Sanguineto.[135] Detailed accounts of their property interests are contained in a number of lengthy letters and other documents written from Padua where a family member was living in the Saracinesca quarter.[136]

The family of Isabetta Barbarigo, also relatives by marriage of the Priuli, were among the first Venetians to recommend abandonment of trade (which they conducted with Spain) in favor of agriculture.[137] They also had ecclesiastical ambitions: Hironimo was apostolic protonotary, *primicerio* of San Marco, and the administrator of the bishopric of Padua on behalf of Cardinal Marco Corner, his uncle.[138] In this last capacity, contingent upon approval by the pope, he was authorized to invest the bishopric's rich feuds, which he did to Marco and Zuan Foscari.

The Pesaro, one branch so connected with northern trade as to be known as 'da Londra' (of London),[139] also offered distinguished service to the papacy. The battle against the Turks led by Bishop Jacopo Pesaro and his cousin Benedetto has been described in Chapter 1. His family and the Grimani were related and he had been a high-ranking member of Cardinal Domenico Grimani's staff.[140] Francesco Pesaro, Archbishop of Zara, would become governor of Rome under Adrian.[141] The Pesaro were known not only for fighting the Turk but for defense of the mainland, where they had extensive properties.[142] As noted in Chapter 1, they also had financial relationships with leading mainland families. Francesco Pesaro qu. Marco, who assumed extensive responsibilities for mainland defense, including some together with Andrea Magno in Verona in 1519, was married to another daughter of Francesco Foscari.[143] Piero Pesaro 'da Londra', a procurator and elector of Doge Grimani, had first married a member of the Diedo family and

134 Gaetano Cozzi and Michael Knapton, *Storia della Repubblica di Venezia dalla Guerra di Chioggia alla riconquista della terraferma* (Turin, 1986), p. 127; Sanuto, 25: 530; PBUC, ms. 996, Marin Sanudo, *Itinerario*, fol. 39ᵛ; ASVe, *AGRM*, busta 223, printed fascicle, pp. 1–35.

135 PBC, B.P. 1422, Antonio Fassini, *Genealogia della grande famiglia Conti e sue diramazioni*, doc. 2, table 101a; Sanuto, 7: 693.

136 ASPd, *Notarile*, busta 1291, fols 12ʳ–13ᵛ, 18ʳ–19ʳ, 20ʳ⁻ᵛ, 21ʳ⁻ᵛ, 22ʳ–8ᵛ, 29ʳ⁻ᵛ, 64ʳ, 69ʳ–70ᵛ, 266ʳ, 420ʳ, 422ʳ; busta 1292, fols 121ᵛ–6ʳ, 126ᵛ–42ʳ, 153ʳ–8ʳ, 469ᵛ–71ᵛ.

137 Lorenzo Finocchi Ghersi, *Il Rinascimento veneziano di Giovanni Bellini* (Venice, 2003–4), pp. 110–15; Sanuto, 36: 497; Cozzi and Knapton, p. 125; Frederic C. Lane, *Andrea Barbarigo, Merchant of Venice* (Baltimore, 1944), p. 122.

138 ASVe, *AGRM*, busta 66, fasc. 5, document dated February 13, 1518; PACV, *Acta capitularia*, vol. 11, fol. 87ʳ; Sanuto, 39: 240–2.

139 Sanuto, 28–33, *s.v.* Alessandro Pesaro.

140 Rona Goffen, *Piety and Patronage in Renaissance Venice. Bellini, Titian, and the Franciscans* (New Haven, 1986), p. 122.

141 Sanuto, 34: 216.

142 See *e.g.* ASPd, *Estimo 1518*, busta 352, fol. 303ʳ⁻ᵛ.

143 Sanuto, 28: 60, 68, 102, 241; ASVe, *AGRM*, busta 251, unnumbered item dated 7 September 1520; Ennio Concina, *La macchina territoriale. La progettazione della difesa nel Cinquecento veneto* (Bari, 1983), p. 17.

then a Priuli.[144] His Priuli in-laws were included in his extensive commerce with northern Europe, whose London branch was saved from failure by Henry VIII himself after the Venetian defeat at Agnadello.[145]

One of the leading members of Lucrezia Zorzi Venier's paternal family, the distinguished diplomat Marin Zorzi, was one of the first patricians to recognize the magnitude of Charles's power, arguing in the Senate that Venice should endeavor to find a *modus vivendi* with him. Shortly thereafter he was elected *podestà* of Padua, including in his entourage numerous women; his term overlapped with that of Andrea Magno as *capitanio*.[146]

The Zane connection to this group is manifest in Antonio Zane's role as *signor di la festa* (lord of the festivities) of the 1521 Ortolano soirée for the Prince of Bisignano, who was honored not only by the presence of over forty of the city's most beautiful women but by their participation in the *ballo del cappello* (hat dance).[147] The dance, while considered scandalous by some because the woman chooses her partner, was frequently offered to visiting dignitaries as an honor and a diversion. As the *signor*'s relative, Elena was likely among the women participants. Her activities in the turn to mainland investments would emerge later when, as wife of a member of the 'dal Banco' branch of the Pisani family, she was intimately involved with their redirecting of investments from sea trade to land, adding to their properties near Montagnana that would later be adorned by a Palladian villa.[148] Her awareness might have been heightened by her ancient family's loss of status with the decline of the spice trade,[149] which included the reassignment of important benefices of the influential cleric Bernardo Zane to Andrea Corner, the illegitimate brother of Cardinal Marco, after Zane's death in 1514.[150] This is the same Andrea Corner to whom Daniello would later dedicate his *Poetica*.

On the other hand, Maria Corner Caravello and the women whose names follow hers belonged to families with reasons to support Marco Grimani, a Marco Corner papacy, or a move toward a French-oriented foreign policy. These included families who saw their commerce in northern Europe served by the land route through

---

144   Sanuto, 30: 473, 474; Barbaro, 6: 83.

145   Girolamo Priuli, *I diarii*, ed. Arturo Segre et al., *Rerum Italicarum Scriptores*, 2nd ed. (Città di Castello and Bologna, 1912–33), vol. 4, fasc. 326, pp. 204–5; Mueller, p. 349 Table 8.8; Sanuto, 24: 327–30, 329, 26: 500.

146   Sanuto, 27: 455, 28: 324; da Corte, fol. 134ʳ; for further efforts in Senate, Sanuto, 34: 295, 311, 383.

147   Sanuto, 29: 543, 546–7; Carroll, "Introduction," pp. 24, 59.

148   Kolb.

149   Cf. Sanuto 35: 146–7.

150   Sanuto, 17: 414, 425, 457; Edward Surtz, S.J., *The Praise of Pleasure. Philosophy, Education, and Communism in More's* Utopia (Cambridge, 1957), p. 81; Edward Surtz, S.J., *The Praise of Wisdom. A Commentary on the Religious and Moral Problems and Backgrounds of St. Thomas More's* Utopia (Chicago, 1957), p. 225; Fabrizio Cruciani, *Teatro nel Rinascimento. Roma 1450–1550*, "Europa delle corti" Centro studi sulle società del antico Regime Biblioteca del Cinquecento 22 (Rome, 1983), p. 363.

France as an alternative to the coastal route with which Charles and Henry had repeatedly interfered.[151] Those with property along the Adriatic coast, relatively recently added to the Venetian dominions and surrounded on the south and west by papal territory, felt that their interests were better served by a pope looking to France than by the Medici, who preferred Charles's support and aimed to consolidate control over central-eastern Italy.

Maria's was a cadet branch of the Corner family; her father, Alvise Corner qu. Donà of the parish of S. Beneto, had only obtained an undesirable office on Cyprus through a loan to the state. After his death in 1517, his widow had her dowry repaid out of the funds of his office, a sign of impoverishment.[152] That sum likely contributed to the dowry for Maria's sister's marriage to Ortolano Agostino Contarini in 1521, which was at the heart of another scandalous episode involving the Prince of Bisignano. At a supper celebrating the couple attended by the prince, a second inductee, the *condottiero* Antonio da Martinengo, arrived with an armed force because of insulting words directed at him by other Ortolani. The prince, seeing their arms, drew his sword, as did twenty other guests. Amidst the fears of the women, the party was terminated.[153] Maria's own marriage was to Moro Caravello, of one of the smallest Venetian patrician clans; he too had property in Cervia, where he had lived prior to the war of the League of Cambrai. Driven back to Venice by the fighting, he volunteered for the defense of Padua. At the war's close, he was among those who agreed to the payment demanded by the pope for the return of his land.[154] The couple's families thus seem to number among those who believed that their Adriatic properties would be less threatened by a French-leaning pope.

'La Querineta' has been hypothesized as Marco Grimani's sister. If so, through her aunt Isabetta Soranzo she was a relative by marriage of the Lucietta (Capello) Soranzo named in the *capitolo*. The Marietta Capello also named in the *capitolo* was as well if she was the wife of the great maritime hero Vicenzo Capello qu. Nicolò, who as *capitanio* of Cyprus had reported on the shipwreck of the Magno galley and who refused election as ambassador to Adrian.[155] A member of the important banking family, Lucietta was the sister of Filippo Capello; their father was Polo Capello, prominent in military affairs and in this period a proponent of alliance with France.[156] As Lucietta and Filippo's mother was a sister of the great Zorzi Corner and Caterina Corner queen of Cyprus, Lucietta and Filippo were cousins of Cardinal Marco. Filippo had shared an investment in the northern galleys with Marco Foscari, whose wife was a Capello.[157] Lucietta had been among

---

151 Sanuto, 30: 154–5.
152 Sanuto, 21: 450–51, 452, 515; 24: 15, 213–14, 221–2, 598, 599–601, 627, 650, 651; 25: 51; 26: 417; 27: 78, 81.
153 Sanuto, 29: 567.
154 Sanuto, 8: 378 (see correction of name in index); 17: 291; 25: 194.
155 Sanuto, 24: 22–3; 34: 108, 135.
156 Gullino, *Marco Foscari*, p. 27; Sanuto, 7: 158–9; 34: 314–15; ASVe, Dieci Savi alle Decime, *Redecima 1514*, busta 45; ASVe, *AGRM*, busta 246, unnumbered fascicle dated February 1507.
157 Gullino, *Marco Foscari*, p. 13.

the women accused of excessive spending on clothing along with the next named, Marina (Capello) Emo.

The daughter of the powerful and wealthy Lorenzo Capello qu. Zuan (and thus first cousin of Marco Foscari's wife), Marina Emo was also granddaughter of Doge Antonio Grimani.[158] She continued to dress luxuriously after her marriage to Zuan Emo, scion of another wealthy family. Her husband fled to his properties in Ravenna after an accusation of embezzling from the state; she joined him later when he became ill. They eventually established themselves in Padua, returning to Venice at the conclusion of the exile. She died suddenly in 1520,[159] perhaps the reason for the lack of description of her in the *capitolo*.

While no member of the Barozzi family has been identified, the lack of description with her name may be attributable to the excommunication of two relatives in 1520.[160] Bianca Grimani has been hypothesized as Marco's wife. Laureta Foscari belonged to a leading family in the French-affiliated group. Maria was a da Leze either by birth or by marriage, possibly the wife of Zuan da Leze. One of the family's most prominent members, he showed French leanings,[161] including membership in the Immortali, hypothesized as fundamentally pro-French despite a willingness to bend toward the empire when advantageous. That Zuan had a relative at the papal court may explain the *capitolo*'s reference to seeing Maria with the pope.[162] Members of the birth family of Isabetta Gussoni Venier had married with those of the 'dal Banco' branch of the Pisani family, whose patriarch Alvise, despite his heavy investments in the northern galleys, was one of the most ardently pro-French patricians.[163] Isabetta herself paid a *livello* on one of her properties to Alvise Pisani.[164] Marieta Bibbiena's family, with strong ties to the papacy, was seeking the renewal of a French benefice for her relative that had been obtained by Cardinal Bernardo while on a mission to France that resulted in his changing his affiliation from imperial to French.[165]

In summary, Marco Grimani's party, the tarring episode, and the *capitolo* all give signs of being intimately connected to the kaleidoscope of loyalties and alliances of individual Venetian patricians and their families that fragmented and varied as they attempted to divine and ally with the eventual winner of the mortal combat among the major external national and international powers. In the conflict between an effort to rally forces on the part of the French, who had many

---

158   Sanuto, 2: 1363; 7: 158–9.
159   Sanuto, 19: 418; 22: 365, 498, 548; 23: 89, 237, 588; 28: 566.
160   Sanuto, 29: 504.
161   Sanuto, 21: 267.
162   Sanuto, 41: 288.
163   Barbaro, 6: 123; Rodolfo Gallo, "Una famiglia patrizia. I Pisani ed i palazzi di S. Stefano e di Strà," *Archivio Veneto* 5ª serie, 35 (1944): 65–228, 89.
164   ASPd, *Estimo 1518,* busta 352, fol. 85ᵛ.
165   Giuseppe Lorenzo Moncallero, "La politica di Leone X e di Francesco I nella progettata crociata contro i turchi e nella lotta per la successione imperiale," *Rinascimento* 8 (1957): 61–109, esp. 75–83.

adherents among his closest Venetian peers, and what appeared to be the tired and thus losing forces of his paternal imperial alliance, Marco Grimani seems to have been considering affiliation with the former and abandonment of the latter. Through his party and the guest list, he signalled his new predilection and invited others to show their similar preference or to join him. Marietta Caravello, whose slender patrimony depended on a combination of Venetian defense and papal good will, then took it upon herself to punish those women who eschewed the invitation. Among the houses tarred were those of bankers Pisani and Capello who, despite personal preferences for French affiliation, owed much of their ongoing generation of wealth to imperial favor of their commerce and thus did not publicly and forcefully advocate for a French alliance. That they were perceived to favor the empire is indicated by the tarring of their houses together with those of the Besalù-Beltrame, Sephardic bankers who served the pope, and Andrea Diedo, whose beautiful wife Isabeta was a member of the Priuli banking family that made their money with the northern galleys (see also Chapter 3).[166] The author of the *capitolo* and Magno as its copyist, in declaring Isabeta Diedo the most beautiful, seem to be throwing their lot in with those continuing to favor the imperial-papal faction, which did force Venice into an alliance in July of 1523 and in the event emerged as the victorious power, their victory sealed with the 1529 Peace of Bologna.

The section of Canonician 36 dedicated to *capitoli* continues with relatively traditional literary works, one attributed to Navagero (presumably Andrea) (53^{r-v}), one by Bernardino da Lucca (Daniello) (53^{v}–4^{v}), one by Onofrio (presumably Onofrio Veronese) (54^{v}–5^{r}), one in the female voice to the Virgin Mary whose verses follow the letters of the alphabet (55^{r}–7^{r}), and one attributed to Bellisario Laura (57^{v}). Magno's characteristic τελωσ signs the bottom of fol. 59^{r}, but then he apparently found an additional work of interest, because it is followed by instructions to turn the page and, on fols 59^{v}–60^{r}, by a *capitolo* in the form of a dialogue between a woman confessing infidelity to her lover and the priest advising her to always do what her lover tells her. The definitive conclusion of the section is marked on fol. 61^{v} with τελωσ.

The Remaining Sections

After four blank folios (62–6), entries resume with *canzoni* on folio 67^{r}, which originally bore the number 73. Although the first (*Ochi miei ch'al mirar foste si pronti*; My eyes, you were so quick to gaze) is anonymous here, it was often attributed to Girolamo Verità.[167] The second (*Amor da che'l te piace*; Love because it pleases you), again here anonymous, is by Ariosto, as is the sixth (*Dappoi mio*

166 See Chapters 3 and 4 for subsequent developments. They did so at the time of the League of Cognac and related wars, by then the northern galley routes having been abandoned as impossible to conduct. For Diedo, see Barbaro, 3: 233–4.

167 Massimo Castoldi, *Per il testo critico delle rime di Girolamo Verità* (Verona, 2000), p. 172.

longo amor mia longa fede; Because of my long love and long fidelity).[168] The third (*Giogia m'abonda al cor tanta et si pura*; Joy abounds in my heart so great and so pure) and fourth (*Ben ho da maledir l'empio signore*; Truly must I curse the cruel lord), both anonymous here, are by Bembo. The fifth (*Perche perche il vigore*; Because because the vigor) is attributed here to Brocardo. The seventh (*Ombre secrete et voi taciti boschi*; Secret shadows and you, silent woods) is anonymous here but elsewhere attributed to Verità or to the Bergamasque poet Nicolò Amanio.[169] The eighth (*Se'l pensier che dal core*; If the thought that from the heart) is correctly attributed here to Verità.[170] The ninth (*Mentre nel vostro viso*; While in your face) is here anonymous, as is the tenth (*Occhi vaghi lucenti*; Lovely, shining eyes) but both are by Francesco Maria Molza.[171]

The eleventh through the seventeenth (and final) *canzoni* are all attributed to Bernadino da Lucca. The first of these (fols 82^r–3^v) is in praise of "q. mio padre se[n]do capitanio d[e] padoa" (my late father, being [= 'in his capacity as' or possibly 'during his term as'] captain of Padua). Presuming the compiler to have been Stefano Magno, whose father Andrea died in 1525, the *canzone* could be assumed to have been composed or at least copied after that date. However, the curious 'sendo' and the triumphalist tone of the work may indicate that it was at least partly composed or perhaps commissioned during Andrea's time in office in Padua. Another curious detail is that the rubrication at the top of fol. 83^r mistakes the work's genre, terming it a madrigal: "Jesus 1520 venet[iarum] Madrial d[e] bernardi[n] da lucha." Announcing that Homer and Virgil would not be capable of adequately praising the greatness, rectitude, and intelligence of this man, the author compares him to Alcide and Massinissa, heroes of works by Garisendi and Trissino that Magno copied into IX, 71 in 1523 and 1524 respectively. Against the background of a rapidly spreading Lutheran movement, the *canzone* also praises the elder Magno's exercise of the three theological and four cardinal virtues (as codified in Catholic belief).

Two *canzoni* by Bernardino on love themes are followed by the second one praising the compiler's father: "Ca[n]zo[n] d[e]l med[e]simo al q. mio padre ut sup[r]a" (Canzone by the same [poet] to my late father as above) (fols 84^v–6^r). The sequence of the four works and the mournful tone of the second *canzone* point to a date of composition subsequent to Andrea's death. Closing the series attributed to Bernardino are a *canzone* on death and two on tormented love. There is rubrication for a fourth (86^r–90^r) that was never copied; eight blank folios follow, apparently indicating that the copyist anticipated additional works in this genre.

168 Mortara, col. 44.
169 Castoldi, pp. 175–6.
170 Castoldi, pp. 113–14.
171 Mortara, col. 43; Giuseppe Mazzatinti, *Inventarii dei manoscritti delle biblioteche d'Italia* (Forlì, 1890–), 13: 78 citing Magliabecchiana Cl. VII, no. 371, although *Mentre nel vostro viso* is attributed to Luigi Alamanni in Luigi Alamanni, *Versi e prose di Luigi Alamanni*, ed. Pietro Raffaelli, 2 vols (Florence, 1859), 2: 158–60.

Writing resumes with eclogues (pastoral dialogues) on a folio bearing the inked number '104' in relatively modern hand, which has been corrected in pencil to '99'. However, in the upper right corner appears the truncated original number '10', which apparently has lost a final '0': if one counts backward from the later folio where the original numeration is still complete, one arrives at '100' for this folio. The handwriting here, while most probably that of the same copyist, is rather different in appearance, perhaps indicating that this section was copied at a different time. Two works in the vernacular compose the eclogue section. The first (99ʳ–112ᵛ) is based on the usual Arcadian themes, but with a note of earthiness closer to Ruzante's *Pastoral*; the second (112ᵛ–20ᵛ) teaches that young women need to be kinder to the men in love with them to keep them from committing suicide for love.

Madrigals on typical Petrarchan love themes follow (121ʳ–3ᵛ), some of which are ascribed to Bernardino of Lucca (although *Venuta era madonna al mio languire* [My lady has come to my languishing] is attributed elsewhere variously to Sannazaro and to Amanio[172]) and one to Onofrio Veronese. The madrigal entries end in the middle of fol. 123ᵛ; the lack of final rubrication and the blank folios 124–30 indicate that the compiler originally intended to copy more works into this section.

Entries resume with five *frottole*,[173] which initiate a series of works in non-aulic genres (*frottola, novela, stanza, lettera d'amore, epitafio*) whose subjects and language are at times extremely earthy. The first, *Frotola d[e]le tasche e scarsele* (Frottola of the pockets and the pouches; fols 131ʳ–4ᵛ), immediately indicates the change in tone, as the clearly erotic anatomical referents of 'pockets' and 'pouches' are spun out in a lengthy metaphor.[174] The following *frottola* is even more explicitly addressed to the "putane" (whores) of Padua, asking them what they will do now that the soldiers are gone (fols 135ʳ–6ᵛ). Its topic raises the issue of the works' date, given that there was only one brief period prior to the general peace of 1530 in which this was the case: from 1518 to 1520.[175] Combined with the adolescent nature of the first *frottola*, this consideration may point to Stefano's collection of some of the works during sojourns in Padua or on the family property near there prior to Andrea's time in office.

A *frottola* of typical Petrarchan love topoi follows, structured in verses of five lines followed by the *ritornello* (fols 136ᵛ–7ʳ). Next is one with a bitter account of how Padua is cursed because all the city's beautiful women are unhappily married (fols 137ʳ–8ᵛ). After a blank section (fols 139–46), texts resume with a lengthy *novella* (fols 147ʳ–56ʳ), and then what appears to be a rare glance into Carnival or other kinds of informal patrician entertainment, a "Sta[n]za da recitar 4 co[m]

---

172 Castoldi, p. 175.
173 On this genre see Prizer, pp. 92–6.
174 Cf. Jean Toscan, *Le carnaval du langage. Le lexique érotique des poètes de l'équivoque de Burchiello a Marino (XVe–XVIIe siècles)*, 4 vols (Lille, 1981).
175 Carroll, "Dating *La Veniex[ia]na*."

pagni maschar[at]i i[n]sieme cu[m] u[n] capit[ano]" (Stanza to be recited by four masked *compagni* together with a captain; fols 156ᵛ–7ᵛ) in which the four declare to a woman that they are the heralds of love. The next two works are love letters full of exaggerated expressions of sentiment to a cold and haughty lady, of the kind that Ruzante satirizes in his *Lettera giocosa* (fols 158ʳ–9ʳ). Invective asserts itself in the subsequent group of satirical epitaphs that conclude the manuscript. They excoriate with equal vehemence Paduan women who are prostitutes, or at least do not observe norms of chastity, and Paduan men who pursue the erotic life too vigorously (fols 161ʳ–2ᵛ).

Magno as Compiler of Texts

Canonician 36's date of 1520 may be combined with the dates inscribed by Magno in his other manuscript collections to give some idea of his history as a compiler of texts. The text whose copying he began next, to the extent that it can be ascertained, was Ruzante's *Pastoral*. It is currently part of manuscript IX, 288, a collection of comedies completed by three anonymous plays (*Bulesca*, *Veniexiana*, and *Ardelia*), to which have been added numerous poems including ones by Girolamo Verità.[176] The manuscript's importance is increased by the fact that the copies of the comedies are the sole known ones.[177] The precise role of Stefano Magno in the creation of the manuscript, beyond copying the *Pastoral*, remains unclear. Emilio Lovarini was of the opinion that he copied the *Bulesca* as well, but that each of the other two works was copied by someone different (*i.e.* three hands total). He identified a watermark on some of the paper of the *Bulesca* as dating to 1518, which induced him to view the *Bulesca* as the first work to be copied.[178] Padoan believed that each of the four was copied by a different hand and saw a different watermark in the *Bulesca* folios that put it much later.[179] After a close examination of the manuscript, the present author concurs with Lovarini on the watermark (though not necessarily on the conclusion that its date and the date of the transcription of the *Bulesca* correspond) and with Padoan on the presence of four hands. Padoan also noted that folii 48 to 51 of the *Pastoral* manuscript had no watermark and that they constitute their own, very short quire at the end of the play, theorizing that Magno had removed unneeded sheets to use in a different manuscript (but they may be the sheets removed from

---

176 VBM, Ital. Cl. IX, 288 (= 6072); Anon., *Bulesca*, Da Rif, ed.; Anon., *La venexiana*, ed. Emilio Lovarini (Bologna, 1928); Anon., *La Veniexiana*, ed. G. Padoan; Anon., *La commedia Ardelia*, Edizione, introduzione e commento a cura di Annalisa Agrati, Biblioteca degli Studi mediolatini e volgari, Nuova Serie XIII (Pisa, 1994).

177 Emilio Lovarini, "Introduzione," in *Antichi testi di letteratura pavana*, ed. E. Lovarini (Bologna, 1894), pp. III–CXVI, LXIV–LXVI; Lovarini, "La *Pastoral*," pp. 271–92, esp. pp. 271–7.

178 Lovarini, "La *Pastoral*," pp. 273–4 identifying Charles-Moise Briquet, *Les filigranes. Dictionnaire historique des marques du papier dès leur apparition vers 1282 jusqu'en 1600*, 4 vols (Paris, 1907), no. 3502 found in Udine in 1518 in a public document.

179 Padoan, "Nota ai testi," identifying Briquet no. 3407 found between 1527 and 1536.

Canonician 36). Padoan, Da Rif, and Annalisa Agrati, editor of the *Ardelia*, document annotations to the manuscript's other texts in the hand that transcribed the *Pastoral* (*i.e.* Magno's).[180] As noted above, Padoan deduced that the *Pastoral* had originally belonged to a different manuscript (IX, 71) that includes a segment of the *Deifira* attributed to Leon Battista Alberti,[181] a group of poems including ones by Girolamo Verità, Jacopo Dal Legname's *Tragedia*, Gian Andrea Garisendi's *Dialogo overo Contrasto de Amore*,[182] and Gian Giorgio Trissino's *Sofonisba*. Padoan theorized that Magno, who styled IX, 288 a "libro de comedie de più hautori" (book of comedies by several authors) transferred the *Pastoral* there because of its genre.

Magno recorded in his copy of the *Pastoral* that he transcribed it from one he had obtained in Padua when his father was *capitanio* there, inscribing the folios with the date '1521'. Stefano could have witnessed the *Pastoral*'s Venetian performance of the preceding year: his father gave his report to the Senate as the returned *podestà* of Verona the same day. In 1521 his father arrived in Padua at the height of Carnival, when the *Pastoral* might have been repeated after its glorious Venetian performance of the year before.[183] *La Pastoral*'s contrasting groups, Arcadian shepherds who lament in Tuscan the sorrows of unrequited love and the uncouth dialect-speaking peasants whose practical knowledge saves the life of one of the Arcadians, not only reflect the mixed genres more popular on the mainland but exhibit an eclecticism and a taste for high-low juxtaposition similar to Magno's. Its love plot is also the most chaste of Beolco's early plays, limited to Ruzante's besottedness with a Betia who refuses his timid advances.

The manuscript of which the *Pastoral* originally formed a part (IX, 71) then continues (fols 59^r–74^r) with an untitled text that Giorgio Padoan identified as the second half of Leon Battista Alberti's *Deifira*.[184] Magno limits his annotation

---

180 Padoan's hypothesis that Magno formed the definitive manuscript subsequent to 1524 relies on a date of the mid 1530s for *La veniexiana*. However, the dates in the second decade of the sixteenth century of the *Bulesca* (probable) and *Pastoral* (certain) provide indirect support for the hypothesis of 1516 for *La veniexiana* presented in Carroll, "Dating *La Veniexiana*." Agrati sees no clear evidence for the *Ardelia*'s date, citing reasons why it could be 1522 and would not be after the late 1520s: Agrati, pp. 9, 51–3, 60–61. It could also have been between 1517, the year in which the war ended, and 1521 and perhaps particularly 1520, in May of which year Federico II Gonzaga was fêted for the second time in Venice by the Immortali (the play is set in May in Mantua and involves the herding of sheep outside the town, which could only have occurred in peacetime).

181 Leon Battista Alberti, *Deifira* in *Opere volgare*, ed. Cecil Grayson, 3 vols (Bari, 1973), 3: 221–46.

182 Ludovico Frati, "Gio. Andrea Garisendi e il suo *Contrasto d'Amore*," *Giornale storico della letteratura italiana* 49 (1907): 73–82; Giovanni Andrea Garisendi, *Ioannes Andreae Garisendi bononiensis opus. Dialogo overo contrasto de amore. Interlocutori: Antiphylo et Phylero extemporalmente cantanti*, in *Rimatori bolognesi del Quattrocento*, Ludovico Frati, ed. (Bologna, 1908), pp. 275–334.

183 Sanuto, 29: 566; da Corte, fols 140^v–1^r; Mario Baratto, "L'esordio del Ruzante," in *Tre studi sul teatro* (Vicenza, 1968), pp. 11–68; Sanuto, 28: 252–6; for further bibliography and information, see Carroll, "Venetian Attitudes."

184 Padoan, "Introduzione," p. 31; Alberti, pp. 234–45.

to the fact that he received the source text from his cousin Lorenzo Dolfin (for whom see above). The date and place of the copying are unrecorded. Padoan's list of pre-existing manuscript and print editions available in both Padua and Venice demonstrates that Magno could have undertaken it in either location. Also remaining unsolved is the mystery of why so meticulous a manuscript curator, even at the beginning of his endeavors, left the text incomplete. The manuscript exhibiting more than one hand, it is possible that the missing section was given to someone else to copy or that the segments forming the current manuscript were bound together later, possibly by someone other than Magno. Following the fragment (fols 74–6) are four poems by Girolamo Verità, identified by Padoan, that complain of tormenting thoughts, decry human hunger for money and glory, warn of the variability of fortune, and lament the coldness of the object of his affections: *Datemi pace o voi pensier molesti* (Give me peace, O you trouble-some thoughts), *Perché sete sì accese o genti insane* (Why do you burn so, O unhealthy people), *Questo è pur ver nisuna sorte è lunga* (This yet is true, no fate lasts long), *Qual cosa al mondo esser potea più strana* (Nothing in this world could have been stranger).[185]

Dramatic works resume with the *Tragedia* of Jacopo Dal Legname which, as Magno notes, he began copying in Venice on January 20, 1522 (Magno's fidel-ity to the dating practice of the city of copying means that this was most likely *more veneto* and thus 1523 *more comune*, subsequent to his father's return from Padua). It had been staged in Treviso on February 15, 1517 in the main palazzo of the city by the *podestà-capitanio*, Nicolò Vendramin. Given that Vendramin completed his term of office in the summer of 1517,[186] this detail proves that the performance year was given in the *more comune* used widely on the mainland (*i.e.* the year must have been 1517 and not a Venetian-style 1517 to be converted to common-style 1518, because by then Vendramin no longer held that office). At the conclusion of the play, Magno adds that he had the copy of it from his aunt Chiara, the wife of his uncle Lunardo Giustinian (Barbaro's genealogy records their marriage in that year).[187] The tragedy, which is preceded by a justification of drama ("Per che lexempio piu chel parlar move"; Because example is more mov-ing than words) unites two literary conventions normally separate, tragedy as the prerogative of the ruling class and the sorrows of unrequited love.

A summary of the play, which has not yet seen print, will be provided here because of its unusual content and because of the presence in the manuscript of the full *intermezzi*. Philippo, a duke (head of state), becomes enamored of a woman and speaks of her glowingly to his servant Scythio, who arranges an encounter through the woman's maidservant. Comic relief is provided after this first act by *intermezzi*: a jolly *frottola* about the happiness of those who fall in love performed by four rustics—two men and two women—under the leadership of Mercury, a *moresca* (Morris dance), and a *homo salvatico* (wild man). In the second act

185   Verità, pp. 67, 63, 63, 18.
186   Sanuto, 24: 433.
187   Barbaro, 7: 456; Sanuto, 26: 147.

Philippo meets Aurora, his beloved, and declares that he loves her, but she does not believe him. The following *intermezzo* consists of a triumphal float ridden by Cupid and accompanied by four nymphs carrying torches. They are led by Mercury, who pronounces the stanzas of a *frottola* exalting the triumph of love, repeated in song by the nymphs. It concludes with Jove, changed into a bull, a shower of gold, and a warning to women to eschew detachment and welcome those who are constant. The play resumes with an elderly procuress meeting Philippo's servant in the palace; they consult and she promises that she will do what she can to obtain a sign of interest from Aurora. She hastens to Aurora's house, where she presents herself as a seller of thread. Penetrating the ruse, Aurora sends her away. After Philippo receives the bad news from Scythio, he instructs the servant to take the palace musicians to Aurora's house to play for her in the hope of placating her. Despite their playing of a *mattinata* and other pieces, she is steadfast in her indifference. Plunged into despair by her rejection, Philippo resolves to deal himself 'obscura morte' (dark death). In the following *intermezzo* a chorus of four women nobly dressed in courtly fashion and led by Mercury repeats in song the stanzas of a *frottola* pronounced by him expressing pity for the lord's suffering, which will cause him to lose his state. Silenus then appears on his ass with his flask, led by satyrs playing bagpipes; they are followed by some laughing nymphs, as the fable tells. The tableau is clearly inspired by the painting *The Feast of the Gods* executed by Giovanni Bellini for Alfonso d'Este Duke of Ferrara only a few years prior.[188] Philippo wounds himself mortally in the fourth act; a hermit appears, and, seeing the inert body, laments that the prince is in hell with no chance of salvation. Roused from his death throes, Philippo accepts the hermit's instruction that he forgive the one who harmed him and confesses that he wounded himself. In the *intermezzo*, the four nymphs return, without the float. Again Mercury speaks the verses of a *frottola* which they then sing, lamenting that the state might be lost through the death of the duke and predicting that Aurora will suffer greatly when she learns of it so that all may understand the consequences of their actions. The characters, however, assure the audience that all will conclude with music and festivities. A *moresca* follows, with "in strumentj d[e] tela depintj de / varij colorj co[n] balzi antiqui i[n] capo / et i[n] mano uno festone co[n] foco ar / tificiato i[n] cima" (instruments [costumes? puppets?] of canvas painted various colors and [the dancers had?] old-fashioned headdresses on their heads and in their hands a wreath with fireworks [make-believe fire?] on top) (fols 100ᵛ–101ʳ). A bear comes out and attacks a combatant, causing the others to flee. The bear is frightened off by a "homo sylvaticho" (wild man), which allows the morris dancers to return, dressed as sailors, to carry off their fallen companion. (Because of the importance of the sea to Venice, the presence of sailors at a patrician's funeral was a sign of honor.[189]) As the fifth act begins, Aurora realizes that Philippo's death has deprived her of all comfort. Proclaiming that she will follow Dido, she kills

---

188 For the painting see Finocchi Ghersi, p. 134.
189 ASVe, *AGRM*, busta 95, fasc. 9; the comedian and comic impresario Zuan Polo was paid to organize this aspect of the funeral of Doge Antonio Grimani in 1523. Cf. Sanuto, 30: 399.

herself.[190] The servants bury the pair. The play concludes with a speech by Poeta, who exhorts the audience to be well and enjoy the festivity and, in a reference to Aristotelian views, wishes the spectators to be saved from bad things by the prudence engendered in them through observing the price paid by others. Magno then adds his characteristic τελωσ and the date and source of the copy (see above).

An unpublished madrigal by Girolamo Verità follows (fol. 105^v). Although untitled in the manuscript, the next piece is Giovan Andrea Garisendi's *Contrasto d'amore* (Debate about love), a dialogue between a character who disparages love and one who exalts it, with the latter having the last word.[191] At its conclusion Magno writes τελωσ and states that he received the work from his cousin Lunardo Coco, but does not include the date. Following it are two additional unpublished madrigals by Girolamo Verità.

The last lengthy work is Gian Giorgio Trissino's tragedy *Sofonisba*. Magno's marginal annotation that it is in print indicates that he preferred a manuscript source; he added "1524 adi otub.e Venetiis" (1524, on the day [blank] October, Venice). At the conclusion, after additional poems by Girolamo Verità, Magno notes that the texts were copied from originals provided by Jacopo Marcello. The simple name 'Jacopo' was not common in the Marcello family at the time; one of the few was Jacopo di Bernardo, whose father followed shortly upon Andrea Magno as *podestà* of Verona in 1521.[192] It is noteworthy that although Marcello returned from Verona in 1522,[193] Magno did not execute the copy until autumn of 1524, weeks after the appearance of two editions of the work and weeks before the author's arrival in Venice as papal nuncio on the delicate and vital diplomatic mission of convincing Venice to join an alliance including France.[194] Trissino, a member of a rebel imperialist Vicentine noble family whose kinsman Lunardo had been imperial governor of Padua during its brief freedom from Venetian rule in 1509, had composed the work after he was exiled from the Venetian dominion. Having been given refuge at the papal court, he dedicated the work to Leo X to express his gratitude. One of the first tragedies of the Italian Renaissance revival, it deals both with the heart-wrenching humiliation of the Carthaginians by the conquering Romans and with the uplifting restraint of a Roman who salvages Carthaginian honor by sacrificing his interests. The resonances for Italian leaders facing a renewed and fierce battle between Charles V and Francis I for the domination of the peninsula could not have been clearer, especially in the

---

190   Interest in the *Aeneid* was then increasing in Venice along with interest in the city's founding, believed by many to have been by Aeneas. Shortly thereafter the figure of Dido proliferated in Ferrarese art, possibly inspired by the arrival from Rome of a cartoon by Raphael for the *Stanze dell'Incendio*: Alessandro Ballarin, *La pittura a Ferrara negli anni del ducato di Alfonso I*. Register of documents by Alessandra Pattanaro. Catalogue by Vittoria Romani with the collaboration of Sergio Momesso and Giovanna Pacchioni, 2 vols (Cittadella, 1994–5), 1: 43, 79, 315. Vendramin may have learned of it earlier through his connections to Rome: Sanuto, 25: 92.

191   Padoan, "Nota ai testi," pp. 32–3; Lodovico Frati, ed., *Rimatori bolognesi del Quattrocento* (Bologna, 1908), pp. 283–327.

192   Sanuto, 31: 99.

193   Sanuto, 33: 476.

194   Sanuto, 37: 277.

context of Trissino's mission to convince Venice to abandon its formal but hollow alliance with Charles to join Clement and Francis.[195] One may only imagine the resonances for Jacopo Marcello's father Bernardo, governor of a mainland city coveted by the empire at a time when the war was intensifying, and for Trissino, whose loyalty to the Medici papacy required him to betray the earlier one that had created so much turmoil in his life.

The miscellany's termination coincides with Andrea Magno's concerted but fruitless efforts to crown his *cursus honorem* with election as procurator, possibly defeated because of his lack of wherewithal for a loan.[196] Shortly thereafter, and a month prior to the Triumphante festivity with the Ruzante performance that will be the subject of Chapter 3, Stefano married the daughter of Francesco Mocenigo qu. Piero, who brought him a dowry of 8,000 ducats. Within months his father Andrea died.[197] Four years later, Stefano's wife, in the late stages of pregnancy, was taken suddenly ill while visiting Padua and died.[198] Stefano later remarried, fathered numerous children, acquired an admired collection of medals,[199] and redirected his manuscript efforts to histories of Venice and its patricians.

Conclusions

Canonician 36, both in its contents and in its physical features, opens up new perspectives on Magno as a literary copyist and on the other manuscripts that he created. One notes his sense of authorship of the manuscript as a collection, beginning with its material form. The varying length of quires with the obvious removal of folios, the presence in a single manuscript of varying papers, the relocation of a work from one manuscript to another all provide evidence that he frequently manipulated the manuscripts just as authors rewrite their texts. His custom of inscribing the initial date and place on his manuscripts and the inclusion of information about his sources also belie an authorial attitude.

That custom also provides precious information about the chronology of the copies and Magno's literary tastes. The inscription in Canonician affirms it as his first known manuscript, begun the year before the transcription of the *Pastoral*. Its inauguration in Venice with works by Pietro Bembo says much about the birth of Magno's interest in lyric poetry. Canonician 36's strict division by genre differs from the careful choices and interleaving of texts that shape Magno's other literary manuscripts into chapbooks. Canonician 36 is also free from the contemporary exile from the attention of serious people of all poetry beyond the bounds of Petrarchism. These two characteristics together seem to indicate that Magno intended the collection for his personal use and perhaps as a repository

195 Setton, pp. 225–7.
196 Da Corte, fol. 140ᵛ notes that he was not rich.
197 Sanuto, 37: 7, 9, 11–13, 16, 440; 39: 335.
198 Da Corte, fol. 286ʳ.
199 PBC, *C.M.* 168 *Indice dei codici e medaglie esistenti appresso il N.H. s. Pietro Gradenigo fu de s. Giacomo in Venezia*, p. 15 "Memorie di scriverle [sic] Lettere iniziali all'uso antico scritto, e dimostrato di proprio pugno da Stefano Magno P.V. q. s. Andrea 1515."

from which to draw. His other two literary manuscripts, by contrast, seem more intended for circulation, as is also indicated by the preponderance of theatrical texts. That Magno's interest in realistic theater may have arisen even earlier than his interest in poetry may be indicated by the copy of the *Bulesca*, which is set in Venice and generally dated to about 1514. The plot centers on the competition of working-class men for a woman's favors and its resolution by a patrician. The inclusion next of *La veniexiana*, which has recently been shown to date to about 1518, further supports the hypothesis of an early interest in theater. This, the most openly erotic of any known sixteenth-century Italian play with its competition between the young and disappointed patrician wife of an elderly husband and a patrician widow for the favors of a young foreign man, is followed by *Ardelia*, in which a married woman at first resists temptation and then decides that because her marriage occurred without her consent it poses no obstacle to her following her desire. Its date of about 1522 confirms the chronologically and thematically tight organization of the manuscript around subjects and attitudes attractive to a very young man. That the *Pastoral* is placed first seems to say that Magno's taste or aesthetic judgment privileged those works that include at least some element of humanism or high culture and its traditional morality.

In all of these early literary manuscripts, to varying degrees, Magno mixes earthy themes with ethereal ones. He juxtaposes with apparent nonchalance highly formal or conventional Tuscan literary texts in the Petrarchan and humanistic traditions with texts in a rough vernacular or dialect that give extremely realistic portraits of contemporary life in all of its officially condemned, hidden or eschewed aspects. He thus manifests the high spirits and openness to all cultural levels characteristic of a young man attentive to the full range of developments in the vernacular cultural world. In addition, Magno's role as editor of eclectic works has a more serious side in its correspondence with the dual patrician habit of maintaining stable patrician authority while seeking and promoting cultural renewal through the importing to Venice of the best of innovative cultural production arising elsewhere. It is in this realm that his habit of providing paratextual information proves especially revealing. Important shared features of the works were their connectedness to Magno's circle of family and friends and the connection of the staging or copying of the works to their mainland governance duties. That the authors of the works were largely from mainland towns that had rebelled during the war and even from members of rebel families (Beolco, Trissino) shows the effort on the part of the Venetian ruling class and Magno as an exponent of it to use literary and theatrical culture to knit Venice back together with its mainland dominion at the war's end. It may also show their interest, in the brief period between 1518–20 and 1526, to open some channels to imperial supporters and possibly even back channels to the emperor.

The survival of both Venetian patricians and citizens of mainland towns depended on their ability to cooperate with one another. Literature and theater promoted such cooperation by helping the Venetian ruling class understand the lives and concerns of those they governed and to allow at least some of the governed to believe that they had been heard.

3 *Concordiae dedicatum*
The Triumphanti, the Beolco, and the Politics of Prosperity in Renaissance Venice

The Founding of the Triumphanti

On January 2, 1516, as Marin Sanudo recorded in a diary entry heretofore unnoted by scholars, a new *compagnia della calza* named the Triumphanti formed by 20-year-olds gave a supper hosted by Antonio Mocenigo di sier Alvise cavalier. The membership roll consisted of Hironimo Bernardo di Nicolò, Zuan Barbo di Benedeto, Lorenzo Bembo qu. Hironimo, Nicolò Arimondo di Piero, Hironimo Grimani di Marin, Tomà Malipiero di Hironimo, Andrea Marzelo di Bernardo, Antonio Mocenigo di Alvise cavalier, Nicolò Morosini di Zacaria, Andrea Sanudo qu. Alvise, Ferigo Valaresso di Polo, Fantin Zorzi di Nicolò, Andrea di Renier qu. Jacomo, Almorò Morosini qu. Antonio, Zuan Francesco Salamon di Zuan Nadal, and Albertin Badoer di Piero. Antedating by four years the information in the classic study of the *compagnie* by Lionello Venturi, the entry also gives a much fuller (though not complete) list of members.[1] The present analysis will provide new data gathered from the *Diarii* and numerous primary sources about the Triumphanti, their interests, and their connections that will illuminate the strategies that they chose in constructing their careers and their influence on public life and policy, including through festivities. As the generation coming of age in the new climate of austerity, they provide an excellent case study in coping strategies. New background information about their famous 1525 festivity, at which Angelo Beolco performed a scandalous play, includes the discovery in Foscari account books that Beolco's great-uncle and uncle had provided critical investment to an earlier threatened Venetian galley round in which numerous patrician families, including many represented among the Triumphanti, held stakes (see Chapter 1). A wealth of new information documenting the many connections linking Beolco and his affines to the Triumphanti and their affines over the preceding decades will be presented and analyzed for political and cultural strategies.

The information detailed below may be summarized as follows: the Triumphanti entered their adult years contemporaneously with the resumption—after the war-related

---

1 Marino Sanuto, *I diarii*, ed. Rinaldo Fulin et al., 58 vols (Venice, 1879–1902), 21: 436; Lionello Venturi, "Le Compagnie della Calza (sec. XV–XVI)," *Nuovo Archivio Veneto* n.s. 16.2 (1909): 3–157, 87–8, 138.

eight-year hiatus—of Venice's western galley commerce, which produced much of the city's wealth. Although the wars had concluded, commerce continued to face threats from both the continuing Habsburg-Valois conflict, which also posed dangers to Venice's mainland dominion, and from the Turkish Porte, whose aggression in the waters of the Mediterranean and its surrounding lands also menaced Venice's *stato da mar*. Triumphante members, along with their families and allies, developed strategies to minimize such dangers while broadening the range of opportunities for wealth and status; the means they used to achieve their goals included festivities. In these endeavors they were often in competition, and sometimes in cooperation, with other prominent *compagnie*, especially the Immortali, Ortolani, and Zardinieri. As detailed below, they were chiefly concerned to regain control of their mainland properties and possibly increase them, to reassert governance and defense of the mainland state to protect them, to restart the lucrative commercial western-northern galley rounds suspended during the Cambrai wars, and to inaugurate their careers in government. Profitable commercial rounds were of crucial importance because they would provide the cash needed for both the purchase of additional property and the loans that were becoming a prerequisite to state office. However, the rounds also faced numerous grave challenges.

That mainland matters were from the beginning among Triumphante concerns may be deduced from the group of them now identifiable among the young patricians welcoming Federico II Gonzaga in 1517 when he came seeking a military *condotta* of the Republic, as those of the Immortali and Ortolani have been.[2] Federico, also extremely young and having just inherited the marquisate of Mantua, faced many of the same issues as the *compagni*. Venice was intent on keeping his friendship because of the strategic location of his state in the south central Po Valley, critical to the conflicts among both Italian and transalpine states, especially France and the empire, fighting for control of the peninsula. Both of their monarchs presented daunting profiles. The youthful Francis I, after assuming the throne in 1515, had helped the Republic regain its mainland state and held Gonzaga for three years at his court, while the Emperor Maximilian had only recently returned to Venetian control Verona and the Veronese, whose southern border abutted the Gonzaga marquisate. The boundary was protected by the fortress of Legnago, to the command of which Antonio Capello had been elected in 1516; Antonio was the brother of Triumphante Marin and cousin of Ortolano Bernardo, who figured among Gonzaga's greeters.[3] Facilitating the election of Capello, whose family was among the many in the patriciate having important

---

2 Linda L. Carroll, "Venetian Attitudes toward the Young Charles: Carnival, Commerce, and *Compagnie della Calza*," in Alain Saint-Saëns, ed., *Young Charles V, 1500–1529* (New Orleans, 2000), pp. 13–52.

3 Sanuto, 23: 489, 491; Legnago: M.E. Mallett and J.R. Hale, *The Military Organization of a Renaissance State. Venice c. 1400 to 1617* (Cambridge, 1984), pp. 264, 299, 389, 391, 410–11, 414, 425; Ennio Concina, *La macchina territoriale. La progettazone della difesa nel Cinquecento veneto* (Bari, 1983), pp. 6, 8–9, 11; Bruno Rigobello, "Modi di intervento del capitale veneziano nel polesine e l'insediamento agricolo dei Loredan, dei Corner, dei Badoer, e dei Grimani," in *Palladio e palladianesimo in Polesine* (Rovigo, 1984), pp. 21–35, 34; Sanuto, 23: 312–13.

holdings in the Veronese, had been a significant loan to the state. At the moment of Federico's visit, the Capello and other families were trying to wrest the rents that had remained uncollected during the war from the Veronese imperial nobles who had usurped them while free from Venetian control. However, on the recommendation of *provveditore generale* in the Veronese Zuan Polo Gradenigo, the Signoria stopped the effort to avoid irritating Maximilian. Gradenigo was the father of later Triumphante Zusto, who had recently returned from the war badly injured.[4]

In the following years, family members of Triumphanti, in addition to holding a variety of entry-level judicial and bureaucratic offices,[5] achieved election to governorships of towns such as Piove di Sacco and to the commission conducting the reassessment of taxable real estate (*Estimo*) of Padua and its territory.[6] The family of Triumphante Vicenzo Contarini, whose brothers included the future cardinal Gaspare, followed a typical strategy. In 1517, the brothers inherited the patrimonial land in the region of Piove di Sacco. Originally enfeuded to the bishopric of Padua, it was agricultural property acquired by their grandfather Ferigo and their father Alvise over the course of the fifteenth century with the profits of maritime commerce and leased to peasants. Some parcels were held in common with the Dandolo or the Gussoni[7]; one of the latter was the subject of a 1507 transaction in Padua involving Alvise Contarini and Alvise Anzelieri, uncle of later Ruzante patron Alvise Cornaro.[8] When the Contarini brothers inherited the land in 1517, Gaspare, who felt an especially strong connection to the family villa there,[9] undertook to resolve several boundary disputes that had arisen over the years involving the Conti di Collalto, who also owned land in the region, and the community of Rosara. The peasant community, which had its own legally-recognized corporate structure, did not remain passive in the face of the action by patricians and nobles. In a procedure possibly providing a model to Beolco for his *Prima oratione*, the *visinanza* (council of male heads of families) of Rosara elected representatives to a meeting to resolve the conflict, a procedure involving a legal consultant and local officials. The notarial acts recording their agreement, which include a statement by Contarini apparently written in his own hand (fig. 3.1), were witnessed by important figures: Pietro Bembo's brother Bartolomeo and the Immortale Francesco Sanudo, who also owned land in the area.[10]

4   Sanuto, 22: 450; 23: 312, 583; 24: 250–51; Mallett and Hale, 264, 299, 389, 391, 410–11.
5   Sanuto, 22: 192, 527; 23: 196–7, 212, 225, 226, 242, 243, 260–61, 280, 313, 338, 368, 376, 428; 24: 514; 26: 232; 28: 336; 29: 502; 30: 20; 33: 574, 586.
6   Sanuto, 22: 657; 23: 223–4, 226, 241, 411, 412, 434–5; 25: 543, 565.
7   ASVe, *AGRM*, busta 223, unnumbered printed fascicle: pp. 1–35; busta 250, first *vacchetta*, fols 15ʳ, 26ʳ, 70ʳ⁻ᵛ, second *vacchetta*, fol. 9ᵛ; ASPd, *Estimo 1518*, busta 352, fols 238ʳ, 346ᵛ; ASPd, *Notarile*, busta 1531, fols 111ʳ⁻ᵛ, 113ʳ⁻ᵛ.
8   ASPd, *Notarile*, busta 1389, fols 614ʳ⁻ᵛ; see Chapter 1, note 53.
9   Elisabeth G. Gleason, *Gasparo Contarini. Venice, Rome and Reform* (Berkeley and Los Angeles, 1993), pp. 6, 25.
10 ASPd, *Notarile*, busta 2727, fols 36ʳ⁻ᵛ, 38ʳ–44ʳ (38ʳ the apparently autograph portion), 48ʳ–50ʳ; on the *visinanza*, see Emilio Menegazzo, "Stato economico-sociale del padovano all'epoca del

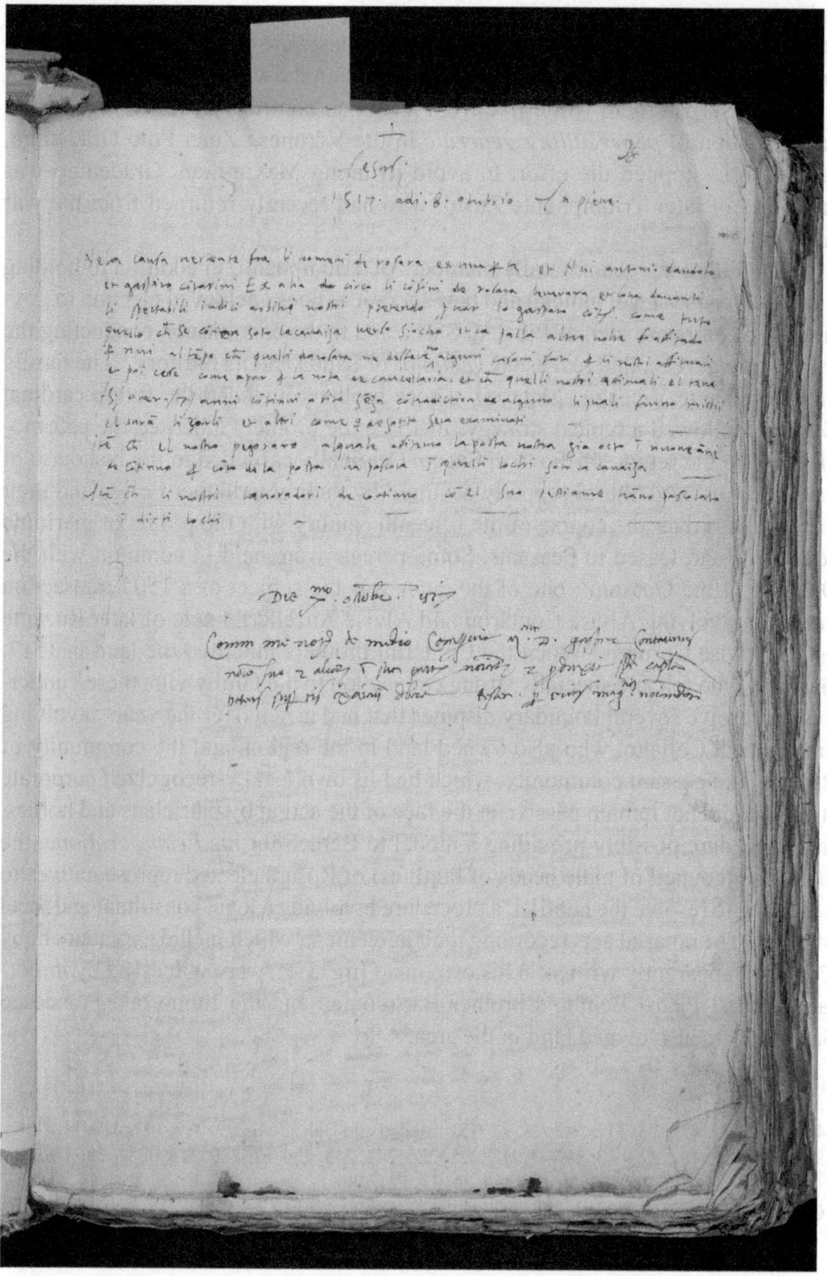

Figure 3.1 Archivio di Stato, Padova, *Notarile*, busta 2727, fol. 38ʳ, Archivio di Stato, Padua. (Photo: Sezione di Fotoriproduzione dell'Archivio di Stato di Padova su concessione del Ministero per i Beni e le Attività Culturali, Archivio di Stato di Padova, n. 6 del 8 luglio 2015 prot. n. 2331 sez. 28.13.07 / 1.2)

Soon after, Gaspare was elected to the commission measuring state-owned plots on the mainland that the government planned to sell to resolve the war debt (*Monte Nuovo*).[11] Accurately-drawn property lines were critical to potential purchasers because the sale represented an important opportunity for acquiring land, including many parcels confiscated from the war's imperial rebels and the enemy Este of Ferrara. The sales were important to the state as well because the looming war between Charles and Francis I for dominance of the peninsula made evident the need for long-term mainland defense and, to finance it, a complete updating of state landholding records for tax purposes. The updating was undertaken in 1518, and a commission to conduct the sale was authorized in 1519. Gaspare's election to the measurement commission may reflect in part respect for the expertise he demonstrated in the Piove dispute. In the following years he and his brothers, chiefly through Tommaso, purchased numerous *livello* rights and parcels in the area.[12]

Triumphante Hironimo Grimani di Marin also epitomizes the contemporary trends in economic activities, as documented by records including his account book.[13] He belonged to the Santa Maria Zobenigo branch of the family, more closely associated with the S. Cassian branch to which one of the Immortali belonged than to Doge Antonio's Santa Maria Formosa branch that was the backbone of the Ortolani. The Grimani family was a principal in northern trade; Marin, probably the Triumphante's father, was involved in the voyage assisted by the Beolco.[14] Their associations with other Triumphante families ran deep. Through his maternal Capello uncles, Hironimo was related both to the Ortolano Bernardo Capello and to his fellow Triumphante Marin Capello qu. Battista.[15] Marin's mother had been Paula Garzoni, daughter of Procurator Marin, of the family that managed the Bernardo bank.[16] When Marin's brother Antonio became commander of the fortress of Legnago, he continued in the family military tradition exemplified by Polo Capello qu. Vetor, *provveditore* or civilian overseer of the army, during the wars.[17] In 1502, Hironimo's sister Chiaretta had married Francesco Mocenigo qu. Piero, the marriage arranged by Vicenzo Contarini's

Ruzante," in *Colonna, Folengo, Ruzante e Cornaro. Ricerche, testi e documenti*, ed. Andrea Canova (Padua, 2001), pp. 304–37; see in general Lorena Favaretto, *L'istituzione informale. Il Territorio padovano dal Quattrocento al Cinquecento* (Milan, 1998).

11 Gleason, pp. 7, 27–8; Sanuto, 26: 129, 483, 27: 111; 28: 120, 137, 197, 236, 237, 270, 549, 620–21; cf. 38: 284.
12 ASPd, *Notarile*, busta 2733, fols 126ʳ–30ʳ, 142ʳ–5ʳ, 297ᵛ–9ᵛ, 306ʳ⁻ᵛ, 365ᵛ–7ʳ, 493ᵛ–4ᵛ; ASPd, *Estimo 1518*, busta 352, fol. 238ʳ; busta 354, fol. 111ʳ; ASVe, *AGRM*, busta 223, unnumbered printed fascicle; ASPd, *Notarile*, busta 1389, fol. 614ʳ⁻ᵛ.
13 ASVe, *AGB*, busta 9.
14 ASVe, *AGRM*, busta 250, second *vacchetta*, fols 9ʳ (Gussoni), 42ᵛ (Grimani); cf. ASVe, *AGB*, busta 40, unnumbered folio of 1478; Sanuto, 8: 213.
15 Marco Barbaro, *Arbori dei patritii veneti*, copied by Tommaso Corner and Antonio Maria Tasca (1743), ASVe, *Misc. Codici I, Storia Veneta* 17 (hereafter Barbaro), 2: 250–1.
16 ASVe, *AGB*, busta 22, unnumbered folio dated October 17, 1507.
17 Angelo Ventura, "Cappello, Paolo," *DBI*, 18 (1975).

maternal uncle, Nicolò Malipiero qu. Tommaso, also kinsman of Triumphante Tomà Malipiero.[18]

In 1519 Hironimo Grimani married a member of another wealthy Santa Maria Zobenigo merchant banking family, Donada Pisani, daughter of Almorò and niece of Alvise. The bride's mother was the granddaughter of Doge Leonardo Loredan and the daughter of another merchant in northern trade, Giacomo Gussoni, who had long-standing relations in Padua with the family of Alvise Cornaro and co-owned property with Alvise Contarini in Codevigo. The Pisani also owned property in Pernumia bounding that of the Beolco family of which Donada appears to have been particularly fond, choosing it in the 1526 *divisio* of her father's inheritance.[19] Hironimo borrowed significant sums for his wedding finery, probably because his father, known for his miserliness, kept him on a limited allowance.[20] In 1520 Hironimo recorded dowry payments and the profits of spices from the Alexandria galleys and in 1521 from cloth of the Flanders galleys, investments that he continued to pursue through 1526 and that probably allowed him to invest in the Priuli bank. He had regular transactions with the banks of the Garzoni and of Alvise Pisani, including as treasurer of the Triumphanti probably for their 1522 *festa*. In the Monte Nuovo sale he bought a farm near Padua confiscated from the rebel Buzzacarini and another one in Frassinella, the latter together with his maternal relatives Pangrati and Lorenzo Capello, merchant bankers who had been involved in the Foscari voyages and more recently in commercial dealings with Alvise Pisani. Hironimo and his father may also have been involved in the purchase of the great feud of Bagnolo by Alvise Pisani.[21] Hironimo continued such agricultural purchases for years, often using Paduan nobles as his agents and doubling his agricultural income over the 1520s.[22]

The reactivation of the lucrative commercial galleys toward the close of the Cambrai wars offered patrician merchant families a potential financial bright spot, but one that was clouded by the significant difficulties facing them. The Alexandria galleys, with the shortest and most profitable route, were the first authorized for departure, in 1515, at the request of the sultan of Egypt and of towns along the north African coast.[23] Their backlog of goods promised high yields, as the Alexandria market offered a range of merchandise that could include spices and other Asian products despite Portuguese competition. However, the galleys' departure was repeatedly delayed by complications. On

18 ASVe, *AGB*, busta 8, unnumbered document dated February 1502.
19 Sanuto, 28: 66, 71; ASPd, *Notarile*, busta 1389, 614ʳ⁻ᵛ; ASPd, *Estimo 1518*, busta 341, fol. 121ᵛ; busta 352, fols 266ʳ, 238ʳ; busta 358, fols 38ʳ, 204ʳ; busta 35, fols 51ʳ–3ʳ. For Pernumia, see also Linda L. Carroll, "Introduction," in Angelo Beolco (Il Ruzante), *La prima oratione*, ed. and trans. Linda L. Carroll, MHRA Critical Texts vol. 16 (London, 2009), pp. 5–74, 5, 6, 11.
20 ASVe, *AGB*, busta 3, unnumbered folio dated 1525, Dec. 20; Sanuto, 29: 630.
21 Sanuto, 29: 545; 32: 450; 36: 351; ASVe, *Ufficiali alle Rason Vecchie*, reg. 48, fol 38ʳ; ASVe, *AGRM*, busta 250, second *vacchetta*, fols 42ᵛ, 44ʳ, 55ʳ, 57ʳ, 80ʳ; ASVe, *AGB*, busta 19, busta 30; ASPd, *AO*, *ASC*, busta 231, fol. 34; Sanuto, 27: 241.
22 ASVe, *AGB*, busta 19, busta 21; VBMC, ms. Malvezzi 144, fols 93ᵛ–5ʳ.
23 Sanuto, 19: 41, 43–5, 360; 20: 54, 69, 72, 82–3.

the African end these included local restrictions, duties, and dangerous corsairs, as the Senate was warned by *provedador sora il cotimo di Alessandria* (overseer of the Alexandria trade) Andrea Arimondo, relative of Triumphante Nicolò. On the Venetian end, departure was obstructed by the *cotimo*'s accumulated debts and the poor condition of the galleys. They posed risks so grave that various patricians spoke in the Collegio (the steering committee of the Senate with particular jurisdiction over military matters) against sending them, including Gaspare Contarini, whose brother Tommaso was one of the *patroni* (investors) and whose brother Vicenzo at some point joined the Triumphanti. Despite these and additional difficulties and dangers caused by the 1516 Ottoman conquest of Egypt, the Collegio ordered the galleys' departure that autumn. The results were disastrous: one galley, rotten inside, broke apart in a winter storm and many of its men, including patron Vicenzo Magno (kinsman of Stefano Magno), died. The other ship was captured, sacked, and detained by Ottoman Egyptian authorities. Finally, through the intervention of Tommaso Contarini and the ambassador to the Ottoman Porte Alvise Mocenigo (the father of Triumphante Antonio), the surviving galley was released.

A fresh round was authorized in 1518 under *capitanio* Marco Gradenigo, uncle of Triumphante Zusto. After organizers and officials had overcome numerous difficulties in locating investors and obtaining the repaired galleys from the Arsenal, it sailed in October. After a temporary reassignment to fighting corsairs along the Barbary coast, it returned with a respectable cargo. The 1519 round, despite encountering some of the same problems, came back well laden. The next round was successfully auctioned to Vetor Garzoni and Zuan Alvise Badoer, a relative of Triumphante Albertin. This more fortunate situation continued through the first half of the 1520s, with Vetor Garzoni, whose sister Paula was the mother of lord of the 1525 festivity Marin Capello, repeatedly purchasing the galleys. Triumphanti and their relatives became even more closely involved in the galleys' functioning: Nicolò Morosini and a relative sailed on the 1522 round, Vicenzo Contarini's uncle Antonio served as *patron* on the 1523 round, and Michiel Capello served as a member of the commission governing the Alexandria *cotimo*. This pattern repeated the one evident in which the Beolco participated in the late fifteenth century, also a time in which they and their in-laws the Pernumia used the Garzoni bank for their financial dealings and in which Vetor's father Marin was *podestà* of Padua, where the Garzoni home flanked the Beolcos'.[24]

24 Sanuto, 20: 168–71, 171–4; 21: 7, 9, 32, 34, 35, 74, 74–5, 231, 250, 252–3, 285, 286; 22: 80, 180–81, 216, 253, 272–3, 288, 290–92, 327, 641, 641–2; 23: 14, 127, 453–4; 24: 11–12, 18, 22–31, 42–4, 135–7, 211, 378, 434, 545–6, 569, 599–601, 602, 606; 25: 38–9, 50, 123–5, 148, 186–7, 194, 439, 441, 453–4, 583, 595; 26: 25, 27, 126, 239, 388, 390; 27: 106, 114, 116, 129, 502, 511–13, 525, 528, 529, 658; 28: 119–20, 135, 139–40, 154, 197, 216, 217, 219–20, 266–8, 286, 314, 315–16, 334, 369, 379–80, 441, 457–60, 511, 545, 560, 563, 679; 29: 139–40, 141, 186–7, 203, 365, 545, 608, 647, 654; 34: 51, 467; Garzoni: ASVe, *AGB*, busta 22, unnumbered folio dated 1507 October 17; ASVe, *AGRM*, busta 238; busta 250, second *vacchetta*, fols 1ʳ, 2ʳ, 8ᵛ, 9ʳ; ASPd, *Notarile*, busta 1759, fols 436ʳ–7ʳ; busta 1760, fols 21ᵛ, 23ᵛ–4ᵛ, 392ʳ⁻ᵛ, 393ʳ⁻ᵛ, 394ʳ–5ʳ; *Estimo 1518*, busta 35, fols 46ʳ–7ʳ; busta 356, fols 165ʳ–6ʳ.

The Triumphanti Embark upon Governance Careers

During the period of the galleys' renewal, Triumphanti were also embarking upon the administrative careers assuming greater importance in patrician lives as trade declined. Fantin Zorzi di Nicolò and Hironimo Grimani provide important examples. More than a year before Gonzaga's visit, Zorzi, whose uncle Marin was then ambassador to the papal court, had made an early entrance into the Maggior Consiglio through a loan to the state.[25] Such a prerequisite to exemptions to minimum ages and candidacy for public office was increasingly imposed in the years after the financially draining war and with the prospect of a new one looming. Shortly thereafter Zorzi became a candidate to the *savi ai ordeni*, the commission on maritime commerce that was the province of young patricians staking out their generation's endeavors. The *savi* were then involved in the resumption of the Alexandria galleys, including the one bought by the Contarini.[26] Although Zorzi did not win that election, fellow Triumphante Hironimo Grimani was successful in early 1516, giving the loan required by the Council of Ten.[27] The difficulties of the job soon manifested themselves in a dispute in the Senate between some *provedadori sora la mercadantie* (overseers of commerce), who proposed a lucrative western extension of the Alexandria galley route, and senior patricians, who opposed it because of dangerous corsairs in those waters. Grimani, after joining Luca Tron in his bill to defer the decision, moved to a more tranquil bureaucratic office, his election facilitated by a loan from his father.[28]

Late in 1516 as the Barbary and Flanders galleys prepared to resume sailing, Fantin Zorzi was elected *savio ai ordeni* in an election in which two other Triumphanti also stood. The *compagni* seem to have chosen this strategy to ensure the success of at least one of their number at this critical time. That they applied it globally is hinted in their name, whose meanings included 'to play cards of a particular suit in a series as a winning strategy'.[29] Zorzi, who would prove a leader in resolving conflicting patrician interests, would be re-elected to the commission twice.[30] Over the next several years, an additional five Triumphanti (Nicolò Arimondo, Antonio Mocenigo, Andrea Renier, Albertin Badoer, and Lorenzo Bembo) were elected *savi ai ordeni* and thus participated in the decisions over galleys. In 1521, as *savi*, Fantin Zorzi and Triumphante cousin Cristoforo Barbarigo greeted the ambassador from the Duke of Ferrara, Giacomo Alvaroto, whose father Conte had died in a Venetian prison for his role

---

25 Sanuto, 19: 70.
26 Sanuto, 1: 943–4, 2: 461, 845; 20: 72, 387; 21: 143.
27 Sanuto, 22: 10–11, 98–9, 142, 290–92, 445.
28 Sanuto, 22: 290–92, 527.
29 Sanuto, 23: 254; Angelo Beolco (Il Ruzante), *La Pastoral*, in *Teatro*, ed. and trans. Ludovico Zorzi (Turin, 1967), hereafter *RT*, Scene 19 (p. 125); Ludovico Zorzi, "Note a *La Pastoral*," in *RT*, p. 1306, note 222. This instance of *trionfo/trionfare*, as well as another in the *Pastoral*'s Tuscan Prologue (par. 2; *RT*, p. 17) and one in the *Betia* Act III, v. 94 (*RT*, p. 301) are missing from Ivano Paccagnella *et al.*, *Vocabolario del pavano (XIV–XVII secolo)* (Padua, 2012).
30 Sanuto, 29: 530, 30: 19, 76.

in the 1509 Padua rebellion and whose (somewhat distant) cousin Marc'Aurelio was Ruzante's stage partner.[31]

Among the duties of the *savi ai ordeni* was the resolution of conflicts among backers of the galley routes. Such arose with the request of north African towns to extend the Alexandria galleys to them, creating competition with the Barbary galleys. The further request to allow them to carry Moorish traders and goods risked increasing the hostility of Charles of Spain, who accused Venice of supplying arms to Muslims along the African coast that he was intent on conquering. His hostility was of concern because, while his control of increasing stretches of that coast protected the Barbary and Flanders galleys from predators, it also gave the Spanish control over the galleys' access to those ports as well as to the ports of Spanish-controlled southern Italy where the galleys also traded. Thus the conclusion of a peace treaty with Charles's grandfather Maximilian in January 1517 had resulted immediately in proposals to resume the Barbary and Flanders galleys. The obtaining of the all-important safe-conducts permitting entry to ports was entrusted to Zuan Badoer, Venice's ambassador to the French court, where he invoked French support when Charles deferred their issuance to gain the upper hand in negotiations with Venice over war reparations. Badoer's assistant, the trusted chancellery secretary Hironimo di la Vedoa, succeeded in obtaining the passes by emphasizing to Charles the income he would perceive from the duties. The Barbary galleys were immediately authorized and found purchasers; the Flanders galleys, however, had to overcome the preference of some in the Senate to send them to Beirut to salvage Venetian goods from the Turkish onslaught. Having sailed, the Barbary galleys encountered an uprising in Sicily, corsairs and pirates along the coast, and hostility from Charles himself, who threatened to withhold the safe-conducts in continued pressure on Venice. Finally, however, they returned, well laden.

Captained by another Triumphante Contarini brother, Francesco, the 1519 round left richly provided with goods desired in Africa. It unfortunately encountered very dangerous conditions; its return with disastrous results during the debates to authorize the 1520 round aroused opposition to the new round. In response, Fantin Zorzi, then a *savio ai ordeni*, achieved approval of it by pledging

---

31 Sanuto, 22: 527, 657; 23: 212, 223–4, 225, 226, 241, 242, 243, 254, 260–61, 269, 280, 313, 338, 368, 376, 411, 412, 428, 434–5; 24: 117, 121, 514; 25: 170, 173, 301, 303, 543, 565, 567, 598; 26: 232, 290–91, 411, 493; 27: 116 (influence), 27: 121–2, 180, 338, 518, 525, 647–8, 657, 658, 669, 679–81; 28: 119–20, 336, 445, 499, 513, 515, 522, 545, 603, 619, 625, 656; 29: 33, 186–7, 203, 255–6, 410–11, 424–5; 30: 18, 21, 125, 151, 154–5, 167, 177, 198–9, 347, 383–4, 471–2; 31: 29–30, 78–9, 82, 83, 84, 85, 139–40, 179, 269, 327, 334, 421–2, 436–7, 490–91; 32: 436, 438–9, 449, 466; 33: 29, 633; 34: 49, 234, 250, 277; 35: 146–7, 337, 338, 467; 36: 79–80, 352–3; Alvaroto: Emilio Lovarini, "Ruzzante a Venezia," in *Studi sul Ruzzante e sulla letteratura pavana*, ed. Gianfranco Folena (Padua, 1965), pp. 81–107, 98–9; Paolo Sambin, "Briciole biografiche del Ruzzante e del suo compagno d'arte Marco Aurelio Alvarotti (Menato)," in *Per le biografie di Angelo Beolco, il Ruzzante, e di Alvise Cornaro*, restauri di archivio rivisti e aggiornati da Francesco Piovan (Padua, 2002), pp. 87–119, 107, 109, 118; Sanuto, 31: 30, 78–9, 82, 84; and see also entries in note 36.

financing from his committee and the *provedadori a l'Arsenal* (overseers of the Arsenal). The measure was not sufficient to attract investors, however. *Savio ai ordeni* Zuan Contarini, of the 'da Londra' (London) branch of the family, then proposed extending the route to Lisbon for the purchase of spices; despite Zorzi's opposition, the measure passed. One of the investors was Vetor Garzoni. But delays in obtaining the safe-conducts prolonged the debates, which pitted merchants with established trade in Africa against those seeking important new opportunities in Lisbon.[32] The Lisbon situation was reported by the Afaitadi, Cremonese bankers loyal to Venice who had early established themselves in Portugal to monopolize the spice trade there. They had augmented their influence in Venice by assisting the Republic in making payments to its soldiers in Lombardy and lending money to important patricians (see Chapter 1 and below). In the end the Lisbon group won.[33]

In 1521, days after captain Francesco Contarini reported to the Senate on his disastrous 1519 round, in Padua Alvise Cornaro received on his behalf payment owed him and his brothers by Marin Bembo, kin to Triumphante Lorenzo. It is likely that losses caused by the round forced the Contarini to call in this outstanding debt, perhaps an investment in it by Bembo. Witnesses to the notarial record were Angelo Beolco and Marc'Aurelio Alvaroto.[34] A few months later, procurator and Ortolano Marco Grimani, whose heavy investments in cotton indicate that he was involved in the round, borrowed from the Afaitadi and the Pisani for his commercial ventures. Serving as broker for one loan was Zuan Manenti, precisely at the moment in which he was organizing Venice's first state lottery (see Chapter 1, this chapter below, and Chapter 4). The loan also occurred a few months after the party of Marco Grimani that gave rise to the scandalous tarring episode.[35] As emerges in the analysis in Chapter 2, the party appears to have signalled his move away from the pro-imperial faction and toward the pro-French one. The other individuals involved in the loan, once more strongly associated with the Spanish-imperial faction, seem to have been doing the same (see below). This perhaps provides a further hint that the tarring episode was revenge for those members of their families not yet willing to openly join or advocate for the French faction.

Following much the same Mediterranean route as the Barbary galleys, the Flanders galleys continued on to northern terminus points in England and Flanders, whose control by Charles as Duke of Burgundy and his then-ally Henry VIII created further obstacles to their successful completion. Nonetheless, the northern galleys remained extremely desirable not only for the profits from the

---

32 Sanuto, 29: 331–2, 338–9.

33 Sergio Bertelli, "Affaitati, Giovan Carlo," and "Affaitati, Giovan Francesco," in *DBI*, 1 (1960); Sanuto, 3: 33; 4: 66–9, 87, 485, 663–6; 5: 129–31, 133–4, 751, 840–43; 6: 25, 26–8, 55–7, 65–6, 74, 75–6, 84, 86–8, 105, 212, 227, 238; 22: 375, 582–3; 23: 157–8, 171–2, 594; 24: 479, 553; 25: 203, 375; 26: 18, 469; 27: 306; 30: 412; 32: 323–4, 467–8, 481, 483; 33: 15; loans to Grimani: ASVe, *AGRM*, busta 9, fasc. 18.

34 Sambin, "Briciole," p. 90 citing ASPd, *Notarile*, busta 1085, f. 75ᵛ.

35 ASVe, *AGRM*, busta 9, fasc. 18.

goods carried north but for the return cargo of wool and tin, materials so vital to Venetian industry that in 1517, when investors and crew for the Flanders galleys were not forthcoming, there were proposals to favor foreigners to supply them. By 1518, the dangers to the Flanders galleys had grown so acute that, cautioned by former ambassador to England Andrea Badoer among others, the Senate did not authorize a round. Very high subsidies were proposed for the next round by the *savi ai ordeni*, including Vicenzo Garzoni, who defended them with the reminder that the war had interrupted them for eight years. A group of purchasers was subsequently organized by the experienced and astute merchant banker Alvise Pisani, and the capable Zuan Moro was named captain.

Shortly thereafter Maximilian died and Charles was elected his successor. Fear of his hostility led three patricians involved in the returning round to persuade the Council of Ten to order the omission of stops in Spanish-controlled ports to avoid endangering a cargo worth 300,000 ducats. In the event, the outbound galleys did not encounter hostilities but loaded little wool. As the Senate prepared for the successive round, which began after Triumphante brother Gaspare Contarini had been elected ambassador to Charles, it entertained rival bills, some favoring western galley commerce with a full round (including Flanders) assisted by large state incentives and some favoring the wool industry by limiting the voyage to England (to bring wool quickly) or other trade routes. Proposers of the latter, who included Alvise Mocenigo and Luca Tron, won initially, but lack of investors prompted new bills facilitating the importation of wool from other sources, even through or by foreigners. *Savio ai ordeni* Fantin Zorzi read one of these on behalf of Mafio Bernardo, already engaged in such measures, and helped the Senate reach a compromise.

Having finally sailed, the galleys encountered great difficulties, one detained by Spanish authorities, one by English authorities along with Bernardo's goods, and one by French authorities claiming that Venice had broken its truce with them. The French were clearly aware that Charles's efforts to pressure Venice into an alliance had resulted in the Senate's election of three patricians, including Alvise Mocenigo, to conduct negotiations with the imperial ambassador to that end. Gaspare Contarini, as ambassador to Charles, constantly intervened at court on behalf of the galleys. In September 1523, after more than two years out and six weeks after Venice had allied with the empire, the galleys finally returned with a valuable cargo.[36]

36 ASVe, Senato, *Secreta*, reg. 50, fols 15ʳ–6ʳ; Lane, pp. 128–31, 145–6, 246, 285–7, 291–2, 304–5, 337–9, 348–52; Frederic C. Lane, "Family Partnerships and Joint Ventures," in *Venice and History* (Baltimore, 1966), p. 47; Peter Gwyn, *The King's Cardinal. The Rise and Fall of Thomas Wolsey* (London, 1990), pp. 144–57; Linda L. Carroll, "Dating the *Woman from Ancona*," *Sixteenth Century Journal* 31 (2000): 963–85; Sanuto, 23: 488–95, 534, 535, 539; 24: 8, 37, 56, 107–8, 131–2, 142, 143, 192, 193, 194, 200, 240, 272, 326–30, 389, 440, 547, 537, 567, 702; 25: 18, 19, 23, 77, 107, 109, 112, 120–1, 161, 162, 165, 174, 177, 190, 191, 243, 257, 258, 279–80, 326, 465, 472, 512, 580, 601, 602, 689–92; 26: 10–11, 46–8, 58, 95–7, 199–200, 213, 224, 237, 252, 289, 290, 297, 299, 306, 313, 328, 390, 438, 450–51, 495, 500; 27: 8–9, 22, 23–5, 45–6, 51–2,

Renewed western trade apparently contributed to the wave of new or reopened banks that occurred in the early 1520s, in addition to the factors identified by Frederic Lane as the "divorce between bank money and coined money arising from the shortage of full-weight coins" and "a considerable increase in the quantity of bank money."[37] Mafio Bernardo inaugurated his in 1521, a few months after Fantin Zorzi had successfully sponsored a bill supporting irregular routes of wool importation by Bernardo and the Immortale Pietro da Molin qu. Marin, whose brother Hironimo was the bank's first investor.[38] As Sanudo notes, Bernardo had grown rich on the Alexandria and Flanders trade; a contemporary chronicle confirms his great wealth and his power in England.[39] Another bank was founded in 1522 by Antonio Priuli, whose family was also deeply involved in galley commerce, as was his father-in-law Alvise Pisani, who provided the bank with significant funds.[40] The following year, Piero Molin and his brother Andrea opened their own bank, with pledges coming from the Bernardo and numerous other merchant-banking families with members in prominent *compagnie della calza*, particularly the Immortali.[41] The weakest of the banks was founded in early 1524 by Andrea Arimondo qu. Alvise, former *provedador sora il cotimo di Alexandria* and a relative of Triumphante Nicolò.[42]

However, the conflicts of the earlier war had also returned; by 1521, the rivalry between Francis I and Charles V for control of Italy created a whirlpool toward which Venice's commercial and territorial interests drove it but that it struggled with every means to avoid, having learned from the devastation of the Cambrai wars. Alliance with France, which had easier relations with the Turkish Porte, benefited Venice's commerce with the eastern Mediterranean and its *stato da mar*; it also provided a bulwark against imperial power in Europe. On the other hand, alliance with the empire benefited Venetian commerce with the western Mediterranean and northern Europe and relieved Venice of the dangers of war against this formidable enemy, with which the republic shared its longest border.

60, 62, 82–4, 84–5, 88, 96, 106, 129, 145, 181, 185, 196–7, 208, 219, 301, 303, 310, 357, 388, 401, 404–5, 407, 430–32, 459, 482, 487, 502, 503, 510, 511–12, 512–13, 525, 528, 529, 535, 544, 558–9, 582, 600, 612, 614, 678, 680, 684; 28: 8, 47–9, 72, 78–9, 86, 96–7, 107–8, 121, 131–2, 135, 153, 205, 216, 266–7, 270, 286, 315–17, 324, 331–3, 369, 379, 381, 397, 415, 432, 441, 457–60, 486, 488, 497, 499, 505, 511, 515–16, 545, 560, 562, 563, 579, 679; 29: 12, 126, 139–40, 141, 153, 160, 186–7, 193, 202, 214, 280–81, 286, 288, 321–2, 331–3, 352, 356, 359, 363, 365, 398–99, 408–12, 412–13, 417, 445, 456, 464, 465–6, 476, 511, 539, 542, 545, 611–12, 647; 30: 18, 21, 60–62, 100, 103, 116–17, 140–41, 154–5, 164, 167, 177, 185–6, 198–200, 203–4, 256–9, 282–4, 353–4, 383–4; 31: 33–4; 32: 405–9, 444–5, 469; 33: 7, 21, 127, 140, 145, 148, 171, 277–8, 295, 341, 376, 390, 407, 416, 424, 453, 475, 478, 681; 34: 53, 230, 265, 401–2.

37 Frederic C. Lane, "Venetian Bankers, 1496–1533," in *Venice and History*, pp. 81–5, quotations 81, 83; see *e.g.* Sanuto, 35: 467–72.
38 Sanuto, 30: 125; 31: 182–3; 36: 203.
39 PBUC, ms. 874, 3: 182ʳ–3ʳ.
40 Carroll, "Venetian Attitudes"; Sanuto, 30: 106–9; 33: 545–6; 36: 350–52, 410.
41 Sanuto, 34: 279–80, 283.
42 Sanuto, 36: 203; 18: 468.

Imperial alliance was not without disadvantages, however, including both feudal claims of Charles over large parts of Venice's mainland dominion and retaliation by the increasingly powerful Turkish empire.

The Creation of the State Lottery

Trade and banking being uncertain, a means of making good earnings on a small investment was invented by the ragpicker Hironimo Bambarara ("è sussità uno novo modo di vadagnar metando poco cavedal a fortuna, e fu comenzà in cosse basse, auctor Hironimo Bambarara strazaruol"). Thus in late 1521 and early 1522 sprang up a number of private lotteries. One involved a 4,000-ducat pool staked by Ludovico Afaitadi. Perhaps not coincidentally, Afaitadi invested the sum only three days before the Senate entrusted him with 4,000 ducats to send to their French allies in Lombardy to pay the troops that they hoped would retake Milan, seized by imperial forces several months before. Almost certainly not coincidental was the move of the Council of Ten, within days, to put all lotteries under their jurisdiction, and to organize their own state-sponsored one immediately. Chosen to run it was Zuan Manenti, a Venetian *cittadino* whose private service as a broker to patricians including Marco Grimani confirmed the level of trust that he enjoyed.[43]

As detailed in Chapter 1, government records show that initially the state lottery was funded principally by a group of Spanish and Florentine investors that Sanudo would list as backers only several years later: Piero Ram or Rames, the *consolo* (representative) of the Catalan merchants in Venice; Gaspare Besalù of the papal banking family; and Ferigo dei Nerli of the Florentine banking family. Given the increasing pressure on Venice by Charles to join him in the Lombard war and the recent election to the papacy of his former tutor, it is reasonable to hypothesize that Venetian leadership decided upon the public lottery to raise funds for the anti-Spanish efforts of themselves and their allies with the least expense to the state and with the risk delegated to Spaniards and other foreigners, as the empire did to Venice itself. However, the financing was soon transferred to locals: Piero di Francesco Dall'Oro with a counter guarantee by Donado Malipiero qu. Pasquale, though the cash may have been provided by the Afaitadi possibly from government funds. The original Spanish-associated and Florentine investors turned to a second state-run lottery, managed by the Bolognese Ludovico di Orazio, whose grand prize of 1,000 ducats was won by the Triumphanti. In the Manenti lottery, which was drawn in the monastery of the Frari during Carnival, the grand prize was won by the son of Venice's Grand Chancellor; the second prize by Piero Gradenigo, member of a Triumphante family who had just returned from service in the armada defending Corfu from the

43 ASVe, Senato, *Secreta*, reg. 49, fol. 56ᵛ–77ᵛ, 81ʳ–2ʳ; *Provveditori di Comun, Atti*, busta 9, fols 81ᵛ–6ʳ; *AGRM*, busta 9, fasc. 18; Sanuto 32: 467 (quotation), 468, 481, 501–4; 33: 13. In this first year, the private lotteries organized prior to the Ten's decision were permitted to complete their course.

Turks; and the third prize by a woman who, as daughter of Donà Marcello (then a head of the Ten) and wife of Jacomo Badoer, belonged to two Triumphante families. The Triumphanti collectively won three prizes; Piero and Hironimo Rames, Ferigo dei Nerli, Gaspare Besalù, and two members of the Afaitadi family all won prizes.[44] The apportionment hardly seems left to chance. Soon several other state lotteries offering large prizes were created, including a new 6,000-ducat lottery to be drawn in the monastery of S. Zanipolo that Sanudo first reported as run by Manenti but later by Orazio.

In the spring of 1523, as Venice's negotiations for an imperial alliance were reaching conclusion, Zuan Francesco and Zuan Jacopo Beolco, Ruzante's father and uncle, reopened the commercial society that had been established with their Milanese family in the previous generation to conduct commerce in Venice and Milan. The Milanese participant was Francesco Beolco, who had served as *questore* in Massimiliano Sforza's administration as his father Zuan had for Ludovico Sforza. In 1512 Venice had parted ways with Milan, ending their shared pro-imperial policy in favor of affiliation with France. Massimiliano Sforza, instead, remained loyal to the empire but lost his state to Francis in 1515. Although Francesco Beolco had been valuable enough to be retained by the French in their earlier Milanese administration, this does not appear to have been the case after 1515. However, Francesco Maria Sforza returned to Milan as duke in 1522 with assistance from Charles. The third party to the 1523 association was the Genoese Agostino Lomellino, who had participated in the 1484 agreement by which Zuan de Beolco formed a society for business in Venice with his nephews.[45] That, a few weeks after the new society was formed, Ruzante was favored by Marco Grimani with the party that allowed the author-actor his only performance in the Ducal Palace at precisely the moment that Grimani was deep in debt to Lombard financiers and that the emperor was pressuring Venice for an alliance does not seem casual. Grimani's ruthlessness and constant need for funds arising from spendthrift habits would be consistent with such a double game.[46]

In late July of 1523, with French forces having largely withdrawn from the peninsula after the defeat of La Bicocca, the Republic under the new Doge Andrea Gritti (Grimani had died in May, days after Ruzante's performance) entered the alliance forcefully proposed by Charles and Adrian. This public action reflected the pragmatism informing Gritti's earlier private oral expression of appreciation

---

44 Sanuto, 32: 125, 500–504; see also Chapter 1, notes 189, 190.
45 ASPd, *Notarile*, busta 1052, fols 102ʳ–3ʳ; busta 1056, fols 188ᵛ–9ᵛ; busta 3969, fols 125ʳ–7ʳ, 214ᵛ–15ᵛ; ASPd, *AO, ASC*, busta 231, fols 17–22; busta 235, pp. 3–5; for Beolco offices in Milan, see also Letizia Arcangeli, "Esperimenti di governo: politica fiscale e consenso a Milano nell'età di Luigi XII," in *Milano e Luigi XII: ricerche sul primo dominio francese in Lombardia, 1499–1512*, ed. Letizia Arcangeli (Milan, 2002), pp. 253–339, esp. pp. 312–28. The renewed connection did not bear fruit, as both died in 1524.
46 See Giuseppe Gullino, *Marco Foscari (1477–1551): l'attività politica e diplomatica tra Venezia, Roma, e Firenze* (Milan, 2000).

to a Mantuan contact for the need to find a *modus vivendi* with Charles's power.[47] Allied forces captured Milan a few months later. Humiliated by the loss, Francis regrouped during early summer 1524, attracting the interest of the Republic and the new pope, Clement VII (elected November 18, 1523), with his proposed campaign to retake the wealthy city and its territory.

This period saw the prospects of the western galleys diminished by several factors. After reports that Henry VIII would invade France in the spring of 1524, a proposal by Luca Tron and others for a round of Flanders galleys failed. A second attempt at the end of the summer garnered even less support. Troubles in Alexandria required extra incentives before *patroni* could be attracted to those galleys, including Hironimo Gradenigo, a Triumphante kinsman.[48] Mafio Bernardo closed his bank after learning that the French had countered Charles's pressures by capturing one of his ships and attacking another, his wealth permitting him to satisfy his creditors.[49] The one bright spot on the economic scene was the 1524 round of Barbary galleys, whose *patroni* included Zuan Antonio Contarini and for which his brother the ambassador Gaspare managed to secure safe-conducts from Charles.[50]

As the needs of the Lombard war grew, the government created more lotteries, including as prizes shops at Rialto and the jewels of the Duke of Milan that Venice held as collateral to an earlier loan. The Spanish ambassador even offered a diamond to help raise money to build a ship for their joint forces. When ticket sales fell short, authorities increased the value of the prizes and included desirable state income streams such as boat fee stations and state lands such as the Legnago forest.

For much of 1523 and 1524, Manenti's services were used almost exclusively and the good fortune of the Triumphanti continued, with one lot of the Legnago forest going to Andrea Marcello di Bernardo. Over the course of 1524, with reports of Francis's powerful army reaching Venice, Charles pressed his reluctant ally to fight their now-common enemy. The Republic's governing councils relied on a strategy of deflecting his requests while waiting for news of a French victory in Milan. When that came in late October, the Senate moved immediately toward a new French alliance with a necessary partner, Clement VII; the agreement was kept secret to forestall imperial and Turkish hostility and also, according to the Senate record, to permit modifications should the balance of power shift.[51] Indeed, between that point and December, the Venetian Senate revised the direction of the Republic's external alliances several times. Save slight variations that will

47 Linda L. Carroll, "The Shepherd Meets the Cowherd: Ruzante's *Pastoral*, the Empire and Venice," *Annuario dell'Istituto Romeno di Cultura e Ricerca Umanistica* 4 (2002): 288–97, citing Mantua, Archivio di Stato, *Archivio Gonzaga, Da Venezia, Carteggio G.B. Malatesta*, busta 1454, fols 47ʳ, 284ᵛ, 353.

48 Sanuto, 36: 79–80, 86, 302, 352, 362, 363, 381–2, 388, 462, 467, 468, 469, 514, 551, 582, 622.

49 Sanuto, 36: 401, 484.

50 Sanuto, 36: 64, 86, 181, 202, 267–8, 305–6, 381–2, 514, 582.

51 ASVe, Senato, *Secreta*, reg. 50, fols 107ᵛ–21ʳ; Sanuto, 37: 109–10.

appear in the more detailed account given below, the same core group of Senators proposed all of the major developments: *savi dil consejo* Domenico Trevisan, Lunardo Mocenigo, Polo Capello, Luca Tron, Alvise Mocenigo, Andrea Trevisan and Nicolò Bernardo; *savi di terraferma* Marc'Antonio Contarini, Domenico Venier, and Zuan Francesco Badoer. As will be shown, the constant factor behind the adjustments was their publicly stated desire for peace.

The French captured Milan on October 22; when the news reached Venice the following day, the Senate, having previously avoided voting on a proposed bill to remain united with the pope in dealings with France, immediately wrote to the Venetian ambassador in Rome. The letter instructed him to emphasize to the pope the importance of common protection, although the proposal of the group of leading senators to add a clause explicitly promising that Venice would join him in any negotiations with France was defeated. The matter of negotiations with France soon returned, the capture of Milan being too significant to ignore. On October 29, the Senate approved a letter instructing the ambassador to encourage the pope to negotiate a peace pact with France and to try to extend it to the emperor, given the pope's earlier claims of his ability to do so.[52] By mid November, Venetian resolve was shaken by reports that imperial forces had fought back so energetically that the French might not succeed in capturing Pavia (another crucial Lombard town) and that an English invasion of France might draw them away from northern Italy. Many of the senators who had favored an agreement with France now made attempts to formulate a letter telling the ambassador to modulate his efforts according to the outcomes of battles in Lombardy; their proposals, however, failed to muster adequate votes. When, for an extremely brief period, the pope contemplated bringing about peace between Francis and Charles by dividing Milan between them and forming an Italian confederation, the same group of senators proposed supporting the plan but could not garner a consensus.[53]

Decisions over the running of the lottery took several odd turns in early November that prove congruent with the changes in foreign policy. Although the Collegio had begun negotiating with Manenti to organize a new lottery, they gave it instead to Hironimo Bambarara, who was backed by the same group of Spanish and other foreign merchant bankers who had backed Manenti in 1522 (Besalù and Beltrame, of Spanish origin, papal financiers, and connected with the imperial-leaning Ortolani; Nerli, the successor of a Florentine with whom the Beolco had conducted business and a relative of the merchant who that year sponsored the restoration of the Frari altarpiece, probably Ferigo, who had obtained an indulgence from Clement VII to benefit the *scuola*; Piero Ram, in 1523 the imperial functionary receiving the payment of 30,000 ducats to the emperor to which Venice had agreed as a stipulation of the league with Charles and Adrian). Three days later, however, the Collegio declared that Bambarara

52   ASVe, Senato, *Secreta*, reg. 50, fols 107r–22v.
53   Sanuto, 37: 183, 196, 203; ASVe, Senato, *Secreta*, reg. 50, fols 113ʳ–17ʳ.

had failed to obtain financing and reassigned the lottery to Lodovico Orazio, with no backers named. The sudden switch was probably triggered by Venice's covert move, under the protection of the pope, to an alliance with France. Spanish-associated investors had likely gotten wind of it and were concerned about the loyalties of Manenti, a faithful son of Venice who had spent years at the court of Clement's cousin Leo X, while Venetian authorities apparently had their own second thoughts about Spanish investors and suspicions about Manenti (see below). The drawings were moved to S. Zanipolo, another sign of a change of (political) orientation of the lotteries.[54]

Similarly, the final turn in international relations came toward the end of November when, after important successes by the French forces, the Senate decided to join the pact being formalized by the pope with France, which at first was glossed as a union of Christian nations to fight the Turks. The Senate insisted, however, on modifications to the wording designed to avoid incurring the wrath of Charles and the Turkish Porte, who menaced the Venetian dominion along two lengthy borders, land and maritime, and its merchants within their states. On December 13, nonetheless, the Spanish ambassador came before the Collegio demanding the 25,000 ducats that Venice had owed for its support of the imperial army for almost a year. Possibly having gotten wind of the negotiations but at a minimum having understood Venice's reluctance to support the Spanish effort, he referred to Venice's 'pratiche che va atorno' (undertakings/negotiations that are going on) and warned that if Venice did not pay the sum, the Spanish would come up with it themselves. The Collegio, understanding this as a threat that the Spanish governor of Sicily would do so by impounding the Barbary galleys making port there, wrote to *capitanio* Alexandro Contarini advising him to avoid that stop.[55]

By December 17 the pact was ready. Reference to action against the Turks was omitted from the statement of purpose, which was given as achieving peace among all Christian nations. In addition, Francis promised to undertake no campaigns against the emperor without the assent of the pope and Venice. Venice was omitted from the list of signatories, though an eventual announcement of the Republic's participation was covered by the convention of 'leaving a place' for potential future adherents. An olive branch was extended to Charles and Henry through similar spaces left open for them.

An analysis of the evolving Senate proposals described above indicates that what appears to be a fluctuation in alliance preferences of the group of senators

54 ASVe, *Consiglio dei Dieci, Miste*, filza 52, fols 4ʳ, 166ʳ, 177ʳ, 178ᵍ; *Collegio, Notatorio*, reg. 20, fol. 27ʳ⁻ᵛ; Sanuto, 32: 502, 503, 509; 33: 13, 14, 15, 19, 92, 243, 250–51, 255–6, 371, 401–2, 406, 408, 442, 448, 499–500, 501, 521, 531, 532–3, 537, 542, 547, 595, 629; 34: 20, 102, 237, 284, 288, 381, 394, 401, 408, 429–30, 440–41; 35: 66, 203, 269–70, 314, 317, 319, 324, 341–2, 364–6; 36: 144, 243, 265, 266, 307, 330–31, 400, 411, 423, 427, 439–40, 468, 484, 488, 519, 520, 549, 550, 557, 561, 562; 37: 119, 146, 165, 166, 191–2. For overview of international developments, see Kenneth M. Setton, *The Sixteenth Century to the Reign of Julius III*, Memoirs of the American Philosophical Society vol. 161 (Philadelphia, 1984), pp. 225–40.

55 Sanuto, 37: 319.

was in fact the product of a commitment to peace dictated by economic considerations. The extent of the Senators' and their affines' investments in the north
African galleys had become all the more important with the abandonment of the
Flanders route. As is evident in the Sicilian example, the yield of the galleys
depended on Charles's good will for the necessary port permits and freedom from
harassment. The investments of these senators and their families in mainland
properties were also considerable. Some of those properties still had formalized
feudal ties to the empire, and all of them risked devastation in a war for control
of the mainland state. Thus the senators' multiple sources of wealth could be
protected only by peace among the three major external powers—France, the
empire, and the papacy.

The congruity of lottery and alliance events supports the hypothesis that
Manenti, who directed numerous lotteries during the period in 1523 and early
1524 when Venice was aligned with the empire, was more strongly associated
with a faction willing to deal with the empire. Such an orientation was consistent with his time at the court of Leo X, who had re-established the Medici in
Florence with the assistance of Ferdinand of Aragon. That the Collegio swiftly
and silently shifted the direction of the new lottery to Bambarara after the October
1524 French victory but before a formal change of alliance is consistent with a
covert effort to draw financial resources from the officially-allied Spanish financiers and redirect them to the Venetian army, which the Senate was keeping distant
from battle to avoid taking sides. The failure of the lottery financing in this itera-
tion seems clearly attributable to the withdrawal of the Spanish financiers because
of their assumption or knowledge that Venice saw the French victory in Milan as
motivation for changing alliances. That the financiers even received information
about the Senate decisions from their extensive contacts with important patricians
or other sources is consistent with the Spanish ambassador's hint that he knew
about negotiations. That the Collegio then entrusted the lottery to Orazio, with
his origins in the capital of the Papal State, conforms with Venice's growing rap-
prochement with the papacy.

After the holidays, events quickened their pace. The pact was signed by the
doge in January of 1525.[56] When it was learned shortly thereafter that Francis
intended to turn the league to war against Charles, the desire for peace was reiterated by most of the group in the Senate discussed above. As the winter wore on,
interest in a general peace grew because of the fear that the spring would bring an
attack on France by Henry VIII that would draw French troops away from northern Italy and give Charles the victory. Charles and Henry rejected the invitation to
join; Henry, instead, sent his special envoy, Richard Pace, to pressure Venice to
maintain its 1523 commitment. After stopping in Padua, Pace arrived in Venice
on February 7, 1525.[57]

---

56   ASVe, Senato, *Secreta*, reg. 50, fols 122^v–4^v; Setton, pp. 224–8; Gullino, *Marco Foscari*, pp. 45–88;
       Sanuto, 37: 319 (quotation), 416–20 (text).
57   Sanuto, 37: 521–2.

The Triumphanti, the 1525 Audience, and the Beolco

On February 11, Sanudo records a Triumphante festivity as follows:

Da poi disnar, pochi di Collegio si reduse, perchè parte di Savii dil Conseio, tra li qual sier Lorenzo Loredan procurator, sier Hironimo Justinian procurator, sier Luca Trun, sier Nicolò Bernardo savii dil Consejo andono a veder provar una comedia a cha' Arian a san Raphael, si farà Luni a li 13 di questo, per la festa fanno li compagni *Triumphanti*, di la qual è autor Zuan Manenti. È signor di la festa sier Marin Capello qu. sier Batista. Poleno menar do done per compagno parente, et una in numero di belle da esser conossuta per tre di loro compagni, a questo deputati sier Vicenzo Contarini qu. sier Alvise *Minoto*, sier Hironimo Grimani di sier Marin et sier Justo Gradenigo qu. sier Zuane Paulo, zoè per do ballote di loro sono compagni. E faze la cena a persone 300; preparà la cena benissimo et fu un bel concier, con lettere: *Concordiae dedicatum*. Il concier fu bellissimo. Vi vene altri procuratori, sier Jacomo Soranzo, sier Andrea Justinian, sier Marco da Molin, sier Marco Grimani, sier Francesco di Prioli, sier Andrea Gusoni, sier Antonio Mozenigo, ch'è compagno et per il grado de la procuratia non si spoglioe. Era do Cai di X, sier Polo Donado et sier Hironimo Barbarigo, sier Lazaro Mocenigo consier da basso, sier Andrea Badoer el cavalier, sier Zuan Dolfin fo savio a terra ferma, sier Fantin Valaresso fo al luogo di procurator, sier Nicolò Trivixan, e sier Piero Badoer governadori de l'intrade. Altri di Pregadi più di 40, di altra età assà, e di condition, tra li qual io Marin Sanuto. Et si andò con pioza, e per tempo la sala fo piena. Et però non fu fato Pregadi nè Consejo di X. Erano do fradelli dil Serenissimo, sier Michiel e sier Polo Malipiero. Et fo principiada a hore 24; duroe fino a le 6. Fo 9 intermedii, et tre comedie per una fiata in prosa per Zuan Manenti, ditta Philargio et Trebia et Fidel. Poi Ruzante et Menato padoani da Vilan feno una comedia vilanesca et tutta lasciva, et parole molto sporche, *adeo* da tutti fo biasemata, et se li dava stridor. Quasi erano da done 60 con capa sul soler, et scufie le zovene, che se agrizavano a quello era ditto per so' nome. Tutta la conclusion era de ficarie, et far beco i so' mariti. Ma Zuan Polo si portò benissimo, et li intermedii fonno molto belli, de tutte le virtù de soni e canti ch'è possibil haver, vestiti in vari habiti da mori, da todeschi, da griegi, da hongari, da pelegrini, et altri assà habiti senza però volti, et Zan Polo con l'habito prima de tutti si messe nome Nicoletto Cantinella. E infine venino 8 da mate con roche, qual fe' un bel ballo in piva. Et fo compita la prova di la ditta comedia con biasmo de tutti, non a li compagni che spendeno ducati . . . , ma di chi è stà l'autor, e fo danari vadagnati mo' un anno al loto.

After dinner only a few members of the Collegio gathered, because part of the Savi del Conseio—including procurator Lorenzo Loredan, procurator Hironimo Giustinian, and the savi del Conseio Luca Tron and Nicolò Bernardo—went to see the rehearsal of a comedy at Ca' Arian at San Raphael that will be staged on Monday, the 13th of this month, for the festivity of the

Triumphanti, and whose producer-director is Zuan Manenti. The Lord of the
Festivities is Marin Capello qu. Batista. Each Triumphante may bring two
women relatives and one as a *bella*, to make the acquaintance of three other
Triumphanti, and Vicenzo Contarini qu. Alvise *Minoto*, Hironimo Grimani
di Marin, and Justo Gradenigo qu. Zuane Paulo were put in charge of this,
that is by two ballots of the group's members. And they provided a supper
for 300, which was very well prepared and had lovely decorations, with
the words *Concordiae dedicatum*. The decorations were quite lovely. Other
procurators attended as well, Jacomo Soranzo, Andrea Justinian, Marco
da Molin, Marco Grimani, Francesco Priuli, Andrea Gusoni, and Antonio
Mozenigo, who is a member of the group but because of his rank of procurator did not wear their outfit. Also present were two Heads of the Council
of Ten, Polo Donado and Hironimo Barbarigo, as well as Lazaro Mocenigo
consier da basso, Andrea Badoer the knight, Zuan Dolfin the former member of the mainland governance council, Fantin Valaresso the former substitute procurator, and the governors of state revenue Nicolò Trivixan and
Piero Badoer. More than forty additional senators were there, and many of
a certain age and status, including myself Marin Sanudo. And it was raining
as we went and the room filled early. And for this reason neither the Senate
nor the Council of Ten met. Also present were two of the doge's brothers,
Michiel and Polo Malipiero. The festivity began at sunset and lasted for six
hours. There were nine *intermezzi* and three comedies in prose presented
together by Zuan Manenti, called *Philargio and Trebia and Fidel*.[58] Then
Ruzante and Menato the Paduans as peasants staged a country comedy that
was totally lascivious and had very dirty words, such that it was condemned
by everyone, and they were yelled at. About sixty married women with their
hair veiled, along with young women with their hair in caps, were seated on
the riser, and they shrieked at what was said in their name. The whole conclusion was about screwing and cuckolding their husbands. But Zuan Polo
behaved admirably and the *intermezzi* were very nice, with all the virtuosi
of instruments and song that it is possible to have, dressed in various costumes as Moors, Germans, Greeks, Hungarians, and pilgrims, and a variety
of other costumes, but no masks, and Zuan Polo with the appropriate cos-
tume placed himself at the head of them with the name Nicoletto Cantinella.
And last of all came eight as madwomen with distaffs, who did a nice dance
to a bagpipe. And at its conclusion this comedy was criticized by all, not
the Triumphanti who spent . . . ducats, but the producer-director, and it was
money won a year ago in the lottery.[59]

58 The first of these had been staged at the 1518 wedding of Lorenzo de' Medici Duke of Urbino,
    prior to which Lorenzo's cardinal cousins had visited Venice: Anthony M. Cummings, *The Politi-
    cized Muse. Music for Medici Festivals, 1512–1537* (Princeton, 1992), pp. 102–3, 113; Carroll,
    "Introduction," pp. 22–4.
59 Sanuto, 37: 559–60; a *consier da basso* was a *capo di quarantia criminal*: Giuseppe Cappelletti,
    Relazione storica sulle magistrature venete (Venice, 1873; repr. Venice, 1992), p. 84.

The fact that the rehearsal was attended by so many government officials who were led from the Ducal Palace by four of the six *savi dil consejo* or Savi Grandi, the elective office just below the Council of Ten in prestige and of whom two were Procuratori di San Marco, seems to indicate that there was more to attendance than simple entertainment. Can it be demonstrated that those attending shared economic and political interests that were somehow served by the performance? A correlation of their careers with their voting records available in the *Diarii* of Marin Sanudo and the registers of the *Senato Secreta* provides information concerning not only financial interests in the web of commerce, mainland holdings, and ecclesiastical benefices that are the subject of the present study but their connections to Padua, to the Beolco, and to other Ruzante affiliates in the patriciate. One may begin by noting the importance of the peace-seeking senators and their affines among the officials named and the families of the Triumphanti.

Lorenzo Loredan, Hironimo Justinian, Luca Trun, and Nicolò Bernardo, *savi dil consejo*, had all borne important governmental responsibilities, especially during the wars of the League of Cambrai. Moreover, they and their affines largely derived their wealth from the western galleys and/or from agriculture in the mainland state and some even had explicit ties to the empire. The Senate record shows that all four would be among the senators who, at the Senate meeting of February 27, would successfully propose a congratulatory letter to Charles on the victory at Pavia in which his forces captured Francis I. That these four formed a deliberate group may be deduced from Sanudo's record that after that meeting they stayed on in the Ducal Palace and were entertained by an eclogue, rather than hurrying with their Senate colleagues to a much-heralded performance sponsored by another *compagnia della calza*, the Valorosi.[60]

As the son of Doge Leonardo (1501–21), Lorenzo Loredan had followed closely the brutal twists and turns of the wars of the League of Cambrai. Kin to Lorenzo di Marco Loredan, who had made significant investments in the vexed 1492 western galleys, he was familiar with their troubles as well.[61] The family had imperial connections. Marco di Antonio Loredan married a Neapolitan noblewoman who was the widow of the imperial noble Ulaticò Cosaza.[62] He thereby became the stepfather of Zuan Cosaza, a member of the Immortali who played an important role in Ruzante's first recorded Venetian performance and who was the only one who also was a member of the Ortolani, the *compagnia della calza* that most frequently invited Ruzante to Venice. Loredan family members held large amounts of mainland agricultural property, including in the *padovano*.[63] Lorenzo himself had recently added a rich former Este holding in the Polesine, the important agricultural region between the Adige and the Po rivers that Venice had taken from Ferrara in the late fifteenth century, while his son-in-law Zaccaria Priuli

---

60 Sanuto, 37: 671; ASVe, Senato, *Secreta*, reg. 50, fols 132^v–3^r.
61 ASVe, *AGRM*, busta 250, second *vacchetta*, fols 58^v, 60^r, 61^v; VBMC, ms. Cicogna 3533, Stefano Magno, *Annali Veneti*, fols 125^v–6^r.
62 Sanuto, 2: 505, 510, 1047.
63 ASPd, *Estimo 1518*, busta 352, fols 87^{r-v}, 120^v, 148^v, 156^v.

bought property confiscated from the Paduan rebels in the Monte Nuovo sale.[64] Around the time of the rehearsal, Loredan co-sponsored bills that favored the empire, peace with the empire, or peace between the two sides more consistently than bills favoring the French or the Turks.[65]

Hironimo Giustinian qu. Antonio, the second of the procurators and himself wealthy, was the husband of the enormously wealthy heiress Agnesina Badoer, on whose family estate they had built the Villa Giustinian.[66] Prior to the wars of the League of Cambrai, he had been elected to numerous commissions governing the trade routes until he was banned from office for bribery.[67] After the war began, he and fellow convicted officials proposed to the Council of Ten that they be readmitted on payment of a large loan to the state, eventually offering an even larger loan to enter the Senate without the vote. Giustinian was the first to achieve this objective, and continued to make large loans to the state over the course of the war, eventually being twice elected *savio a terraferma*.[68] Although this commission was not charged with maritime matters, Giustinian was among its members proposing a controversial bill requiring the 1515 Alexandria galleys to sail despite a delay, which passed with the support of Cristoforo Capello, kinsman of an Ortolano and a Triumphante.[69] By 1516, Giustinian had determined to follow in the footsteps of the wealthy banker Alvise Pisani and offer the spectacular sum of 10,000 ducats to be elected procurator, a goal quickly achieved and the sum immediately being sent to the field via Padua for defense expenses.[70]

Giustinian was subsequently elected to the Zonta of the Council of Ten along with Luca Tron and Nicolò Bernardo.[71] It may have been there that the three began to articulate strategies for achieving shared objectives. When, at the war's conclusion, the government decided to sell confiscated rebel properties to resolve old war bonds (the Monte Nuovo), Giustinian was elected to the commission. He also served on one of the committees electing Antonio Grimani doge. Praised by Marin Sanudo for his deportment on it, he was almost immediately elected to the Zonta (the 'Addition' to the Council of Ten), along with Lorenzo Loredan. He attended the inauguration of the new Bernardo bank and the entrance of Cardinal Marco Corner as Bishop of Padua, at which Ruzante recited his *Prima oratione*.[72] He was also the brother-in-law

---

64   Rigobello, "Modi," pp. 21–3; ASPd, *Estimo 1518*, busta 352, fol. 202ʳ.

65   ASVe, Senato, *Secreta*, reg. 50, for the former: fols 16ᵛ, 17ʳ, 72ᵛ–3ʳ, 130ᵛ–32ʳ; for the latter: 14ᵛ–15ʳ.

66   Carolyn Kolb-Lewis, *The Villa Giustinian at Roncade*, Distinguished Dissertations in the Fine Arts (New York and London, 1977).

67   Sanuto, 4: 587, 617; 5: 982.

68   Sanuto, 7: 606, 609–11; 8: 133; 9: 194; 10: 51–2, 10: 595; 14: 139, 487; 16: 509; 17: 44, 249; 18: 24; 18: 307, 334, 347; 19: 72–3, 80, 153, 292, 299; 20: 78, 102, 113–14, 148–51, 153–4, 243, 448, 456.

69   Sanuto, 21: 9, 35, 74–5.

70   Sanuto, 22: 262, 266, 269.

71   Sanuto, 23: 5; 25: 9.

72   Sanuto, 24: 340; 30: 474, 480; 31: 165, 182, 235.

of Francesco Donà el cavalier (the knight), probably the Francesco Donà greeted in Ruzante's *Lettera giocosa*.[73] Giustinian's daughter married the new doge's grandson Vetor Grimani, whom Giustinian provided with funds for the loan enabling Vetor to become a procurator.[74] As a new war grew more likely, Giustinian was elected to the Savi a trovar danari (Committee to Find Money) and then to the commission for taxation of properties in the Paduan and Trevisan territories, whose proceeds would be used to defend the mainland from anticipated imperial aggression.[75] When the Capello and Vendramin bank opened in early 1524, he made a pledge of 1,000 ducats. Weeks later he, Luca Tron, and Polo Capello proposed a new round of ships to Flanders, though the bill was defeated because of the modifications that they proposed adapting the terms to current circumstances.[76] Even more than Loredan he tended to favor actions that preserved peace, not only with the empire but with France, especially with the increasing Habsburg-Valois conflict of the early 1520s.[77]

The most volatile of the four in his views was Luca Tron, member of a small family whose brief moment of glory begun by his uncle Doge Nicolò (see Chapter 1) would die with Luca. To quote Robert Finlay, Luca and his cousin Antonio "were masters at political maneuverings on the margin between tolerated opposition and outrageous dissent." Luca's advocacy for "an aggressive military policy," for which he assumed some governmental responsibilities during the wars of the League of Cambrai, brought Venice one of its signal victories.[78] Signs of tempering appear in the early 1520s, however, in Luca's caution about opposing the emperor, perhaps inspired in part by his interest in continuing the journeys of the western galleys but also by the difficulties of dealing with both Turkish aggression to the east and the impending land war to the north, west, and south.[79] Luca's willingness to pivot with changing circumstances manifested itself in October 1524 as soon as the imperial forces showed weakness in defending Milan. He joined Nicolò Bernardo, Lunardo Mocenigo, Polo Capello and other *savi grandi* in proposing to the Senate the letter to Venice's ambassador to the pope stressing unity with him and containing a secret clause promising to follow him if he approached the French king. The proposal failed, as did one they advanced after the French captured Milan to add to a bland letter of unity with the pope a codicil hinting at a new alliance with France.

Success came finally when Clement advanced the latter proposal, and the four, together with *savio a terraferma* Zuan Francesco Badoer, joined the Collegio

---

73 Sanuto 19: 334; Barbaro, 3: 335.
74 Sanuto 31: 466; 33: 289, 294, 347.
75 Sanuto 31: 275, 33: 45–6.
76 Sanuto, 35: 473; 36: 86.
77 Sanuto, 32: 344 and see ASVe, Senato, *Secreta*, reg. 49, fol. 75[r–v] for letters; busta 50, fols 69[r], 70[r–v], 72[v]–3[r], 73[r–v], 81[r–v], 106[r–v].
78 Robert Finlay, *Politics in Renaissance Venice* (New Brunswick, 1980), pp. 231–42; quotations 231, 236; Sanuto, 9: 183; 12: 460; 19: 80.
79 See note 83; ASVe, Senato, *Secreta*, reg. 49, fols 146[v]–50[r]; reg. 50, fols 47[r], 60[r], 73[r–v], 94[r]–6[r].

majority in an affirmative response. However, as noted above, the five reversed their position only weeks later after imperial forces made stronger efforts, proposing to refrain from the new alliance until the French had given proof of their superiority. Their bill failed, as did a similar one proposed by Alvise Mocenigo and Zacaria Bembo. A third bill aimed at constructing an alliance with France finally passed on the second ballot, as did approval of the pope's new plan to settle the two kings' differences by dividing Milan and Naples between them and stipulating Venice's secret participation and exemption from the requirement to fight the Turks. The five (excepting Zacaria Bembo) were among its proposers. As Kenneth Setton noted, secrecy about this pro-French plan was so effectively maintained that the imperial commanders believed that Venice would join them at the Battle of Pavia (Spanish officials resident in Venice apparently did not share their doubts about Venice with their battlefield colleagues either).[80]

Completing the group of four *savi* leading the way to the rehearsal was its senior member, Nicolò Bernardo, grandson of Doge Francesco Foscari and nephew of procurator and former *podestà* of Padua Marin Venier. He was also the father of Triumphante Hironimo.[81] The Bernardos' important role in banking was funded by the wealth of the western galleys, including the round assisted by the Beolco in which several family members, chiefly Nicolò, partipated (see Chapter 1).[82] When the journeys resumed after the war, Nicolò's somewhat distant kinsman Mafio Bernardo went to Flanders to engage in the work directly. Even after Mafio closed his bank in 1524, the family remained engaged in commerce. They were also committed to mainland defense, particularly Nicolò. Early in the Cambrai wars he was elected *savio a terra ferma* "ma per dir meglio di la guerra" (but more correctly termed [*savio*] of war), was sent on several important defense missions, and eventually was elected to the Conseio and the Council of Ten—even as one of its Heads—despite his (relative) youth. His uncle, Marc'Antonio Loredan, was *capitanio* of Padua at the end of the wars and also the father of Immortale Zuan Francesco. Nicolò's habit of remaining in chambers after Senate meetings meant that he was often the only one available when pressing news arrived unexpectedly, which gave him an important role in formulating the response. In Senate debates over defense issues, he took a prudent approach, especially on questions of when to engage in battle and on maintaining a balance between pro-French and pro-imperial measures, but tended to favor the sovereign strongest at the moment. These views sometimes put him in opposition to more fiery patricians including

---

80 ASVe, Senato, *Secreta*, reg. 50, fols 107^r–10^v, 113^r–21^r; Setton, pp. 227–8.

81 Barbaro, 2: 13–14; PSVBA, ms. 555, Antonio Monterosso, *Reggimenti di Padova dal 1459 sino al 1533* (cited hereafter as Monterosso, *Reggimenti*), vol. 3, fasc. VIII, fols 20^r–21^v.

82 Reinhold C. Mueller, *The Venetian Money Market. Banks, Panics, and the Public Debt, 1200–1500*, Vol. 2 of *Money and Banking in Medieval and Renaissance Venice* (Baltimore, 1997), pp. 60–61, 195, 219–20; Sanuto, 2: 391–2; ASVe, *AGRM*, busta 250, second *vacchetta*, fols 6^v, 9^r, 11^r, 12^r, [e compagni] 13^v, 14^r, 16^v, 18^v, 22^r, 24^r, 25^r, 25^v, 26^r, 41^r, 48^v, [e compagni] 52^v, 53^v, [e compagni] 54^v, 57^r, 66^r, 68^v, 69^r, [e compagni] 84^v, 85^v.

Luca Tron and Antonio Grimani, though he joined them in some proposals such as one to inquire if the Turkish Porte would side with Venice. As a member of the Zonta in 1514 he heard the successful petition of the rebels Giacomo and Francesco qu. Conte Alvaroto to be readmitted to Padua and in 1521 as *consigliere* a petition concerning the assigning of the Paduan canonry of their late brother Alvaroto.[83] As a *savio grande* in 1522, he joined others including Lunardo Mocenigo, Polo Capello, and Lorenzo Loredan in successfully proposing a commission to evaluate the numerous patrician claims of exemption from taxation on real property in the *padovano* and *trevisano*.[84] In early 1524 he made a significant investment in the Bernardo bank, helping Mafio to deal with the losses that would lead to its closing a few months later.[85]

Despite or perhaps because of his heavy responsibilities, Nicolò Bernardo loved a good party and, as a shrewd businessman, also may have been among the first to recognize their potential for profit. In 1518, he succeeded in having the Sunday meeting of the Maggior Consiglio cancelled to allow patricians to attend a Carnival festival given in Campo S. Polo where he lived; rooftop seats to observe it cost a pretty penny and one is justified in wondering if he received some of the proceeds.[86]

The group of procurators that Sanudo names next among the attendees of the 1525 festivity—Jacomo Soranzo, Andrea Justinian, Marco da Molin, Marco Grimani, Francesco di Prioli, Andrea Gusoni, Antonio Mozenigo—had achieved that office at an early age with large loans to the state. They shared many family ties and belonged to or had connections to the prominent *compagnie della calza*. Mocenigo was a member of the Triumphanti, Molin of the Immortali, and Grimani of the Ortolani; Priuli, Grimani's cousin, was the brother of an Immortale. Soranzo, whose family had married with the Grimani, the Priuli, and the Capello and who himself had married a Giustinian, was related to several Ortolani.[87] Giustinian, part of a network of in-laws with numerous connections to the Ortolani, was brother of Paduan canon Hironimo, who was acquiring property for the family there; both were the maternal uncles of Stefano Magno.[88] The Gussoni were in-laws of the Contarini brothers, with whom they co-owned some of their properties in Padua and the *padovano* acquired through Alvise Cornaro's

83 Sanuto, 18: 232; 30: 361.

84 Sanuto, 33: 45–6; Favaretto.

85 The preceding is based on a reading of all entries in Sanudo's *Diarii* through vol. 37; particularly relevant are: 6: 236; 7: 288; 8: 334, 442, 473 (quotation), 507–8; 9: 104, 129, 281, 424; 10: 442, 469, 647, 773, 822, 827, 876; 11: 80, 111, 204–5; 13: 473–4; 14: 38, 194, 252; 15: 452, 508, 571; 16: 363; 17: 44, 250, 366, 432; 18: 56, 198, 232, 311, 385; 20: 469; 21: 163, 494; 24: 307; 26: 17; 27: 569–70; 29: 331–2; 30: 256–9; 31: 182–3; 33: 288, 341; 35: 470; 36: 146, 148–9, 203, 344, 349, 350, 399–400, 401, 484; 37: 154; 39: 338; Lane, "Venetian Bankers," p. 84; Sanuto, 33: 313; ASVe, Senato, *Secreta*, reg. 50, fols 34^{r-v}, 60^r, 73^{r-v}, 107^{r-v}, 109^r–10^r, 113^r–14^r, 116^v–21^r, 122^r–3^v, 124^v, 125^v–8^r, 129^r, 130^v–32^r, 132^v–3^r.

86 Sanuto, 25: 216.

87 Barbaro, 7: 50; Mueller, pp. 645–6.

88 Sanuto, 24: 32; 33: 344, 347; for purchases see *e.g.* ASPd, *Notarile*, busta 1310, fol. 50^r, 102^{r-v}, 125^v.

uncle Alvise Anzelieri, and Andrea Gussoni was the uncle of Donada Pisani Grimani, wife of Triumphante Hironimo Grimani.[89] Involved in the 1480s voyage had been Soranzo's grandfather and great-grandfather, Giustinian's brother, Molin's kinsmen Marco and Hironimo, Grimani's kinsmen Alvise and Lunardo, and Gussoni's family.

The two *capi di dieci* and their families had similar connections: the Donà, related to Mafio Bernardo by marriage, were invested in the 1480s galleys, in a Barbary galley, and in the galley confiscated by the English in 1522, which was captained by Vicenzo Priuli.[90] The family had provided numerous governors to Padua including Polo himself from 1517 to 1519 and Francesco, mentioned in Ruzante's 1524 *Lettera giocosa*.[91] Polo's son had participated in a hunt with Alvise Cornaro and some members of the Immortali.[92] The Barbarigo family's involvement in northern commerce in the early half of the fifteenth century was studied by Frederic Lane and their subsequent turn to landed investment by Gaetano Cozzi and Michael Knapton.[93] Hironimo was the grandson of Doge Agostino, who had served as *capitanio* of Padua and favored the development of silk cultivation on the mainland.[94] During his *dogado* the Beolco had been most involved in Venetian commerce.[95] Hironimo had large agricultural holdings in the *padovano*, especially the Piovato, and owned properties in Padua, where his homonymous cousin, who was also the *primicerio* of San Marco, held the offices of canon and administrator of the bishopric, and where his uncle had numerous properties in the quarter where the Beolco lived.[96] Hironimo's brother had overseen the drawing of a 1524 lottery. One young kinsman was involved in the Barbary galleys and another was a *savio ai ordeni* at the time of Henry's confiscation of a Flanders galley, while a kinswoman had married a Fugger.[97] Very recently Hironimo had returned from

---

89 Emilio Menegazzo, "Altre osservazioni intorno al Ruzante e al Cornaro," in *Colonna*, pp. 267–303, p. 288, note 59; ASPd, *Notarile*, busta 1532, 133ᵛ; ASPd, *Estimo 1518*, busta 352, fols 85ᵛ, 120, 266ʳ, 346ᵛ; busta 353, fols 33ʳ, 45ʳ.

90 Sanuto, 27: 219; 31: 182–3; 32: 405–6, 408–9; 33: 21, 103, 127, 129–30, 145, 277, 278.

91 The repetition of the names Francesco and Alvise in the family led to the (mis)identification of this Francesco qu. Alvise, the future doge, with one who was accused of extortion (Sanuto, 2: 1093): Giuseppe Gullino, "Donà, Francesco," in *DBI*, 40 (1991) but a comparison of Barbaro, 3: 335 Francesco di Alvise qu. Andrea dottore e cavaliere and 3: 317 Francesco di Alvise with ASPd, *Estimo 1518*, busta 352, fols 223ʳ–4ʳ; ASVe, *AGRM*, busta 79bis, fasc. 4; busta 200, fasc. 1; busta 357, unnumbered pergamena of 1512; VBMC, mss. Provenienze Diverse, c, 1297 / II; mss. Provenienze Diverse c, 1350, docs 12, 13, 14, 15, 16, 17, 20, 21, 22, 23 shows that it was most likely this latter, homonymous kinsman who was accused.

92 Sanuto, 26: 397; ASPd, *Estimo 1518*, e.g. busta 352, fols 162ᵛ–3ʳ, 237ᵛ, 229ᵛ.

93 Frederic C. Lane, *Andrea Barbarigo, Merchant of Venice* (Baltimore, 1944); see also ASVe, *AGB*, busta 42; Gaetano Cozzi and Michael Knapton, *Storia della Repubblica di Venezia dalla Guerra di Chioggia alla riconquista della terraferma* (Turin, 1986), p. 125; Favaretto, p. 213.

94 Luca Molà, *The Silk Industry of Renaissance Venice* (Baltimore and London, 2000), p. 219.

95 Monterosso, *Reggimenti*, vol. 3, fasc. VII, fol. 12ʳ–ᵛ; ASVe, *AGRM* 250, first *vacchetta*, fol. 114ᵛ, second *vacchetta*, fol. 71ᵛ.

96 ASPd, *Estimo 1518*, busta 352, fols 111ʳ, 206ᵛ; ASVe, *AGB*, busta 45, unnumbered register, fol. 10ʳ; ASVe, *AGRM*, busta 66, fasc. 5; PACV, *Acta Capitularia*, vol. 11, fols 87ʳ, 91ʳ, 157ʳ–ᵛ.

97 ASVe, Senato, *Secreta*, reg. 49, fols 78ᵛ–9ʳ; Sanuto, 36: 243, 33: 270; 28: 208–9.

duty as *podestà* of Bergamo, on the western boundary of the Venetian state where war was already under way, reporting the great danger that it posed.[98]

Lazaro Mocenigo, kin to a Triumphante, had been *luogotenente del Friuli* (governor of the province of Friuli) at the time of Maximilian's death and was well aware of imperial loyalties in that region, which bounded the empire and contained numerous imperial enclaves, and also supplied Venice with food-stuffs.[99] As ambassador to England during the wars of the League of Cambrai, Andrea Badoer had been charged with setting Henry VII and his son against Louis XII. On his return, he was elected to various responsible offices, being a *capo di dieci* when the treaty with Maximilian ending the wars was ratified.[100] Several of his kin were subsequently involved with the galleys, including a Triumphante who as a *savio ai ordeni* posted Barbary galleys.[101] Aggregated to the Paduan nobility in 1180, the Badoer had immense holdings on the mainland, particularly near Mirano, Gambarare, and San Bruson.[102] A Badoer had married a relative of Alvise Cornaro in the late fifteenth century; another Badoer was married to Immortale Zuan da Leze.[103] Piero Badoer, the father of Triumphante Albertino, had been acquiring important income-producing property on the mainland in the early 1520s and owned property in Padua's *granze* (a country granary that also became a toponym).[104] Documents concerning a possibly ille-gitimate descendant of a branch established in Padua were notarized in the home of Ruzante's uncle in 1522.[105]

Zuan Dolfin, whose family members had been involved in the 1480s voyage, was the brother-in-law of another Gaspare Contarini, of the 'da Londra' branch, the Zardiniere who hosted Beolco's 1522 performance.[106] His brother was then involved in the Barbary galleys, as were the Dolfin including Zuan's son and grandson.[107] Zuan too owned numerous properties in Padua and its *territorio*, including the Polesine di Rovigo.[108] His kinsman Zaccaria became *capitanio* when Padua was retaken in summer 1509.[109] As a *savio a terra ferma*, he had proposed

---

98 Sanuto, *s.v.* 33, 34, 35, 36, esp. 36: 388–9.

99 See especially Sanuto, 26: 474–5; 27: 31–2, 471–2.

100 Angelo Ventura, "Badoer, Andrea," *DBI*, 5 (1963); Sanuto, 23: 398.

101 Sanuto, 29: 186–7; 24: 23–6; 27: 529, 614, 678, 680; 28: 8, 135, 197, 352, 361–2, 369, 379, 381, 415, 433, 441, 457–60, 494, 495, 563, 36: 584.

102 PBC, ms. B.P. 137, Benetto Bertoldi, *Historia cronologica di Padova*, fol. 50ᵛ; ASPd, *Estimo 1518*, busta 352, fols 289ᵛ–290ʳ; busta 358, fol. 122ʳ; Sanuto, 17: 108.

103 Emilio Menegazzo, "Alvise Cornaro: un veneziano del Cinquecento nella terraferma padovana," in *Colonna*, pp. 425–66, 429–34; ASPd, *Estimo 1518*, busta 352, fol. 112ʳ.

104 ASVe, *Archivio Tiepolo, Iª Consegna*, busta 65, unnumbered item dated 8 June 1523; ASPd, *Estimo 1518*, busta 145, fol. 3ʳ.

105 ASPd, *Notarile*, busta 1056, fols 102ᵛ–3ᵛ; ASPd, *Notarile*, busta 1052, fols 14ʳ⁻ᵛ, 15ʳ.

106 ASVe, *AGRM*, busta 250, second *vacchetta*, fols 69ʳ, 84ᵛ.

107 Barbaro, 2: 505; Sanuto 27: 23–5; 34: 277; 36: 32, 64, 267–8, 327, 381–2; 37: 661, 38: 195.

108 ASPd, *Estimo 1518*, busta 352, fols 245ᵛ–6ʳ, 352ʳ; busta 356, fol. 137ᵛ; PBUC, ms. 996, Marin Sanudo, *Itinerario*, fols 11ʳ, 20ʳ⁻ᵛ; Bruno Rigobello, *Lendinara Estense*, Vol. 2 of *Storia antica di Lendinara* (Lendinara, 1977), p. 100.

109 Sanuto, 9, *s.v.*

a strong relationship with the emperor as the instrument of peace with France.[110] Dolfin's kinsmen were involved in a literary network around the families of the Giustinian sisters that included Stefano Magno (see Chapter 2).[111]

Fantin Valaresso, now known to be connected to the Triumphanti through his kinsman Ferigo, had served as proveditor on the Lombard front in 1499. At the time, Venice was allied with Louis XII in his war on Ludovico Sforza, whose financial need compelled him to seek a loan from Venice through Zuan de Beolco.[112] Valaresso's kinsman Polo was at Coron when it was captured by the Turks,[113] and participated in the defense of the mainland in numerous ways during the Cambrai wars. The family apparently abandoned their commerce in London early in the century.[114] Family members held land in Codevigo, in Padua near the Alvaroto, in Pernumia, and in Arquà bounding land of the Castegnola, Paduan nobles with a long association with the Beolco including an actor in his group.[115] Nicolò Trevisan, possibly one of the many Trevisan involved in the 1480s voyage,[116] was then *governador di le entrade*, an office with a close view of the great financial difficulties that a new war would create for the Republic, still suffering from the severe drain of the Cambrai wars. When in 1521 the Alvaroto family appealed their Estimo terms, the commission hearing the petition numbered six Triumphante kinsmen including Fantin Valaresso and Nicolò Trevisan, both of whom were absent from that meeting (possibly respecting the Venetian norm of avoiding conflicts of interest).[117] Piero Badoer, like his kinsman, had large holdings in the *padovano*, to which he added the boat station at S. Zulian.[118] Sanudo attributes his own presence at the festivity to the broad presence of patricians of respectable status and age, rather than to his being kin to Triumphante Andrea.

The last of the rehearsal's attendees to be mentioned, the doge's half-brothers Michiel and Polo Malipiero, were the maternal uncles of Zusto Gradenigo; they were also related to two other Triumphanti: Tomà Malipiero di Hironimo, whose family home had hosted the *compagnia*'s 1522 Carnival supper, and Vicenzo Contarini.[119] The family had many connections to the commercial galleys. Two of

---

110 Sanuto, 33: 540–42; ASVe, Senato, *Secreta*, reg. 49, fols 133ᵛ–4ʳ, 152ᵛ.
111 Giorgio Padoan, "Fortuna della *Pastoral*," in *Momenti del Rinascimento veneto* (Padua, 1978), p. 203; Brian Richardson, *Print Culture in Renaissance Italy: The Editor and the Vernacular Text 1470–1600* (Cambridge, 1994), p. 60.
112 Sanuto, 2: 1096–7, 1386.
113 Sanuto, 3 *s.v.*
114 Sanuto, 1: 50, 80, 125, 380–81.
115 ASPd, *Notarile*, busta 2734, fols 56ʳ–7ʳ; ASPd, *Notarile*, busta 247, fol. 175ᵛ; busta 250, fols 140ᵛ–41ʳ; busta 255, fols 310ʳ–12ʳ; ASPd, *Estimo 1518*, busta 358, fol. 55ᵛ; ASPd, *Notarile*, busta 1116, fol. 296ʳ⁻ᵛ.
116 ASVe, *AGRM*, busta 250, second *vacchetta*, fols 69ʳ, 85ᵛ.
117 Sanuto, 31: 397.
118 ASPd, *Estimo 1518*, busta 352, fols 162ᵛ–3ʳ; ASVe, *Archivio Tiepolo, Iᵃ Consegna*, busta 65, unnumbered item dated 8 June 1523.
119 Sanuto, 32: 450; 37: 17–19; ASVe, *AGB*, busta 9, unnumbered account book of Hironimo Grimani di Marin: 15 Feb. 1521 *m.v.*; Barbaro, 4: 72.

its members were invested in the 1480s voyage. Michiel had had a tragic role in the shipwreck of the Alexandria galley: as *patron al Arsenal*, he had pronounced it fit to depart. Their kinsmen were among contemporary galley owners, and used the profits to add to already large mainland holdings by acquiring properties of Paduan rebels in the Monte Nuovo sales.[120] Another relative, married to Bishop Marco Corner's sister, was an administrator of the Paduan diocese.[121] Matteo Malipiero was involved in a 1523 inheritance dispute with Alvise Cornaro.[122] Erotically-tinged festivities were not a novelty to Polo Malipiero: in 1520 he had invited prostitutes to his Carnival party.[123]

Betia and the 1525 Performance

Two intertwined questions about the performance remain: the identity of the 'dirty comedy' and the identity of the person blamed for it. Beginning with the evidence provided by Emilio Lovarini supporting its identification as *Betia*, there has been an almost universal consensus that this was the play staged. It fits Sanudo's description in its concluding agreement by Zilio, Betia, Nale and Nale's wife Tamia to an equalized erotic sharing, further challenged by the resolve of Tamia's lover Menegello to join the arrangement even without a wife.[124] It includes numerous place and personal names resonating with Triumphanti and their families. Many are found in the list of girls who will help Betia prepare for her wedding, which will be given by her mother Donna Menega Bastia, whose surname is the toponym for a fortified tower such as the one at Strà where the family of Hironimo Grimani's wife Donada Pisani had a farm.[125] In addition to three characters in known Beolco plays (Gnua, Fiore, Trese), they include Colda Beolca d'i Scanfarlati. 'Beolca' is too obvious to require comment. 'Colda' is attested in the Euganean hills, where Alvise Mocenigo, the Trevisan, the Gradenigo, the Morosini and others had property. Nearby Riscossa counts numerous Scanferlati; other Scanferlati worked the farm of Alvise Mocenigo el cavalier near the Brenta.[126] Mocenigo had a curious connection to another woman referred to in the play, Tamia's former employer the Venetian courtesan Anzola Caga-in-Calle. In real life, Anzola had been among

---

120 Sanuto, 24: 29–30, 31; 30: 471–2; ASPd, *Estimo 1518*, busta 352, fols 259ʳ, 350ʳ⁻ᵛ; ASVe, *Ufficiali alle Rason Vecchie*, reg. 48, fols 22ᵛ–3ᵛ, 24ᵛ–5ʳ, 25ᵛ–6ʳ, 30ᵛ–1ʳ.

121 Sanuto, 12: 16; PACV, *Actorum civilium*, vol. 191, fasc. 3, fol. 20ʳ; fasc. 7, unnumbered folio at date of March 11, 1523.

122 ASPd, *Notarile*, busta 1116, fol. 433ʳ⁻ᵛ.

123 Sanuto, 28: 271.

124 Emilio Lovarini, "Ruzzante a Venezia," in *Studi*, 88–93; Emilio Lovarini, "La *Betia*," in *Studi*, pp. 293–317; Pattini. While Giorgio Padoan objected that *Betia* is too long to have been the play in question ("Angelo Beolco," pp. 112–22), the festivity's six hours sufficed for the play and the other entertainment. The play's aspects relevant to the topics of this study will be considered here; given its 180 pages and range of topics from theoretical disputes on love to peasant customs, a full discussion of the play requires a separate study, which is planned.

125 ASVe, *AGB*, busta 5, unnumbered fascicle, accounts of 1520 and 1524.

126 ASPd, *Estimo 1418*, busta 418, fol. 55ᵛ; ASPd, *Estimo 1518*, busta 352, fols 118ᵛ–19ʳ, 136ᵛ, 177ʳ⁻ᵛ, 265ᵛ and 'Coldato' in Oriago; busta 358, fols 9ᵛ, 17ᵛ.

the women fined under sumptuary laws along with the wives of Alvise Mocenigo, father of Triumphante Antonio, and Hironimo Bembo, father of Triumphante Lorenzo. She was also buried in the Frari.[127]

Betia exists in two manuscript forms, one a single-text dedication copy bound in leather with gold decorations discovered by Emilio Lovarini in the Grimani-Morosini archive of the Biblioteca Civica Correr of Venice and the other in the famed Marciana miscellany that contains a large number of Beolco's works.[128] A month before the Triumphante performance, the daughter of Hironimo Grimani's sister Chiaretta and Francesco Mocenigo qu. Piero (kin to Triumphante Antonio and attendee Lazaro) married Stefano Magno, the chronicler and copyist of the *Pastoral*, other theatrical manuscripts, and Canonician 36 (see Chapter 2). Could the Correr manuscript have been produced as a keepsake of that wedding? Hironimo's sons married two Morosini sisters, thus providing one route by which the manuscript may have been included in the Grimani-Morosini archive.[129]

If the inscription on the Correr *Betia* described in Chapter 1 does indeed refer to Antonio Foscarini, it may be the product of the many Foscarini connections with Triumphante families and their activities. They had long been involved in the northern voyages.[130] Zuan Batista Foscarini, whose daughter had married Hironimo Barbarigo, was then invested in the cotton trade, both that conducted by the Marcello through the Capello bank and that conducted by Hironimo Grimani di Marin and his Pisani in-laws, with connections to Milanese merchants.[131] To their land near Bovolenta, the Foscarini added land in the Piovato (Pontecchio) and Polesine di Rovigo in the Monte Nuovo sales of the early 1520s, while Hironimo Grimani and Andrea Foscarini participated in consortial purchases of land in the *padovano*.[132] Antonio Foscarini studied at the University of Padua while Beolco's father was prior; a few years later his father, a military hero, served as *capitanio* of Padua.[133] Antonio followed in his father's footsteps, holding the combined office of *podestà* and *capitanio* of Feltre, in which he was succeeded by Hironimo Barbarigo. In 1523 he served as a government official in Montagnana, where both he and the Beolco had property. He appears in a June 1525 entry in a Paduan notarial register containing many acts witnessed by Beolco, and departed as the *rettore* of the island of Candia in early 1526.[134] It is possible that the Correr manuscript,

---

127 Angelo Beolco (Il Ruzante), *Betia*, Act V, v. 791 (*RT*, p. 1120); Sanuto, 6: 278; 19: 25.

128 VBMC, ms. Grimani-Morosini 4; VBM, Ital. XI, 66. See also Chapter 1 for more about the play.

129 Sanuto, 37: 440; ASVe, *AGB*, busta 24, folio dated 5 May 1539.

130 ASVe, *AGRM*, busta 250, first *vacchetta*, fols 17[r-v], 84[v], 85[r]; second *vacchetta*, fol. 70[v].

131 Barbaro, 1: 172; ASVe, *AGB*, busta 30, unnumbered folio.

132 ASVe, *AGRM*, busta 352, unnumbered fascicle, "Esenzioni sopra beni a Bovolenta di ragione delli NNHH Fratelli Pesaro furono di s. Lunardo"; VBMC, mss. Provenienze Diverse c, 1318, XVII "Inventario di tutte le Scritture del N.H. s. Vicenzo Foscarini," unnumbered folios; ASPd, *Estimo 1518*, busta 354, fols 216[v]–17[r].

133 Barbaro, 3: 541; Monterosso, *Reggimenti*, vol. 4, fasc. IX, fols 5[r]–6[r].

134 Nardi, p. 40; Sanuto, 17: 523, 18: 386; ASPd, *Notarile*, busta 5031, fol. 57; Sanuto, 31: 281; ASPd, *Estimo 1518*, busta 358, fol. 107[v]; Sanuto, 41: 118.

produced as a memento of a wedding at which it was performed, was lent to him for his journey or for a period of *villeggiatura* 'in pavana'.

Of the two manuscripts, the Correr volume is by all indications the earlier. The Marciana text bears the marks of much rewriting; the absence of a large section hints that it was perhaps even occurring during the copying. Several of the differences between the texts seem particularly important. The Correr version contains two prologues, a "Prologo p[er] recitarla in Venetia" (prologue to recite it in Venice; fol. 1ʳ) and "In pavana[,] prologo" (In the countryside of Padua, prologue; fol. 3ʳ); the Marciana version has only an untitled version of the latter. In the Correr version only, stage directions instruct Nale to speak "Voltato i[n] verso el populo" (turned toward the populace) and "Verso el populo (toward the populace)."[135] Documenting an audience that was composed at least in part of non-patrician spectators, the instructions punctuate the most transgressive actions of the married Nale, who has persuaded Betia to marry Zilio by promising himself as second husband. In the first instance, he assures the audience that he will scrub Betia's oven (turning into an erotic metaphor Donna Menega's promise to attend to her daughter Betia, who has faked being scalded, after scrubbing the oven). In the second, Nale proclaims that even if it means banishment from Padua and the *pavan*, he is going to show everyone, including Zilio, that Betia wants him and two husbands.

A third difference between the versions may reflect the sensitivities of distinct audiences. It centers on the salacious metaphor involving the military conquest of Ficarolo,[136] a fortified town on the Po River contended between Venice and Ferrara (see also Chapter 1). The devastating defeat of Venice's efforts to claim it in late 1509, blamed on insufficient effort by *provedador in campo* Zuan Polo Gradenigo, led to the defeat of the Venetian armada on the Po and the subjugation of the Republic to Pope Julius II. Gradenigo, whose military career was intended to reclaim family glory, defended himself by pointing out that the Senate had failed to provide him with adequate forces. The following year, *provedador zeneral* Polo Capello wrested Ficarolo from Alfonso d'Este, a victory that led to the eventual defeat of French forces and stood as one of his signal accomplishments in the war.

The Correr text refers to Ficarolo in a more tentative way; while retaining the reference to the town's conquest, it is missing a line referring to soldierly fear. Such ambivalence could be explained by a performance with a *compagnia* numbering relatives of both Gradenigo and Capello. A reference constant in both versions is that to Soncin Benzon, whose history with Zuan Polo Gradenigo potentially numbers it among the instances of speaking truth to power or perhaps

---

135 VBMC, ms. Grimani-Morosini 4, fol. 57ʳ, III, v. 465 (*RT*, p. 327); fol. 67ᵛ, IV, v. 96 (*RT*, p. 365).

136 *Betia*, IV, vv. 700–23 (*RT*, p. 409); for manuscript versions and historical context, see Linda L. Carroll, "'(El) ge sa bon laorare': Female Wealth, Male Competition, Musical Festivities, and the Venetian patriciate in Ruzante's *pavan*," in Melanie L. Marshall, Linda L. Carroll, and Katherine A. McIver, eds, *Sexualities, Textualities, Art and Music in Early Modern Italy. Playing with Boundaries* (Farnham, 2014), pp. 155–83, pp. 159–66.

testifies instead to Gradenigo's loss of power, which began with his alienation of Benzon from loyalty to the Republic and continued with the Ficarolo defeat and a second defeat. At the outset of the wars of the League of Cambrai, Benzon, of the nobility of Crema on the mainland state's western border, had cast his lot with Venice's enemies, in no small measure because of the harsh treatment that Zuan Polo Gradenigo had meted out to him while Crema's *rettore*. As part of the anti-Venetian league, Benzon participated in the 1510 campaigns near Padua, in which the league inflicted a second defeat on provedidor Gradenigo who, over-estimating the enemy force, ordered the abandonment of Rovigo and failed to protect Montagnana, bastions defending the rich agricultural area south of Padua. When the Senate upbraided Gradenigo, the sole *savio grande* not co-sponsoring the measure was Nicolò Bernardo. Benzon's satisfaction was short-lived, how-ever, as he was soon captured and executed in Padua and, according to Nale in the *Betia*, went straight to his punishment in hell.[137] Gradenigo also had a continu-ing connection with Ruzante's family. In 1516, as *provveditore*, he instructed the *podestà* of Montagnana to exempt the soldier Hironimo Guidoti, the cousin of Ruzante's step-mother Francesca Guidoti in Beolco, from certain assessments. The issue returned in 1523; Hironimo, in the meanwhile having killed Francesca's two brothers and given shelter to outlaws, lost the exemption.[138]

Other multivalent allusions in the *Betia* possibly hint at the war, as well as at Venetian patricians' land investments and connections with the Beolco family. Zilio's list of valiant friends on whom he will call to help him fight for Betia begins with Duozo d'i Botazi and ends with Perduozemo da le Gambarare.[139] 'Perduocimo', of which 'Duozo' is a shortened version, is the most Paduan of names, inspired by the city's early bishop patron saint. It was the original name of the peasant character Ruzante, as he explains in the *Anconitana*, "el me derto nome è Perduocimo" (my proper name is Perduocimo).[140] 'Botazi' was a surname present in various locales, principally Venice.[141] The Pisani holding at Strà was farmed by the Botazo family.[142] A tenant of Alvise Cornaro and before him of his

---

137 Benzon: *Betia*, Act I, v. 1103; Act V, vv. 897–910, 1121–4 (*RT*, pp. 231, 471, 485). Analysis in Carroll, "(El) ge sa bon laorare'"; Linda L. Carroll, "Utopia, Venice and Ruzante's *Pavan*: Venetian and Paduan Connections with Thomas More," *Modern Language Review* 107.1 (January, 2012): 162–81; primary sources include PBUC, ms. 874, 3: 29^v; VBM, Ital. VII 328 (=8513), Andrea Ziliol, *Chronica*, fol. 5^{r-v}; ASVe, Senato, *Secreta*, reg. 43, fols 48^r–9^r; Sanuto, 10: 340–41, 344–5, 439–41; Pietro Bembo, *Della Historia vinitiana di M. Pietro Bembo Card. Volgarmente scritta. Libri XII* (Venice, 1552), fol. 142^r.

138 Sanuto, 25: 535; 26: 61, 122, 396; 27: 337–8; 30: 287; 34: 261; Menegazzo, "Altre osservazioni," p. 268 note 2 for siblings; Linda L. Carroll, "Per un itinerario della Padova del Ruzante," *Padova e il suo territorio* 164 (Agosto, 2013): 6–9.

139 Act IV, vv. 78–88 (*RT*, pp. 363–5).

140 Act IV, v. 65 (*RT*, p. 817).

141 Umberto Simionato, *Cognomi padovani e antiche famiglie di Padova e del suo territorio. Ricerca storico-linguistica sulle antiche famiglie di Padova e della sua provincia*, 2 vols (Padua, 1995–99), *s.v.*

142 ASVe, *AGB*, busta 5, unnumbered fascicle, accounts of 1520 and 1524.

uncle Anzelieri living in Codevigo was Meo (Bartolomeo) Botazo.[143] Gambarare was a village on the boundary dividing the larger mainland state from the *dogado*, the strip of land running along the lagoon, where Venetians, including the Gradenigo, had first bought farmland.[144] Its location just beyond the typical area of exile from Venice meant that it was a hang-out for banished criminals (*banditi*).[145] The peasants there being particularly loyal to Venice, they were among the first to be recruited in wartime as *guastadori* (sappers).[146] There, as *provedador zeneral,* Andrea Gritti planned the retaking of Padua that had been proposed in the Senate by Alvise Mocenigo and Nicolò Bernardo among others. Sebastian Bernardo organized the peasant forces in nearby Strà, where his family had a tavern.[147] Polo Donà's family owned large amounts of land in the Piovato; his granddaughter rented land in Padua to "piero de iratj dale gambarare."[148] 'San Bruson' or 'Brison', the dialect form of Sant'Ambrogio, is often called upon in the play. His feast on December 7 was significant to the agricultural year, with its labors of pruning the *stropari* (wicker-providing plants) and of spinning.[149] He was the patron/namesake of the nearby village of Sambruson, where the Tron had a home but that, more importantly, was a stronghold of the Badoer, including Andrea and his brother Zuan. It had served as an important staging area in the reconquest of Padua, success in which turned Venice's fortunes in the Cambrai wars and led to Gritti's election as doge in 1523.[150] He was also the patron saint of Milan, a subtle hint of Beolco's family background.

Given the buildup to the war for Italy of the early 1520s, was Beolco using Zilio's ability to muster and command peasant forces in *Betia* to propose himself for such a role in the famed Venetian *cernide*? The title 'strenuus' (soldier) that Emilio Menegazzo noted preceding Beolco's name in a document of June 2, 1526, hypothesizing that he served as a soldier in about 1526–27, occurs in an entry following another of the same day recording the sale of a horse by Ambrogio Agugia, a relative of Alvise Cornaro's wife, to 'strenuus' Jacomo da Vicoaro, a *capitanio*

143 ASPd, *Estimo 1518*, busta 341, fols 118ᵛ, 120ᵛ; busta 358, fols 50ᵛ–2.
144 Lesley A. Ling, "La presenza fondiaria veneziana nel padovano (secoli XIII–XIV)," in *Istituzioni, società e potere nella Marca Trevigiana e Veronese. Sulle tracce di G.B. Verci*, ed. Gherardo Ortalli and Michael Knapton (Rome, 1988), pp. 305–16, p. 308 note 17.
145 Sanuto, 36: 128.
146 ASVe, Senato, *Secreta*, reg. 45, fol. 158ʳ.
147 Antonio Bonardi, "I padovani ribelli alla repubblica di Venezia (a. 1509–1530), studio storico con appendice di documenti inediti," *Miscellanea di storia veneta a cura della Deputazione veneta di storia patria* ser. 2.8 (1902): 303–612, p. 373; Favaretto, pp. 119–21; Sanuto, 8: 507–8, 522–5.
148 ASPd, *Estimo 1518*, busta 352, fol. 295.
149 *Viz.* Angelo Beolco (Il Ruzante), *La Pastoral*, Proemio ala villana, v. 1 (*RT*, p. 7); *Betia* Act II, v. 657; Dino Coltro, *Santi e contadini Lunario della tradizione orale veneta* (Caselle di Sommacampagna [VR], 1994), at date.
150 *E.g.* ASPd, *Estimo 1518*, busta 352, fols 100ʳ, 135ʳ⁻ᵛ, 165ʳ, 166ʳ, 178ᵛ–9ʳ, 229ᵛ, 237ᵛ, 268ᵛ, 272ʳ⁻ᵛ, 312ᵛ; busta 356, fol. 99ᵛ; busta 358, fol. 112ᵛ; ASPd, *Notarile*, busta 2909, fol. 155ᵛ–6ʳ; ASVe, *Archivio Tiepolo, Iᵃ Consegna*, busta 64, unnumbered item dated 1511 19 January; PBUC, ms 874, fols 14ʳ⁻ᵛ.

of *stradioti* departing for the front. It was also the date on which the Venetian Senate began imparting to the proveditor general instructions on arrangements for the Republic's entry into the war on the French side. That proveditor general was Piero Pesaro, host of the 1521 Ortolano party to welcome *condottiero* Antonio Martinengo into the *compagnia* enlivened by 'una comedia bella et nova' (a lovely and new comedy) performed by Ruzante and Menato.[151]

Did Beolco have a practical purpose as well for the detailed depiction of the realities of farm life in the play? Many of the Venetian families sponsoring his performances were becoming ever more invested in agricultural properties but knew that they had little expertise in handling them.[152] A kind of land rush for the Paduan territory developed in the early 1520s, with (mostly agricultural) properties purchased by Venetian consortia including many of the families and individuals involved with the 1525 performance: the Capello, the Barbarigo including Jacopo and Marco who were possibly the brothers of Hironimo, the Giustinian, the Trevisan, the Contarini, the Foscarini, the Garzoni, the Grimani, the Marcello among whom an Andrea, the Molin, the Sanudo, the Gradenigo including Zuan Polo, the Bembo, the Priuli, the Morosini, the Mocenigo including Lazaro, the Malipiero, the Bernardo, the Gussoni, the Soranzo, the Badoer, the Zorzi, Santo Tron, the Dolfin, the Procuratori, and Jacopo and Alvise Corner, the latter of whom was probably Ruzante's patron. A distinctive feature of these investments is the number of women undertaking them in their own name, the barriers to female participation lowered by the cost-sharing of consortia and the relative accessibility of land investment as opposed to maritime commerce.[153] This is another detail of the performance that resonates especially with *Betia*, centering on the farm of Donna Menega and her daughter, which they run with a profitability that allows them to 'far beco i so mariti' (cuckold their husbands).[154] Marc'Aurelio Alvaroto would have figured in this context, as his branch of the family, descended from a Paduan canon, lived in a cluster of church properties in the Paduan parish of S. Eufemia (Santa Fomia; between Portello and the Santo) whose *livellari* numbered Triumphante affines including Sebastian Bernardo, Piero Bernardo, Alvise Mocenigo, a Barbo, Domenego Contarini, Zacaria Bembo and Piero Gradenigo.[155]

151 Menegazzo, "Stato," p. 330 note 76; ASPd, *Notarile*, busta 5031, fols 201ʳ–2ʳ [202ʳ published in Paolo Sambin, "Altre testimonianze (1525–40) di Angelo Beolco," in *Per le biografie di Angelo Beolco, il Ruzante, e di Alvise Cornaro*, restauri di archivio rivisti e aggiornati da Francesco Piovan (Padua, 2002), p. 78]; for *cernide*, see Piero Pieri, *Il Rinascimento e la crisi militare italiana*, 2nd ed. (Turin, 1952); Angiolo Lenci, "Agnadello e l'assedio di Padova nel 1509: la prospettiva della *securitas veneta* dopo Cambrai," in Sergio Costa, ed. *L'assedio di Padova e la sconfitta dell'esercito dell'imperatore del Sacro Romano Impero Massimiliano I e del re di Francia Luigi XII*. Atti della Giornata di Studio. Padova, Sabato 3 ottobre 2009 (Padua, 2009; repr. with corrections, 2010), pp. 34–42; ASVe, Senato, *Secreta*, reg. 51, fols 41ʳ–2ᵛ; Sanuto, 29: 536–7.

152 Bembo's letters suffice for all: Pietro Bembo, *Lettere*, ed. Ernesto Travi, 4 vols (Bologna, 1987–93), 2: 244 lett. 526; 291 lett. 586, 293 lett. 590 (silk), 331 lett. 639.

153 ASPd, *Estimo 1518*, busta 354, fols 216ᵛ–49ᵛ.

154 See Carroll, "'(El) ge sa bon laorare'."

155 PACV, *Acta capitularia*, vol. 15, fol. 229ʳ⁻ᵛ.

As Venetians of the time recognized, their lack of acquaintance with agriculture made the assistance of more experienced parties in the acquisition and managing of these new investments of great value. Such were Alvise Cornaro and Angelo Beolco, the former well versed in land management and the latter in peasant language and customs. Some of the families involved in the 1525 performance had already had such dealings with Cornaro or his or Beolco's family members, or other Paduans closely connected to them, and more would follow. Zuane and Bernardo Marcello qu. Andrea, for example, had acquired six *campi* some years before from Alvise Cornaro.[156] Bernardo was the father of Triumphante Andrea, while Zuan Marcello had served as a *capo di dieci* with Zulian Gradenigo and Alvise Mocenigo and gave a *livello* on his Paduan property to the son of the notary who recorded the will of Beolco's uncle.[157] Later in 1525, Zuan Antonio Malipiero, the brother-in-law of the late Bishop Marco Corner, and the Paduan noble Bernardino dei Conti would choose as the mediator of a property dispute between them Alvise Cornaro, Malipiero's neighbor in Padua.[158] In October 1528 in his home in Piove di Sacco, Tommaso Contarini qu. Alvise, brother of Triumphante Vicenzo and of former ambassador and future Cardinal Gaspare, modified a lease for the holder's widow, who was unable to meet the terms. Witnesses to the act were Alessandro Contarini qu. Andrea, captain of the much-vexed 1524 galie di Barbaria; Alvise Cornaro; and Angelo Beolco.[159] The latter two also witnessed a subsequent *soceda* (animal husbandry) contract given by Tommaso Contarini to the widow's in-law involving 20 horses and a herd of 35 cattle. Five days later, in his home in Rosara, Count Rambaldo di Collalto, recent heir to the title at a very young age at the deaths of his father and brother and son of the patrician Lucia Mocenigo qu. Lorenzo,[160] gave a *procura* (power of attorney) for determining the boundaries between his properties and those of the villagers. This document, whose importance was increased by the count's purchase days before of the *livello* rights of many of the peasants, was witnessed by Beolco and village leaders. Was Beolco involved as a kind of mediator between the young noble and the peasant community? Rambaldo's trust in Beolco may have been inspired by the role of Beolco's great-uncle Antonio da Pernumia in a land purchase by Rambaldo's grandfather Vinciguerra in 1467 in Rosara.[161] Of particular interest to patricians was sericulture, whose introduction, stoutly defended by Doge Agostino Barbarigo, helped offset the dearth of Syrian silk caused by the prohibition of export.[162] The cultivation of silk worms is one of the sources of Betia's prosperity in the play.

156 ASPd, *Estimo 1518*, busta 352, fol. 80ᵛ.
157 Sanuto, 28: 46; ASVe, *AGB*, busta 4, unnumbered folio at date of 1522 Aug. 9; ASPd, *Notarile*, busta 3969, fols 15ᵛ–16ᵛ.
158 Sanuto, 12: 16; ASPd, *Notarile*, busta 1315, fol. 516ᵛ; busta 2190, fols 235ʳ–6ʳ.
159 ASPd, *Notarile*, busta 2734, fols 603ᵛ–6ᵛ.
160 Barbaro, 2: 401; see Chapter 1 for additional information on Lucia Mocenigo.
161 ASPd, *Notarile*, busta 2727, fols 435ʳ, 501–12; busta 4010, fols 334ʳ–5ᵛ.
162 Molà, pp. 219–20; cf. Bembo, *Lettere*, 2: 293 lett. 590.

Complications in identifying the 1525 play and author have arisen from Sanudo's account of the substitution between the rehearsal and the formal staging: "non feno recitar la comedia sporca fata per quel da l'Oio, di la qual havia ducati 50, ma ben quella di Ruzante a la villota" (they did not have the performance of the dirty comedy put on [chosen?] by the Oio guy [the guy from around the Oglio River? the oil guy? but see below for another transcription], for which he had 50 ducats, but Ruzante's country one).[163] Some scholars have interpreted the passage as meaning that the 'comedia sporca' had been written by 'quel da l'Oio'. However, a correct understanding of the meaning of 'autor' supports a different interpretation. As attested by the Venetian legislation of 1508 concerning theatrical festivities, as well as other instances, the 'autor' was the person who organized and ran the festivities, what today might be called the 'director', 'manager', or 'master of ceremonies': "li auctorj verame[n]te over maistrj che le [=momarie] facesseno, ordinasseno over guidassesno" (the organizers, that is, or teachers [dance teachers, who frequently organized spectacles] who put on, organize, or conduct them).[164] The term was also used to designate those who ran lotteries, including Manenti.[165] Thus Sanudo's concluding comment, "Et fo compita la prova di la ditta comedia con biasemo de tutti, non a li compagni che spendeno ducati . . . , ma di chi è stà l'autor" indicates that the blame ('biasemo') was on the organizer of the festivity ('la festa fanno li compagni Triumphanti, di la qual è autor Zuan Manenti'). Additional considerations regard the sum of 50 ducats paid to 'quel da l'Oio', a sum consistent with a large spectacle rather just a comedy. For example, the payment that Ruzante received for the performance of his comedy in 1523 at the Ducal Palace was 31 *lire* (about five ducats), while Cherea was paid 82 *lire* (about 12 ducats) for an eclogue and other entertainment.[166]

The verb 'fece' or its passive form 'fata per' was used by Sanudo regularly to indicate who organized and staged a comedy, as is made unequivocal in the penultimate passage quoted below; this was the case even for an *autor-attore* such as Ruzante, who headed an acting troupe and also performed. On the other hand, when the play was staged or directed by someone other than the actors Sanudo used the verb 'recitar'. Compare "una altra comedia a la vilanescha, la qual fece uno nominato Ruzante padoan" (another country style comedy, which was done [=organized and staged] by one under the name Ruzante the Paduan) for the separate comedy staged by Ruzante as the coda to the 1520 Immortale festivity; "et poi cena fu recità una bela et nova comedia per Ruzante et Menato padoani" (and after supper a lovely and new comedy was recited by Ruzante and Menato

163 Sanuto, 37: 572.
164 ASVe, Senato, *Terra*, busta 18, fol. 13ᵛ; cf. Sanuto, 18: 300; 26: 482. For the evolution of theatrical staging in Venice from *compagnie della calza* to professional troupes, see Peter Jordan, *The Venetian Origins of the Commedia dell'Arte* (New York, 2014).
165 Sanuto, 32: 467, 501.
166 ASVe, *AGRM*, busta 9, fascicle 10; cf. busta 28, fols 10ᵛ–11ʳ, 17ᶜ for expenses for another festivity. It could be objected that *Betia* is a long play requiring a large number of actors.

the Paduans) for a festivity run by the *compagni* themselves; "Fu fata certa come-dia a la vilanescha, per Ruzante et Menato di Padoa" (A certain country-style comedy was done [=organized and staged] by Ruzante and Menato from Padua) for the sole entertainment at a festivity; "fo recità una comedia fata per Ruzante" (a comedy was recited that was organized and staged by Ruzante) for a large festivity directed by the Grimani; "se fa . . . a Padoa al Santo, in chà Corner un altra comedia per Ruzante, bellissima" (another comedy is done [=organized and staged] by Ruzante in Padua, at Sant'Antonio, in the Corner house, very lovely) for a comedy as sole entertainment. The distinction between the two activities is clearest when they occur in a single passage: "recitate tre commedie, una per Cherea, l'altra per Ruzante e Menato a la vilanescha, l'altra per el Cimador et fiol di Zan Pollo, bufoni; fato questa festa per il Patriarca di Aquileia" (three com-edies were recited, one by Cherea, another by Ruzante and Menato in the country style, another by Cimador and son of Zuan Polo, buffons; and this festivity was done [=organized and staged] by the Patriarch of Aquileia).[167]

A further clarification of the 1525 passage may result from a corrected tran-scription of 'quel daloio' to 'quel daloro' ('the gold/money guy' or 'the Dall'Oro guy'). The foregoing information converges on Manenti, the *autor* of the festivity and of numerous lotteries bringing money (gold) to the state and the prize win-ners, at least one of the latter being backed by the Dall'Oro family.

The identification of the 1525 play as the *Betia* is further supported by the description of the substitute comedy "ma ben quella di Ruzante," as well as the curious wording of the initial entry, "Ruzante et Menato padoani da Vilan feno una comedia vilanesca," when it is considered that the *Betia* is one of the few Beolco comedies lacking in characters named Ruzante and Menato. Their cor-respondents instead are named Zilio and Nale. In this interpretation, the Sanudo passage means that the dirty Beolco country comedy (*Betia*) chosen by the festiv-ity organizer (Manenti) was substituted by an acceptable Ruzante country comedy (a version of *Fiorina* or something like it).

Whichever play it was, presentation of a "dirty play" is consistent with the "sexual disrespect" that Matteo Casini observed as an occasional manifestation of the erotic element of the *compagnie*.[168] It is also consistent with Beolco's auda-cious articulation of the deviation from official moral codes practiced silently by some of his sponsors, of which one obtains occasional glimpses in references to prostitutes invited to parties, to the presentation of beautiful patrician wives to visiting dignitaries often accompanied by the 'ballo del cappello' (hat dance) in which the woman chose her partner, and possibly to the odd 'una in numero di belle' of the 1525 festivity (who were the *belle*? what was their function?).[169] The new fashion of modestly covering the hair displayed by both the married and the

167 Sanuto, 28: 255; 29: 536; 33: 9; 34: 124 (for payment see ASVe, *AGRM*, busta 9, fascicle 10); 57: 528; 40: 789.
168 Matteo Casini, "The 'Company of the Hose': Youth and Courtly Culture in Europe, Italy, and Venice," *Studi Veneziani* 63 (2011): 1217–37, p. 1236.
169 See Carroll, "Introduction," p. 59.

unmarried women of the audience (*capa, scufie*) may have heightened a Ruzantine impulse to mock hypocrisy. That his impulse may have been related to his uneasiness about his own contemporary hypocrisy will be discussed in Chapter 4.

Concordiae dedicatum

To return to the larger context: how broad was the scope of the festivity's referents and implications? The list of dignitaries and the title *Concordiae dedicatum* provide important clues. A core of the attendees and members of Triumphante families had often acted in concert over the course of the post-Cambrai period, in which the Republic dealt with lingering devastation and faced an expensive new round of wars. In doing so, they expressed their preference for peace over war as providing the conditions for prosperity in both maritime commerce and mainland agriculture. After the election of Charles, who, as the sovereign of the Habsburg holdings bounding the mainland state and Spanish holdings along the maritime route, had the capacity to devastate both, many Venetian leaders, regardless of their personal political preferences, redoubled the effort to find peace with him.[170]

Particularly relevant is the series of Senate debates of August 1519 as France pressured Venice to support military efforts clearly oriented toward war, while Charles's grand chancellor Mercurino di Gattinara was exhorting the Republic to prolong their truce and enter into an agreement of "paxe e intelligentia" (peace and [shared military] intelligence). The proposals cover the range of leading political opinion on the matter. Most of the *savi* advocated a typical response to Francis favoring his strategy but refraining from contributing material support, using the excuse of past war expenses. Zorzi Pisani and Marin Zorzi, both holders of university degrees and experienced diplomats, instead favored a dual strategy that would also extend an olive branch to Charles by prolonging the truce. Pisani's speech in favor of this view led to the approval of a letter reflecting it. The next day, however, Alvise Molin (Marco's father) initiated an effort to substitute it with a new letter to Spain removing the agreement to "paxe et amorevol intelligentia" (peace and loving intelligence), coupled with a new letter to France about this development and swearing allegiance to France. Polo Capello opposed Molin's proposal and the *savi* Alvise Priuli (Francesco's uncle), Andrea Gritti, and Tomà Mocenigo withheld their support. After much debate and many modifications accommodating individual and collective opinions, two principal proposals emerged. Placed by Alvise Molin, Alvise Priuli, Polo Capello, Nicolò Bernardo, and Tomà Mocenigo, one expressed thanks to Charles for the offer of "paxe e amorevol intelligentia" (peace and loving intelligence) and the hope that peace would emerge from planned talks in Verona. From the latter phrase, as Sanudo noted, "intelligentia" (*i.e.* military intelligence) had been omitted, subtly expressing that Venice hoped for peace but would refrain from sharing intelligence.

170 Carroll, "Venetian Attitudes."

The other proposal was advanced by Andrea Trevisan and Andrea Gritti and included both peace and intelligence in Venice's goals to be expressed to Charles, as well as the hope that peace between Venice and the empire would lead to peace among all Christian princes. In other words, Venice wanted peace and would accept the need to share intelligence with Charles, doing so with an eye to avoiding a war between Charles and Francis. Despite his well-known favoring of France, Gritti thus stated in the Senate his favoring of peace with Charles that he communicated privately.[171] After further debate, the latter wording passed, although the ambassador to the French court was separately instructed to affirm to the king Venice's constant fidelity to France. Few better examples exist of what Frederic Lane defined as Venice's "double balancing act."[172]

In early 1525, the same leaders or their close affines continued to exercise governance in the Senate, while the families' younger generations were active in the *compagnie della calza* and had begun to hold office; the Alexandria galleys, while still encountering difficulties, were returning with a rich cargo.[173] Venetian banks, however, were in a much-weakened condition and some had closed. Conflict between Francis and Charles for control of Italy had metastasized into the war raging in Lombardy and threatening to spill into Venice's state, with both monarchs menacing Venetian commerce to exert political influence. The relevance of these last two factors to each other is succinctly stated by Reinhold Mueller: because of the role of private banks in financing Venetian war efforts, "the strength or weakness of the Rialto banks in the marketplace and in their role as 'pillars of the state' would be carefully observed by foreign powers, preoccupied with the question whether to form military alliances with Venice or to wage war against it."[174] In late 1524, the pope's (fleetingly embraced) solution of a pact by which Francis and Charles would settle their Italian claims by dividing Milan and Naples was supported in the Senate by a group either attending the Triumphante festivity or with connections to the Triumphanti: Lunardo Mocenigo, Luca Tron, Alvise Mocenigo, Andrea Trevisan, Nicolò Bernardo, Marc'Antonio Contarini, and Zuan Francesco Badoer (among others). It failed for lack of a vote.[175]

If this was the kind of concord to which the Triumphante festivity's title alluded, the choice of play may also have had a metaphorical role: in a reworking of a traditional metaphor identifying the husband in a marriage with the head of state and the wife with the state or body politic, fidelity to a spouse functioned as an analogue to fidelity to an ally, the concord in both cases requiring an agreement to share rather than to claim exclusive possession. If some leading patricians thought that Venice's best interests would be served by having multiple allies (*i.e.* sharing spouses), the Paduans who earlier had had exclusive imperial affiliations also

171 See note 47.
172 Sanuto, 27: 561–72; cf. ASVe, Senato, *Secreta*, reg. 48, fols 40ʳ–3ʳ. Frederic C. Lane, *Venice. A Maritime Republic* (Baltimore, 1973), p. 246.
173 On galleys, see Sanuto, 36: 388, 462, 467, 468, 469, 551, 622; 38: 153, 167, 171.
174 Mueller, pp. 568–9.
175 ASVe, Senato, *Secreta*, reg. 50, fols 116ᵛ–17ʳ; cf. Sanuto, 37: 251.

appear to have been feeling the need to re-establish connections with Venice in the interest of peace and prosperity. Their number, who included Beolco and Alvaroto relatives and affines and perhaps even Angelo and Marc'Aurelio themselves, had seen how the 1509 rebellion had led to death, exile and ruin. That they had come to an understanding of the advantages of peace with Venice is evident in both the Venetian and the 'in pavana' prologues. The warning that birds do not sing as well in cages harks back to the captured 1509 imperial supporters locked in cages in Venetian prisons ('birds' because of the imperialists' totemic eagle; they included Giacomo Alvaroto's father Conte, who died in the cages). The accompanying warning that cows do not give as much milk in the city cautions against a new war, as livestock were taken to cities for protection when battle grew imminent. The birds' and cows' 'natural' state in the country where they flourish, as the prologues proclaim, thus represents peacetime, as did the tranquil herding of the sheep in the *Ardelia* copied for Stefano Magno.[176]

176   Carroll, "'(El) ge sa bon'"; for *Ardelia*, see Chapter 2 note 180.

4   1526: State Lotteries, the Final Ruzantine Performance, and a Machiavellian Coda

The rejection of the 'dirty' play that Manenti had staged was accompanied by the government's continued rejection of Manenti as lottery organizer. On February 21, the Council of Ten decided to hold another lottery, which they entrusted to Ludovico Orazio.[1]

On February 25, 1525, Carnival Saturday, a messenger arrived at the Ducal Palace with a letter sent from the Lombard front by proveditor general Piero Pesaro, its urgency underlined by its arriving in a single day. In it Pesaro recounted the defeat of the French army and capture of Francis I and important members of the French officer corps by Charles's troops at Pavia on February 24. Although the government meetings had recessed for dinner, the three heads of the Ten (Polo Donà, Pandolfo Morosini, and Hironimo Barbarigo) were still present; they were summoned by the doge and joined by two procurators who lived in the Piazza, Domenego Trevisan and Hironimo Giustinian. Shocked by the gravity of the situation, they immediately sent a courier to Rome to inform Pope Clement VII. On Monday, after the Senate had adjourned and many officials had hurried off to the much-heralded festivity of the Valorosi featuring a comedy, four *savi dil consejo*—Luca Tron, Lorenzo Loredan, Nicolò Bernardo, and Hironimo Giustinian, the same four who had led the way to the Triumphante rehearsal—remained in the Palazzo for a private performance of an *egloga* (rustic comedy).[2]

On March 2, the *savi* proposed to the Senate the election of an ambassador to England, a measure that was favored by the pope and that was clearly intended to heal a rift between Henry and Charles as well as benefit Venice's northern commerce. Its signalling of an overture to Charles was unmistakable. After Alvise Pisani, an ardent French partisan, spoke against it, it was recalled that the Ten had renewed the exclusion of *papalisti*, patricians with close relatives enjoying ecclesiastical benefices, from debates on matters involving the papacy and that Pisani was one of them. The *papalisti* were sent out of the chamber; also excluded were Lorenzo Loredan, Hironimo Giustinian, Andrea Giustinian, Marco Grimani,

---

1   ASVe, Consiglio di Dieci, *Miste*, filza 54, fol. 222^r; Collegio, *Notatorio*, reg. 20, fol. 38^r; Marino Sanuto, *I diarii*, ed. Rinaldo Fulin et al., 58 vols (Venice, 1879–1902), 37: 627; 38: 85.
2   Sanuto, 37: 648–9, 671.

Lazaro Mocenigo and members of the Trevisan, Donà, Marcello, and Barbo families. At the urging of Alvise Mocenigo, the vote was postponed; the measure was
re-proposed on March 6 and passed unanimously.[3]

The Council of Ten and Collegio entrusted Ludovico Orazio with other lotteries through the spring, all drawn at the Scuola di San Marco at San Zanipolo. A
few weeks after the French defeat at Pavia, a drawing assigned an important prize
to Lorenzo Cardinal Campeggio, the papal legate to Germany and Hungary of
unwavering imperial affiliation.

Francis's imprisonment in Spain threw his Italian followers into disarray.
Charles attempted to capitalize on his victory by offering Clement and Venice
an alliance that would require additional war financing. For a few months that
spring, Clement accepted and the peace-oriented senators led a move in Venice to
do the same. In this period Manenti began to be assigned lotteries again. In May
and June, he was entrusted with one for about 50,000 ducats (not coincidentally
the value of Venice's two outstanding annual payments to the emperor for war
expenses), whose valuable real estate parcels included the house of the Duke of
Milan on the Grand Canal. It was drawn at the Scuola di San Marco and was a
success. He was granted another one in August.[4]

The impulse to make peace with Charles was short-lived. By mid July it
was replaced by a concerted effort to defeat him in Italy through a league led
by France and involving Clement. The Venetian Senate exhibited willingness to
join, although it simultaneously took steps to ensure continuing good relations
with Charles.[5] In a letter of September 6, 1525 to Niccolò Machiavelli, Filippo
Nerli refers to Machiavelli's winning several thousand ducats in a lottery while
in Venice on a mission to promote Florentine wool. Nerli's statement was clearly
a joke, as no lotteries were drawn in that period. But prior to going to Venice,
Machiavelli had made an assessment of military matters in Lombardy. Was
Nerli's joke a veiled reference to the success of a covert mission to draw Venice
into Clement's renewed interest in an alliance with France? By November Venice
had agreed on the alliance privately and the lottery that Manenti had been granted
in August was drawn.

During Carnival of 1526, Manenti received a letter from Machiavelli requesting
an account of the staging in Venice of his *Comedia de Calimaco* (*Mandragola*).
While Machiavelli's letter no longer exists, Manenti's response does, although it
has been attributed to him only recently with the correct transcription of the surname.[6] Dated Feb. 28, 1525 *more veneto* and thus 1526, the letter is addressed to

---

3 Sanuto, 38: 26–8, 49–50; cf. ASVe, Senato, *Secreta*, reg. 50, fols 136ᵛ–8ᵛ.
4 ASVe, Collegio, *Notatorio*, reg. 20, fols 47ʳ; Senato, *Secreta*, reg. 50, fols 141ʳ⁻ᵛ, 142ᵛ–3ʳ,
   145ʳ–6ᵛ, 148ʳ–60ᵛ, Sanuto, 37: 627; 38: 100–103; 39: 45, 75–6, 210, 220, 266, 279–80, 281;
   Setton, pp. 232–3. Orazio makes no further appearance in the record and appears to have died
   around this time.
5 ASVe, Senato, *Secreta*, reg. 50, fols 166ʳ–89ᵛ; Sanuto, 39: 281.
6 A hole in the paper of the original eliminating the final letters of the surname resulted in the errone-
   ous transcription 'Manetti', whereas the remaining trace of an 'n' mark over the hole and all of the

"M[issier] Nicolò padrone honorandissimo," the first indication that Manenti had a formal relationship of some dependency on the Florentine. Manenti describes not one staging of the play but two. The first was executed so well that a rival performance of Plautus's *Maenechmi* by some gentlemen was considered a dead thing in comparison. This first performance was not mentioned by Sanudo, perhaps because of the sumptuary legislation of January 25 that included a ban on *momarie*, a broad term including almost all forms of staged presentations, or perhaps because he did not approve of the subject matter.[7] Nonetheless, Franco Gaeta was able to date it to February 5 because Sanudo did record the performance organized to rival it, stating that it involved the Lucchese actor Cherea and took place at Ca' Morosini at San Aponal. San Aponal was the location of Tanai Nerli's home; the only Morosini documented as living there was Silvestro, then among a group of patricians petitioning to be allowed into the Senate under special terms in return for a large loan to the state.[8]

Silvestro Morosini was closely related to Marc'Antonio Morosini, procurator and knight, a leading patrician of the late fifteenth century who had advocated moderation in relations with Florence and the papacy.[9] Marc'Antonio's life had numerous connections with Beolco's circle and with Padua and its region. As Stefano Magno records in his *Annali*, he had been elected ambassador to the Duke of Milan under Doge Marco Barbarigo (1485). He had served as *provveditore* during the war with Ferrara, fortifying the area around Rovigo where Roberto da Sanseverino headed the garrison.[10] Later, in Padua, he caused the paving of the street on which Marc'Aurelio Alvaroto lived and, as *capitanio* under Doge Agostino Barbarigo, protected communal lands from confiscation.[11] He served on the western front as co-*provveditore* in 1498 with Melchiorre Trevisan, one of the war heroes buried in the Frari, when the Franco-Veneto forces defeated Ludovico Sforza and took Cremona.[12] He was interested in classical literature, especially the poetry of Martial.[13]

Silvestro Morosini also had numerous connections to various people and places of the 1526 festivities. These included Beolco, who would stage his last performance in Venice on February 7, and whose first one was at the behest of

---

historical details confirm that it is 'Manenti': Florence, Biblioteca Nazionale, *Carte Machiavelli*, V, 19; Niccolò Machiavelli, *Lettere*, ed. Franco Gaeta, Vol. 3 of *Opere* (Turin, 1984), pp. 575–7 letter 304; see also Sergio Bertelli and Piero Innocenti, "Introduzione," in Sergio Bertelli and Piero Innocenti, *Bibliografia*, vol. 10 of Niccolò Machiavelli, *Opere* (Verona, 1979), pp. XXI–XXII.

7 Sanuto, 40: 749–53.
8 Sanuto, 40: 785; Morosini: Sanuto, 37: 340; 40: 836.
9 ASPd, *Estimo 1518*, busta 352, fol. 170r; Federico Seneca, *Venezia e Papa Giulio II* (Padua, 1962), pp. 19, 39–40.
10 PBUC, ms. 996, Marin Sanudo, *Itinerario*, fols 29r-v, 31r-v.
11 PSVBA, ms. 555, Antonio Monterosso, *Reggimenti di Padova dal 1459 sino al 1533*, vol. 3, fasc. VIII, fols 21r, 23v.
12 PBUC, ms. 392, fol. 1r; Sanuto, vol. 2 *s.v.*
13 Martin Lowry, *The World of Aldus Manutius. Business and Scholarship in Renaissance Venice* (Ithaca, 1979), pp. 20–21.

the Immortali with two Morosini members and whose 1525 one had been at the behest of the Triumphanti also with two Morosini. In 1523, Silvestro Morosini had reinforced the family connection to Melchiorre Trevisan by marrying Trevisan's granddaughter, their wedding celebrated at the home on the Giudecca that would host Beolco's 1526 performance. The following year, Morosini had had a tangential role in a bizarre episode in which Beolco and Cherea were recruited to spy on Vicenzo Grimani by his nephew Marco, he of the Carnival party that had inspired Maria Caravello's revenge. Marco Grimani's purpose was to have the two actors witness proof that his uncle was attempting to force him to pay interest on a larger loan than he had requested. Marco had first asked Silvestro Morosini for the loan, but, considering that a family source would better serve family honor and cost him less, turned instead to his cousin Antonio, Vicenzo's son. He proposed that Antonio would provide him with a loan from the dowry of his wife, the daughter of banker Alvise Pisani, enticing Antonio with a wedding feast at the expense of his (their) grandfather Doge Antonio in the Ducal Palace. It was this wedding festivity at which Beolco performed in May of 1523 for the only time in the Ducal Palace, staging a play on that occasion as well that Sanudo deemed undignified.[14] Marco brought his complaint about his uncle's loan before the Giudici di Petizion in early 1525, with Beolco giving his testimony the day before the rehearsal of the 'dirty' play for the Triumphanti.[15]

Did Silvestro Morosini stage a rival performance to that of Machiavelli's *Mandragola* to satisfy the professional jealousy of the author-actors of his acquaintance, Cherea and Ruzante? If so, he soon changed his mind, for Manenti's 1526 letter goes on to boast that the rival group was so impressed by accounts of Machiavelli's play that they begged for it to be put on in their home where the Plautine performance had occurred. The second performance also went so well that all involved were praised, from the author to Manenti himself, who had served as prompter. Inspired by the success, Manenti tells Machiavelli, the Florentine merchants resident in Venice promised to finance the performance of other Machiavelli works received by the first of May; he begs Machiavelli to send anything he has by then. He goes on to inform Machiavelli that he has not had the opportunity to meet with the doge (Andrea Gritti) since receiving Machiavelli's letter in such a way as to be able to tell him what Machiavelli charged him with but that he thinks that he will soon be able to do so and will let him know what happens.

One may only speculate on the content of the important message to be delivered orally to the doge but, given Gritti's well-known preference for alliance with France and the urgency with which in a letter dated March 15 Machiavelli pressed his military advice on his friend and papal governor of the Romagna Francesco

---

14 ASVe, *AGRM*, busta 258, first fascicle, esp. fols 10[r-v], 12[r]–13[r], 16[v]–17[r]; Sanuto, 34: 124; see a summary in Giuseppe Gullino, *Marco Foscari (1477–1551): l'attività politica e diplomatica tra Venezia, Roma, e Firenze* (Milan, 2000), pp. 116–20.

15 Sanuto, 21: 436; 28: 256; Jacomo di Vetor and Tommaso di Antonio were members of the Immortali.

Guicciardini, some reasonable hypotheses may be made. As Machiavelli told Guicciardini, Italians should arm themselves immediately against a fresh onslaught by Charles, not waiting for Francis because Charles was already organizing his forces and because Francis's previous Italian campaigns had been desultory. The Italian force should be led by Giovanni de' Medici ('dalle Bande Nere').[16] In that same year the Nerli, who hosted the performance of the *Mandragola*, also became involved in the defense effort recommended by Machiavelli when Filippo became governor of Modena under Guicciardini.

Two days after the *Maenechmi* performance, Cherea contributed one of the three comedies to the February 7 entertainment at Ca' Trevisan on the Giudecca sponsored by the patriarch of Aquileia, Giovanni Grimani. Another was by Ruzante, his last recorded performance in Venice. The attendance list provides fertile ground for observations. As was customary, it was attended by 16 of the most beautiful women in the city. The ambassadors present included the papal legate Tommaso Campeggio, whose father had been a lecturer at the University of Padua,[17] and the ambassadors of the empire, France, England, and the Austrian archduke but, significantly, not those of Milan, Ferrara, or Mantua. The ecclesiastics were numerous: the *primocerio* of the basilica of San Marco (Hironimo Barbarigo), the Bishop of Baffo (the Cypriot benefice by which Jacopo Pesaro was known), the Bishop of Concordia (Giovanno Argentino), the Knight of Jerusalem Zaccaria Garzoni, and others. Among the seculars were Agustin Nani and four young procurators: cousins Marco Molin and Francesco Priuli, and brothers Marco and Vetor Grimani. According to Sanudo's account, the many servants of foreign dignitaries present caused confusion and an insolent Spaniard threw a carafe at Nani, whose kinsman (perhaps father) had recently returned from the *podestaria* of Verona, which the Spaniards were rumored to be planning to take in the rapidly-approaching war.[18] Recent events were at the center of a prank: a rooster with its feathers plucked and its comb cropped was released onto the table and dashed about knocking down carafes and glasses. Tumult at the festivity notwithstanding, the young people refused to leave because the comedy was performed after supper. The patriarch's brother Marco, who kept his accounts, duly recorded that some expenses for the festivity cost 83 lire, or slightly under $13,400.[19]

The political overtones of the practical joke serve as a reminder that a performance by Cherea in December 1508 on the eve of the wars of the League of Cambrai had prompted the Council of Ten to ban all theatrical performances then and that a similar ban had been enacted days before in 1526, although the

---

16 Machiavelli would not have been the first to send an amateur on a secret mission with a military purpose. In July 1509, seeking to rebuild its army, Venice utilized the services of a friar for negotiations with *condottieri* of his native L'Aquila secretly enough that they are not reported by Sanuto: ASVe, Senato, *Secreta*, reg. 42, fols 33ᵛ–4ᵛ.

17 Sanuto, 39: 188–9.

18 Sanuto, 40: 46–7.

19 ASVe, *AGRM*, busta 28, fol. 19ʳ; it is not clear if the L. 54 s. 13 mentioned later is part of the 83 lire or an additional sum.

embedding of the 1526 ban in a larger sumptuary bill indicates that the very high expense of such entertainment was also a central concern.[20] The prank's transparent reference to Francis I, still imprisoned by Charles after his capture at Pavia, seems informed by advance knowledge of the league with Francis to oppose the feared Charles that Venice had already secretly concluded and that the pope was within months of publishing. Was it a warning to the French ambassadors that their king would have to improve his military skills and increase his forces if he were to win? A warning against a league with a Francis so feckless as to allow himself to be captured and a pope known for timidity and self-interestedness? Sanudo's remark that the prank was ill-advised because of the presence of the French ambassadors and that there were numerous complaints throughout the city indicates that the latter was the prevalent contemporary interpretation. Bishop Jacopo Pesaro's earlier stout opposition to the Turks, in which he was aided by Spanish rather than French allies, may have put him among those supporting the empire over France in 1526. A preference for the anti-Turkish Charles over the pro-Turkish Francis would have been increased in some Venetians by the obvious contemporary preparations for war of the Turkish Porte and the apprehensions of the Hungarian king that they were directed at him. These were reported by the Venetian secretary in Hungary, Vicenzo Guidotti, who had faithfully served the Republic in many important capacities for decades and who was probably a relative of Beolco's stepmother. If indeed those were the fears being expressed through the prank, they were prophetic. Venice's governing councils, however, either did not share them or preferred to deal with them by other means, declaring adherence to Francis's League of Cognac in June. Hungary fell to Turkish forces shortly thereafter, while the following year saw the brutal Sack of Rome by Charles's troops.

When the Dieci decided on the next lottery, in March of 1526 as Venice was moving to announce its alliance with France in the League of Cognac, they chose Jacopo da Pergo to run it. Hearing of the decision, Manenti presented a rival proposal, claiming that he could provide more money more quickly that Pergo. Bernardo Marconi and Hironimo Bambarara presented a rival proposal of their own, backed by patricians Antonio Priuli dal Banco, Zuan Emo qu. Zorzi, Zuan Capello qu. Lorenzo, Alvise Badoer, Santo Barbarigo, and two non-patricians. Marconi and Bambarara won that competition and another one later that summer. Manenti would not return to running public lotteries for over a year.[21]

Ruzante's named performances in Venice, which began six months after the election of Charles V as Holy Roman Emperor, ended weeks before the publication of the League in June of 1526. The day after Venice began its preparations to fight on that side, "strenuus dominus Angelus de Beolcho" (soldier sir Angelo

20 ASVe, Consiglio di Dieci, *Miste*, reg. 32, fol. 55ᵛ; Senato, *Terra*, reg. 18, fol. 13ᵛ; Sanuto, 40: 749–53.

21 ASVe, Collegio, *Notatorio*, reg. 20, fols 71ʳ⁻ᵛ, 83ᵛ–4ʳ; ASVe, Consiglio di Dieci, *Comuni*, filza 1, fols 73ʳ⁻ᵛ, 79ʳ, 112ʳ and attachments; filza 2, fols 216ʳ, 225ʳ, 230ʳ; filza 3, fols 42ʳ⁻ᵛ and attachments, 43ʳ⁻ᵛ, 79ʳ, 122ʳ; Sanuto, 41: 201, 298 and cf. 493; 45: 669.

de Beolco) bought a horse of high enough quality for military use. Perhaps part of the turmoil of his last performances in Venice was the conflicted choice between employing his energies in the service of his Venetian sponsors and France on the one hand and, on the other, continuing his support of an imperial network that he perhaps hoped still held a place of authority for him. His use of the feudal form of the surname, de Beolco, used by Venetians with his great-uncle and deriving from the family castle near Milan, may indicate his true preference. Yet a perhaps bitterly instructive example before his eyes of the risks of partisan choices was that of his stage partner's cousin, Giacomo Alvaroto. Having joined the Paduan imperialist rebels who threw off the Venetian yoke in 1509, Alvaroto was exiled with Venice's recapture of the city. While he found a niche at the Ferrara court, his employer Alfonso d'Este, in a twist of fate, also then favored the League of Cognac and sent him on diplomatic missions seeking the support not of the empire but of France.

Conclusion

Material presented in the present study supports the interpretation that a large number of patrons of art works in the church of the Frari that date to the end of the fifteenth and the beginning of the sixteenth centuries shared a set of financial and governance goals that they publicized through patronage and sought to advance through governmental office. These goals involved, on the one hand, defense of remaining Venetian Mediterranean commerce and empire from the advancing Turks and, on the other, the cultivation of involvement with the Venetian mainland dominion, with other Italian states, and with the empire. These families were also among those who directed their financial and status ambitions toward the Catholic Church, holding numerous and rich benefices and important offices. Many of them had invested in a troubled Flanders galley round receiving vital emergency financing from the wealthy and powerful Beolco family of Milan, one branch of which was active in Padua and Venice. They were also assisted by the latter branch in making real estate investments in the Paduan territory, often in proximity to the Beolcos' own holdings. Their sons studied at the Università di Padova, where Zuan Francesco Beolco taught and held administrative office.

These sons and grandsons, upon reaching young adulthood, formed *compagnie della calza* whose purposes, beyond the announced one of entertainment, included the advancing of their members' collective financial well-being and election to influential governmental offices. The *compagnie* most conspicuously connected to the Frari patrons were the Immortali (Immortals), Ortolani (Farmers), Zardinieri (Gardeners), and Triumphanti (Triumphants). They attempted to reinstate galley commerce at the end of the wars of the League of Cambrai and when the obstacles and dangers proved too great, they turned ever more to agricultural income, governmental office, and cultural pursuits.

They were also the ones who invited the illegitimate son of Zuan Francesco, Angelo, to perform at their festivities in his rustic character usually named Ruzante from 1520 (or 1518) to 1526. Beolco thus did not need his patron and Venetian *cittadino* Alvise Cornaro to introduce him to prominent Venetian patricians, as is often claimed; his contacts with them were as numerous as Cornaro's, if not more so. He certainly staged in Venice his *Prima oratione* and most probably his *Betia*, which deal with themes of rural life in a way that, beyond pure enjoyment, also suggest the financial value of farms in the rich Paduan countryside and demonstrate the author-actor's talents at managing peasants both as farmers and as a fighting force. In addition, the two theatrical works may be read metaphorically as advancing the views of his Venetian patrician supporters on the best ways of dealing with Venice's precarious position in the face of threats from numerous stronger outside powers: cultivating their own hinterland and seeking peace in the international arena. And they served as vehicles for Beolco's own advice to his audience, that, as life goals, peace and enjoyment are superior to striving and violence even when they require submission to unpleasant overlords or conditions.

What may have been some of the motivations of his patrician sponsors in inviting him? The power of the empire meant that both lingering local sentiment on the mainland and patrician *libido dominandi* could give rise to patrician efforts to make covert connections to it even to the extent of treason, as the Valier case cited in Chapter 2 shows. The mass throwing off of the Venetian yoke after the Republic's defeat at Agnadello in 1509 demonstrated to Venetian patricians the need to co-opt or dominate influential figures on the mainland, to reinforce their connections to the capital and to patricians who owned land in their areas. Patrician landowners' own loyalty to the Republic also required reinforcement, as some of their properties were imperial enclaves for which the emperor exacted oaths of fealty. Perhaps those staging Beolco's works in Venice for that brief period were signaling to the emperor and to those favoring him that—despite belonging to constituencies of Venice and of the mainland, of the patriciate and of other political and social groups, that often maintained their distance from one another and from him—they were willing to work together in working with him.

A point emerging with clarity from the assembled evidence is the extent to which Venice's state lotteries served not only to fund its war obligations but to show affiliations with and direct money toward outside powers through the choice of organizer. There even seem to have been attempts to use the financing to induce the empire, while a covertly-abandoned official ally, to underwrite military efforts designed to serve its enemy, France.

Beolco's last two Venetian performances, staged in 1525 and 1526 as Venice was moving away from the empire and toward France, scandalized first sexually and then politically. Was his audacity generated at least in part by his own conflicted choice between following personal pro-imperial preferences, with the probable consequence of being forced into exile as many of his associates had been and as his half-brother would be, and accepting the pro-French choice of his Venetian superiors, with the consequence of betraying himself and perhaps others? If so, he followed his own advice and accepted the path of least resistance in order to remain in his beloved *pavan*, the Paduan countryside, exile from which is one of the greatest fears expressed by his peasant character in his final plays.

Bibliography

Archival Sources

Mantua, Archivio di Stato, Archivio Gonzaga, *Da Venezia, Carteggio G.B. Malatesta*
Padua, Archivio della Curia vescovile, *Acta capitularia*
Padua, Archivio della Curia vescovile, *Actorum civilium*
Padua, Archivio della curia vescovile, *Mensa vescovile*
Padua, ASPd, *Estimo 1418*
Padua, ASPd, *Estimo 1518*
Padua, ASPd, *Notai d'Este*
Padua, ASPd, *Notarile*
Padua, ASPd, *Archivio dell'Ospitale, Archivio della Scuola della Carità*
Venice, ASVe, *Archivio Bernardo*
Venice, ASVe, *Archivio Gradenigo di Rio Marin*
Venice, ASVe, *Archivio Grimani Santa Maria Formosa*
Venice, ASVe, *Archivio Grimani Barbarigo*
Venice, ASVe, *Archivio Tiepolo, I^a Consegna*
Venice, ASVe, Capi del Consiglio di X, *Lettere*
Venice, ASVe, Capi del Consiglio di Dieci, *Lettere di Condottieri di gente d'armi*
Venice, ASVe, Collegio, *Notatorio*
Venice, ASVe, Consiglio di Dieci, *Comuni*
Venice, ASVe, Consiglio di Dieci, *Miste*
Venice, ASVe, Dieci Savi alle Decime, *Redecima 1514*
Venice, ASVe, Provveditori di Comun, *Atti*
Venice, ASVe, Santa Maria Gloriosa dei Frari, *Atti*
Venice, ASVe, Senato, *Secreta*
Venice, ASVe, Senato, *Terra*
Venice, ASVe, *Ufficiali alle Rason Vecchie*

Manuscript Sources

Brno (Czech Republic), Státní oblastní archiv, Rambaldo, Antonio, Conte di Collalto, *Genealogia Rectae, imperturbataeque Lineae Excellentissimi Principis Antonij Rambaldi Collalti Comitis ab anno aesti 930 usque ad annum 1729.*
Florence, Biblioteca Nazionale, *Carte Machiavelli*, V.
Padua, Biblioteca Civica, B.P. 137, Bertoldi, Benetto, *Historia cronologica di Padova.*

Padua, Biblioteca Civica, B.P. 143, Dorighello, Francesco, *Notizie storiche delli collegii d'artisti e medici in Padova.*

Padua, Biblioteca Civica, B.P. 801 V, Lazara, Giovanni, *Memorie di famiglie nobili di Padova descritte nel Collegio dell'arte della lana e di famiglie nobili applicate all'esercizio di banchiere e cambista, raccolte dal c. Giovanni Lazara.*

Padua, Biblioteca Civica, B.P. 802.

Padua, Biblioteca Civica, B.P. 938, Dorighello, Francesco, *Memorie di professori e letterati di Padova, particolarmente di medici.*

Padua, Biblioteca Civica, B.P. 1422, Fassini, Antonio, *Genealogia della grande famiglia Conti e sue diramazioni.*

Padua, Biblioteca Civica, B.P. 3159, da Corte (Cortivo), Zuan Antonio, *Historia di Padova, 1509–1530 (Diario degli avvenimenti padovani dal 13 giugno 1509 al 12 ottobre 1529).*

Padua, Biblioteca Civica, C.M. 168, *Indice dei codici e medaglie esistenti appresso il N.H. s. Pietro Gradenigo fu de s. Giacomo in Venezia.*

Padua, Biblioteca universitaria centrale, ms. 198, *Sentenza arbitrale pubblicata in Trento (a. 1535) per le controversie tra l'Imperatore e la Rep. di Venezia.*

Padua, Biblioteca universitaria centrale, ms. 311, *Privilegi della Famiglia Contarini rispetto ai beni posseduti pel matrimonio di Francesco Contarini con Maria figlia di Jacopo da Carrara.*

Padua, Biblioteca universitaria centrale, ms. 320, Potenza, Gerolamo da, *Cronica Giustiniana o annali del mon[astero] di s. Giustina dala edificat[ion]e de padova et Monast. Insino a questi tempi nostri 1604.*

Padua, Biblioteca universitaria centrale, ms. 380, *Miscellanea di cose venete.*

Padua, Biblioteca universitaria centrale, ms. 392, *Raccolta di notizie storiche Venete dall'anno 1489 all'anno 1553.*

Padua, Biblioteca universitaria centrale, ms. 865, *Galee del traffico, 1507–1508.*

Padua, Biblioteca universitaria centrale, ms. 874, *Cronaca di Venezia dalle origini fino all'a. 1552.*

Padua, Biblioteca universitaria centrale, ms. 996, Sanudo, Marin, *Itinerario.*

Padua, Seminario Vescovile, Biblioteca Antica, ms. 385, Monterosso, Antonio, *Vite dei vescovi di Padova.*

Padua, Seminario Vescovile, Biblioteca Antica, ms. 555, Monterosso, Antonio, *Reggimenti di Padova dal 1459 sino al 1533.*

Padua, Seminario Vescovile, Biblioteca Antica, ms. 568, *Memorie spettanti alla città di Asolo.*

Padua, Seminario Vescovile, Biblioteca Antica, ms. 609.

Vatican City, Biblioteca Apostolica Vaticana, Cod. Urb. Lat. 512.

Vatican City, Biblioteca Apostolica Vaticana, Cod. Urb. Lat. 804.

Venice, Archivio di Stato, Barbaro, Marco, *Arbori dei patritii veneti,* copied by Tommaso Corner and Antonio Maria Tasca (1743), ASVe, *Misc. Codici I, Storia Veneta* 17.

Venice, Biblioteca del Museo Correr, ms. Grimani-Morosini 4, Beolco, Angelo, *Betia.*

Venice, Biblioteca del Museo Correr, ms. Cicogna 3529–3533, Magno, Stefano, *Annali Veneti.*

Venice, Biblioteca del Museo Correr, ms. Malvezzi 144.

Venice, Biblioteca del Museo Correr, mss. Provenienze Diverse c, 599.

Venice, Biblioteca del Museo Correr, mss. Provenienze Diverse c, 833.

Venice, Biblioteca del Museo Correr, mss. Provenienze Diverse c, 1297.

Venice, Biblioteca del Museo Correr, mss. Provenienze Diverse c, 1318.

Venice, Biblioteca del Museo Correr, mss. Provenienze Diverse c, 1350.

Venice, Biblioteca Nazionale Marciana, Ital. VII, 328, Ziliol, Andrea, *Chronica*.
Venice, Biblioteca Nazionale Marciana, Ital. VII, 515, Magno, Stefano, *Cronaca*.
Venice, Biblioteca Nazionale Marciana, Ital. IX, 71.
Venice, Biblioteca Nazionale Marciana, Ital. IX, 288.
Venice, Biblioteca Nazionale Marciana, Ital. XI, 66.

Printed Sources

Agrati, Annalisa, "Introduzione," in Anon., *La commedia Ardelia*, pp. 1–64.
Alamanni, Luigi, *Versi e prose di Luigi Alamanni*, ed. Pietro Raffaelli, 2 vols (Florence: LeMonnier, 1859).
Alberti, Leon Battista, *Opere volgare*, ed. Cecil Grayson, 3 vols (Bari: Laterza, 1973).
Anon., *Bulesca*, in Da Rif, ed., *La Bulesca*.
Anon., *La commedia Ardelia*, Edizione, introduzione e commento a cura di Annalisa Agrati, Biblioteca degli Studi mediolatini e volgari, Nuova Serie XIII (Pisa: Pacini, 1994).
Anon., *La Venexiana*, ed. Emilio Lovarini (Bologna, Romagnoli Dall'Acqua, 1928).
Anon., *La Veniexiana*, ed. Giorgio Padoan (Padua: Antenore, 1974).
Anon., *Merchant Culture in Fourteenth Century Venice. The Zibaldone da Canal*, translated with an introduction and notes by John E. Dotson (Binghamton, NY: Center for Medieval & Renaissance Texts and Studies, 1994).
Arcangeli, Letizia, ed., *Milano e Luigi XII: ricerche sul primo dominio francese in Lombardia, 1499–1512* (Milan: FrancoAngeli, 2002).
——, "Esperimenti di governo: politica fiscale e consenso a Milano nell'età di Luigi XII," in *Milano e Luigi XII*, pp. 253–339.
Arnaldi, Girolamo and Manlio Pastore Stocchi, eds, *Dal Primo Quattrocento al Concilio di Trento*, Vol. 3.1 *Storia della Cultura Veneta* (Vicenza: Neri Pozza, 1980).
Ballarin, Alessandro, *La pittura a Ferrara negli anni del ducato di Alfonso I*. Register of documents by Alessandra Pattanaro. Catalogue by Vittoria Romani with the collaboration of Sergio Momesso and Giovanna Pacchioni, 2 vols (Cittadella: Bertoncello, 1994–95).
Baratto, Mario, "L'esordio del Ruzante," in *Tre studi sul teatro* (Vicenza: Neri Pozza, 1968), pp. 11–68.
Barzon, Antonio, ed., *Libri e stampatori in Padova*. Miscellanea di studi storici in onore di mons. G. Bellini (Padua: Tipografia Antoniana, 1959).
Bembo, Pietro, *Della Historia vinitiana di M. Pietro Bembo Card. Volgarmente scritta*. Libri XII (Vinegia: Gualtero Scotto, 1552).
——, *Prose e Rime di Pietro Bembo*, ed. Carlo Dionisotti, 2nd ed. (Turin: UTET, 1966).
——, *Lettere*, edizione critica a cura di Ernesto Travi, 4 vols (Bologna: Commissione per i testi di lingua, 1987–93).
——, *History of Venice*, edited and translated by Robert W. Ulery, Jr., 3 vols, The I Tatti Renaissance Library 28, 32, 37 (Cambridge: Harvard University Press, 2007–9).
Beolco, Angelo, (Il Ruzante), *La Pastorale*, ed. Emilio Lovarini, Filologia Italiana e Romanza. Biblioteca di Studi Superiori, 14 (Florence: La Nuova Italia, 1951).
——, *Teatro*, ed. and trans. Ludovico Zorzi (Turin: Einaudi, 1967).
——, *L'Anconitana* in Beolco, *Teatro*, pp. 773–881.
——, *La Pastoral* in Beolco, *Teatro*, pp. 3–141.
——, *La Pastoral, la Prima Oratione, Una lettera giocosa*, ed. and trans. Giorgio Padoan, Medioevo e Umanesimo, 32 (Padua: Antenore, 1978).
Berni, Francesco, *Opere*, ed. Eugenio Camerini, 2nd ed. (Milan: Sonzogno, 1874).

Bertelli, Sergio, "Affaitati, Giovan Carlo," in *DBI*, 1 (1960).

——, "Affaitati, Giovan Francesco," in *DBI*, 1 (1960).

——, and Piero Innocenti, "Introduzione," in Sergio Bertelli and Piero Innocenti, *Bibliografia*, vol. 10 of Niccolò Machiavelli, *Opere* (Verona: Valdonega, 1979).

Biadego, Giuseppe, "Notizie," in Ludovico Corfino, *Istoria di Phileto veronese*, ed. Giuseppe Biadego (Livorno: Giusti, 1899), pp. ix–xxvii.

Bloemendal, Jan, Peter G.F. Eversmann, and Elsa Strietman, eds, *Drama, Performance and Debate: Theatre and Public Opinion in the Early Modern Period* (Leiden and Boston: Brill, 2013).

Boerio, Giuseppe, *Dizionario del dialetto veneziano*, 2nd ed. (Venice: Cecchini, 1856).

Bonardi, Antonio, "I padovani ribelli alla repubblica di Venezia (a. 1509–1530), studio storico con appendice di documenti inediti," *Miscellanea di storia veneta a cura della Deputazione veneta di storia patria* ser. 2.8 (1902): 303–612.

Bonora, Elena, *Aspettando l'imperatore. Principi italiani tra il papa e Carlo V* (Turin: Einaudi, 2014).

Branca, Vittore, *Poliziano e l'umanesimo della parola* (Turin: Einaudi, 1983).

Briquet, Charles-Moise, *Les filigranes. Dictionnaire historique des marques du papier dès leur apparition vers 1282 jusqu'en 1600*, 4 vols (Paris: Picard, 1907).

Brognoligo, Gioacchino, "Rime inedite di Girolamo Verità," *Studi di letteratura italiana* 7 (1906): 98–129.

Brown, Rawdon, ed. and trans., *Four Years at the Court of Henry VIII*. Selection of Despatches Written by the Venetian Ambassador, Sebastian Giustinian, and Addressed to the Signory of Venice, January 12th 1515, to July 26th 1519, 2 vols (London: Smith, Elder and Co., 1854; reprint New York: AMS, 1970).

Buranello, Roberto, "(Non) Plus Ultra: Charles V and Sperone Speroni's Bolognese Trilogy," in Saint-Saëns, ed., *Young Charles V*, pp. 113–61.

Calore, Andrea, "Giovanni Foscari, un amico veneziano di Angelo Beolco," in *III Convegno Internazionale di Studi sul Ruzante*, ed. Giovanni Calendoli (Padua: Società Cooperativa Tipografica, 1993), pp. 21–7.

——, and Francesco Liguori, *Le donne di Ruzante* (Padua: Panda Edizioni, 2012).

Cantù, Cesare, *Storie minori*, 2 vols (Turin: UTET, 1864).

Cappelletti, Giuseppe, *Relazione storica sulle magistrature venete* (Venice: Grimaldo, 1873; reprint Venice: Filippi, 1992).

Carroll, Linda L., "'Who's on Top?': Gender as Societal Power Configuration in Italian Renaissance Drama," *Sixteenth Century Journal* 20 (1989): 531–58.

——, *Angelo Beolco (Il Ruzante)* (Boston: Twayne, 1991).

——, "Giorgione's *Tempest*: Astrology is in the Eyes of the Beholder," *Reconsidering the Renaissance. Papers from the Twenty-First Annual Conference*, ed. Mario Di Cesare (Binghamton: Medieval and Renaissance Texts and Studies, 1992), pp. 125–40.

——, "A Nontheistic Paradise in Renaissance Padua," *Sixteenth Century Journal* 24 (1993): 881–98.

——, "Machiavelli's Veronese Prostitute: *Venetia Figurata*?" in *Gender Rhetorics: Postures of Dominance and Submission in History*, ed. Richard C. Trexler (Binghamton: Medieval and Renaissance Texts and Studies, 1994), pp. 93–106.

——, "Dating *The Woman from Ancona*," *Sixteenth Century Journal* 31 (2000): 963–85.

——, "Venetian Attitudes toward the Young Charles: Carnival, Commerce, and *Compagnie della Calza*," in Saint-Saëns, *Young Charles V*, pp. 13–52.

——, "The Shepherd Meets the Cowherd: Ruzante's *Pastoral*, the Empire and Venice," *Annuario dell'Istituto Romeno di Cultura e Ricerca Umanistica* 4 (2002): 288–97.

——, "Dating *La Veniex[ia]na*: The Venetian Patriciate and the Mainland Nobility at the End of the Wars of Cambrai, with a Note on Titian," *Annuario dell'Istituto Romeno di cultura e ricerca umanistica* (Venice) 5 (2003): 511–19.

——, "'I have a good set of tools': The Shared Interests of Peasants and Patricians in Beolco's *Lettera giocosa*," *Theatre, Opera and Performance in Italy from the Fifteenth Century to the Present. Essays in Honour of Richard Andrews*, ed. Brian Richardson, Simon Gilson, and Catherine Keen, Occasional Papers 6 (Egham, UK: The Society for Italian Studies, 2004), pp. 83–98.

——, "A Newly-Discovered *Charles V with Dog*," *Ateneo Veneto* ser. 3, 4.2 (2005): 43–77.

——, "Introduction," in Angelo Beolco (Il Ruzante), *La prima oratione*, ed. and trans. Linda L. Carroll, MHRA Critical Texts vol. 16 (London: Modern Humanities Research Association, 2009), pp. 5–74.

——, "Utopia, Venice and Ruzante's *Pavan*: Venetian and Paduan Connections with Thomas More," in *Modern Language Review* 107.1 (January, 2012): 162–81.

——, "Per un itinerario della Padova del Ruzante," *Padova e il suo territorio* 164 (Agosto, 2013): 6–9.

——, "Venetian Literature," in *A Companion to Venetian History, 1400–1799*, ed. Eric Dursteler, (Leiden; Boston: Brill, 2013), pp. 615–49.

——, "'(El) ge sa bon laorare': Female Wealth, Male Competition, Musical Festivities, and the Venetian patriciate in Ruzante's *pavan*," in Marshall, Carroll, and McIver, eds., *Sexualities*, pp. 155–83.

——, "Ruzante Speaks Truth to Venetian Power: Some Hows, Whys, Whens, and Wherefores," in *Speaking Truth to Power*, ed. Jo Ann Cavallo, forthcoming.

——, and Anthony M. Cummings, "Historical Introduction," in Molino, *Delightful Madrigals*, pp. x–liii.

Casini, Matteo, "The 'Company of the Hose': Youth and Courtly Culture in Europe, Italy, and Venice," *Studi Veneziani* 63 (2011): 1217–37.

Castoldi, Massimo *Per il testo critico delle rime di Girolamo Verità* (Verona: Biblioteca Civica, 2000).

Chojnacki, Stanley, "La posizione della donna a Venezia nel Cinquecento," in *Tiziano e Venezia*, pp. 69–70.

——, *Women and Men in Renaissance Venice. Twelve Essays on Patrician Society* (Baltimore and London: The Johns Hopkins University Press, 2000).

——, "Kinship Ties and Young Patricians," in Chojnacki, *Women and Men*, pp. 206–26.

Cicogna, Emmanuele Antonio, *Delle iscrizioni veneziane raccolte ed illustrate*, 6 vols (Venice: Orlandelli, 1827).

Coltro, Dino, *Santi e contadini Lunario della tradizione orale veneta* (Caselle di Somma-campagna [VR]: Cierre, 1994).

Concina, Ennio, *La macchina territoriale. La progettazione della difesa nel Cinquecento veneto* (Bari: Laterza, 1983).

Cornaro, Alvise and Cristoforo Sabbadino, *Scritture sopra la laguna*, ed. Roberto Cessi (1941; reprint Venice: Ufficio Idrografico, 1987).

Covini, Maria Nadia, *"La balanza drita." Pratiche di governo, leggi e ordinamenti nel ducato sforzesco* (Milan: FrancoAngeli, 2007).

Cozzi, Gaetano, "La donna, l'amore e Tiziano," in *Tiziano e Venezia*, pp. 47–63.

——, and Michael Knapton, *Storia della Repubblica di Venezia dalla Guerra di Chioggia alla riconquista della terraferma* (Turin: UTET, 1986).

Crescenzi, Victor, *"Esse de Maiori Consilio": legittimità civile e legittimazione politica nella Repubblica di Venezia (secc. XIII–XVI)* (Rome: Istituto Storico Italiano per il Medioevo, 1996).

Crollalanza, G.B. di, *Dizionario storico blasonico delle famiglie nobili e notabili italiane estinte e fiorenti*, 3 vols (1886; reprint Bologna: Forni, 1965).

Cruciani, Fabrizio, *Teatro nel Rinascimento. Roma 1450–1550*, "Europa delle corti" Centro studi sulle società del antico Regime, Biblioteca del Cinquecento 22 (Rome: Bulzoni, 1983).

Cummings, Anthony M., *The Politicized Muse. Music for Medici Festivals, 1512–1537* (Princeton: Princeton University Press, 1992).

D'Ancona, Alessandro, *Origini del teatro italiano*, 2nd ed., 2 vols (Turin: Loescher; Rome: Bardi, 1891).

Daniello, Bernardino, *Poetica*. In Vinegia per Giovan'Antonio (Venice: Nicolini da Sabio, 1536) (reprint; Munich: Wilhelm Fink, 1968).

——, *L'Esposizione di Bernardino Daniello da Lucca sopra la* Comedia *di Dante*, ed. Robert Hollander and Jeffrey Schnapp with Kevin Brownlee and Nancy Vickers (Hanover, NH and London: University Press of New England for Dartmouth College, 1989).

Da Rif, Bianca Maria, ed., *La letteratura 'alla bulesca'. Testi rinascimentali veneti* (Padua: Antenore, 1984).

——, "Introduzione," in Da Rif, *La letteratura*, pp. 3–47.

De Gramatica, M. Raffaella, "Daniello, Bernardino," *DBI*, 32 (1986).

Del Bo, Beatrice, *Banca e politica a Milano a metà Quattrocento* (Rome: Viella, 2010).

Del Torre, Giuseppe, *Venezia e la terraferma dopo la guerra di Cambrai. Fiscalità e amministrazione (1515–1530)* (Milan: Franco Angeli, 1986).

Dionisotti, Carlo, "Daniello, Bernardino," in *Enciclopedia dantesca* (Rome: Istituto dell'Enciclopedia italiana, 1970), 2: 303–4.

——, "Nota biografica," in Bembo, *Prose e rime*, pp. 57–60.

Dondi Dall'Orologio, Francesco Scipione, *Dissertazioni sopra l'istoria ecclesiastica padovana*, 9 vols (Padua: Stamperia del Seminario, 1802–17).

——, Francesco Scipione, *Serie cronologico-istorica dei canonici di Padova* (Padova: Nella Stamperia del Seminario, 1805).

Dovizi da Bibbiena, Bernardo, *Epistolario di Bernardo Dovizi da Bibbiena*, ed. Giuseppe Lorenzo Moncallero, 2 vols (Florence: Olschki, 1955–65).

Favaretto, Lorena, *L'istituzione informale. Il Territorio padovano dal Quattrocento al Cinquecento* (Milan: Edizioni Unicopli, 1998).

Finlay, Robert, *Politics in Renaissance Venice* (New Brunswick: Rutgers University Press, 1980).

——, "Fabius Maximus in Venice: Doge Andrea Gritti, the War of Cambrai, and the Rise of Habsburg Hegemony, 1509–1530," *Renaissance Quarterly* 53 (2000): 988–1031.

Finocchi Ghersi, Lorenzo, *Il Rinascimento veneziano di Giovanni Bellini* (Venice: Consorzio Venezia Nuova; Marsilio, 2003–4).

Foà, Simona, "Dolfin, Niccolò," in *DBI*, 40 (1991).

Fogolari, Gino, *Chiese veneziane: i Frari e i SS. Giovanni e Paolo* (Milan: Treves, 1931).

Forman, Valerie, *Global Economics and the Early Modern English Stage* (Philadelphia: University of Pennsylvania Press, 2008).

Frati, Ludovico, "Gio. Andrea Garisendi e il suo *Contrasto d'Amore*," *Giornale storico della letteratura italiana* 49 (1907): 73–82.

——, ed., *Rimatori bolognesi del Quattrocento* (Bologna: Romagnoli Dall'Acqua, 1908).

Gallo, Rodolfo, "Una famiglia patrizia. I Pisani ed i palazzi di S. Stefano e di Strà," *Archivio Veneto* 5ª serie, 35 (1944): 65–228.

Garisendi, Giovanni Andrea, *Ioannes Andreae Garisendi bononiensis opus. Dialogo overo contrasto de amore. Interlocutori: Antiphylo et Phylero extemporalmente cantanti*, in *Rimatori bolognesi*, pp. 275–334.

Gentilini, Graziella, ed., *Il teatro umanistico veneto: La commedia: Tommaso Mezzo, 'Epirota', Giovanni Antono Marso 'Stephanium', Bartolomeo Zamberti, 'Dolotechne'* (Ravenna: Longo, 1983).

——, "Mezzo, Tommaso," *DBI*, 74 (2010).

Giannetto, Nella, *Bernardo Bembo umanista e politico veneziano*, Civiltà veneziana Saggi 34 (Florence: Olschki, 1985).

Gilbert, Felix, *The Pope, His Banker, and Venice* (Cambridge: Harvard University Press, 1980).

Gilliodts-van Severen, Louis, *Cartulaire de l'ancienne estaple à Bruges. Recueil de documents concernant le commerce intérieur et maritime, les relations internationales et l'histoire économique ce cette ville*, 4 vols (Bruges: L. de Plancke, 1904–6).

Gios, Pierantonio, *L'attività pastorale del vescovo Pietro Barozzi a Padova (1487–1507)* (Padua: Istituto per la Storia Ecclesiastica Padovana, 1977).

——, "Nomine canonicali a Padova durante l'episcopato di Pietro Barozzi (1487–1507)," *Studia Patavina. Rivista di Scienze Religiose* 54 (2007): 189–211.

Girgensohn, Dieter, *Kirche, Politik und adelige Regierung in der Republik Venedig zu Beginn des 15. Jahrhunderts*, 2 vols (Göttingen: Vandenhoeck und Ruprecht, 1996).

Gleason, Elisabeth G., *Gasparo Contarini. Venice, Rome and Reform* (Berkeley and Los Angeles: University of California Press, 1993).

Gloria, Andrea, *Il territorio padovano*, 4 vols (Padua: Prosperini, 1862).

Goffen, Rona, *Piety and Patronage in Renaissance Venice. Bellini, Titian, and the Franciscans* (New Haven: Yale University Press, 1986).

——, *Giovanni Bellini* (New Haven: Yale University Press, 1989).

Gouwens, Kenneth, "Female Virtue and the Embodiment of Beauty: Vittoria Colonna in Paolo Giovio's *Notable Men and Women*," *Renaissance Quarterly* 68 (2015): 33–97.

Grafton, Anthony and Lisa Jardine, *From Humanism to the Humanities* (Cambridge: Cambridge University Press, 1986).

Grubb, James S., *Firstborn of Venice. Vicenza in the Early Renaissance State* (Baltimore: Johns Hopkins University Press, 1988).

——, *Provincial Families of the Renaissance. Private and Public Life in the Veneto* (Baltimore: Johns Hopkins University Press, 1996).

Guazzo, Marco, *Historie di M. Marco Guazzo di tutte le cose degne di memoria nel mondo per terra & per acqua successe, qual hanno principio l'anno M.D. IX Ove se conteneno otto giornate o vero fatti d'armi, oltra le grosse scaramuzze, opera nova con la sua tavola novamente & non piu stampata. Con gratia & Privilegio del Senato Venetiano per anni X. In Venetia al signo di San Bernardino M.D.XLVIII.*

Gullino, Giuseppe, "Corner, Andrea," *DBI*, 29 (1983).

——, "Corner, Giacomo," *DBI*, 29 (1983).

——, "Corner, Giorgio," *DBI*, 29 (1983).

——, "Corner, Giorgio," *DBI*, 29 (1983).

——, "Corner, Giovanni," *DBI*, 29 (1983).

——, "Corner, Marco," *DBI*, 29 (1983).

——, "Corner, Marco," *DBI*, 29 (1983).

——, "Corner, Marco," in *DBI*, 29 (1983).

——, "Donà, Francesco," in *DBI*, 40 (1991).

——, *I Pisani dal Banco e Moretta. Storia di due famiglie veneziane in età moderna e delle loro vicende patrimoniali tra 1705 e 1836* (Rome: Istituto Storico Italiano per l'età moderna e contemporanea, 1984).

——, *Marco Foscari (1477–1551): l'attività politica e diplomatica tra Venezia, Roma, e Firenze* (Milan: FrancoAngeli, 2000).

Gwyn, Peter, *The King's Cardinal. The Rise and Fall of Thomas Wolsey* (London: Barrie and Jenkins, 1990).

Hallman, Barbara McClung, *Italian Cardinals, Reform, and the Church as Property* (Berkeley: University of California Press, 1985).

Hallmark, Anne, "*Protector, imo verus pater*: Francesco Zabarella's Patronage of Johannes Ciconia," in *Music in Renaissance Cities and Courts. Studies in Honor of Lewis Lockwood*, ed. Jessie Ann Owens and Anthony Cummings (Warren, MI: Harmonie Press, 1997), pp. 153–68.

Jordan, Peter, *The Venetian Origins of the Commedia dell'Arte* (New York: Routledge, 2014).

King, Margaret L., *Venetian Humanism in an Age of Patrician Dominance* (Princeton: Princeton University Press, 1986).

——, "Book-lined Cells: Women and Humanism in the Early Italian Renaissance," in *Renaissance Humanism: Foundations, Forms, and Legacy*, ed. Albert R. Rabil Jr., 3 vols (Philadelphia: University of Pennsylvania Press, 1988).

——, and Albert R. Rabil Jr., eds, *Her Immaculate Hand: Selected Works by and about the Women Humanists of Quattrocento Italy* (Binghamton, N.Y.: CEMERS, 1983).

Kolb, Carolyn, "New Evidence for Villa Pisani at Montagnana," in *Interpretazioni veneziane. Studi di storia dell'arte in onore di Michelangelo Muraro*, David Rosand ed. (Venice: Arsenale, 1984), pp. 227–37.

Kolb-Lewis, Carolyn, *The Villa Giustinian at Roncade*, Distinguished Dissertations in the Fine Arts (New York and London: Garland, 1977).

La Bulesca, see under Anon.

La commedia Ardelia, see under Anon.

La Venexiana, ed. Lovarini, *see under* Anon.

La Veniexiana, ed. Padoan, *see under* Anon.

Lane, Frederic C., *Andrea Barbarigo, Merchant of Venice* (Baltimore: Johns Hopkins University Press, 1944).

——, *Venice and History* (Baltimore: The Johns Hopkins University Press, 1966).

——, "Family Partnerships and Joint Ventures," in *Venice and History*, pp. 36–55.

——, "Venetian Bankers, 1496–1533," in *Venice and History*, pp. 81–85.

——, "Venetian Shipping," in *Venice and History*, pp. 3–24.

——, *Venice. A Maritime Republic* (Baltimore: The Johns Hopkins University Press, 1973).

Lazzarini, Vittorio, "Beni carraresi e proprietari veneziani," in *Studi in onore di Gino Luzzatto*, 2 vols (Milan: Giuffrè, 1949), 1: 274–88.

Lenci, Angiolo, "Agnadello e l'assedio di Padova nel 1509: la prospettiva della *securitas veneta* dopo Cambrai," in Sergio Costa, ed. *L'assedio di Padova e la sconfitta dell'esercito dell'imperatore del Sacro Romano Impero Massimiliano I e del re di Francia Luigi XII*. Atti della Giornata di Studio. Padova, Sabato 3 ottobre 2009 (Padua: Stamperia Comunale, 2009; ristampa wi corrections, 2010), pp. 34–42.

I libri commemoriali della Repubblica di Venezia. Regesti, Monumenti storici publicati dalla R. Deputazione Veneta di Storia Patria, Serie Prima, Documenti (Venice: R. Deputazione Veneta di Storia Patria, 1876–1914).

Ling, Lesley A., "La presenza fondiaria veneziana nel padovano (secoli XIII–XIV)," in *Istituzioni, società e potere nella Marca Trevigiana e Veronese. Sulle tracce di G.B. Verci*, ed. Gherardo Ortalli and Michael Knapton (Roma: Istituto Storico Italiano per il Medio Evo, 1988), pp. 305–16.

Long, Pamela O., David McGee, and Alan M. Stahl, eds, *The Book of Michael of Rhodes. A Fifteenth-Century Maritime Manuscript*, 3 vols (Cambridge, MA and London: The MIT Press, 2009).

Lovarini, Emilio, "Introduzione," in *Antichi testi di letteratura pavana*, ed. E. Lovarini (Bologna: Romagnoli Dall'Acqua, 1894), pp. III–CXVI.

——, *Studi sul Ruzzante e sulla letteratura pavana*, ed. Gianfranco Folena (Padua: Antenore, 1965).

——, "La *Betia*," in *Studi*, pp. 293–317.

——, "Notizie sui parenti e sulla vita del Ruzzante," in *Studi*, pp. 3–60.

——, "Nuovi documenti sul Ruzzante," in *Studi*, pp. 61–80.

——, "La *Pastoral*," in *Studi*, pp. 271–92.

——, "Per l'edizione critica del Ruzzante," in *Studi*, pp. 109–63.

——, "Ruzzante a Venezia," in *Studi*, pp. 88–93.

Lowe, K.J.P., *Church and Politics in Renaissance Italy. The Life and Career of Cardinal Francesco Soderini (1453–1524)*, Cambridge Studies in Italian History and Culture (Cambridge and New York: Cambridge University Press, 1993).

Lowry, Martin, *The World of Aldus Manutius. Business and Scholarship in Renaissance Venice* (Ithaca: Cornell University Press, 1979).

Machiavelli, Niccolò, *Lettere*, ed. Franco Gaeta, Vol. 3 of *Opere* (Turin: UTET, 1984).

Madan, M.A.F., *A Summary Catalogue of Western Manuscripts in the Bodleian Library at Oxford*, 7 vols (Oxford: Clarendon Press, 1897).

Mainoni, Patrizia, "L'attività mercantile e le casate milanesi nel secondo Quattrocento," in *Milano nell'età di Ludovico il Moro*, Atti del convegno internazionale, Milano 28 febbraio–4 marzo 1983, ed. Giulia Bologna, 2 vols (Milan: Comune di Milano, Archivio storico civico e Biblioteca trivulziano, 1983), 2: 575–84.

——, "Alcune osservazioni sulla politica economica di Milano fra Ludovico il Moro e il dominio francese," in Arcangeli, ed., *Milano e Luigi XII*, pp. 341–52.

Majoli, F., "Della Vope, Taddeo," in *DBI*, 38 (1990).

Mallett, M.E. and J.R. Hale, *The Military Organization of a Renaissance State. Venice c. 1400 to 1617* (Cambridge: Cambridge University Press, 1984).

Marechal, Joseph, "Le Départ de Bruges des Marchands Etrangers (XVᵉ–XVIᵉ Siècles)," *Handelingen van het. Genootschap voor Geschiedenis "Société d'Emulation" / Annales de la Société d'Emulation, Bruges*, 88 (1951): 26–74.

Marshall, Melanie L., Linda L. Carroll, and Katherine A. McIver, eds, *Sexualities, Textualities, Art and Music in Early Modern Italy. Playing with Boundaries* (Farnham: Ashgate, 2014).

Marucci, Valerio, Antonio Marzo e Angelo Romano, eds, *Pasquinate romane del Cinquecento*, 2 vols (Rome: Salerno Editore, 1983).

Mazzatinti, Giuseppe, *Inventarii dei manoscritti delle biblioteche d'Italia* (Forlì: Bordandini, 1890–).

Menegazzo, Emilio, *Colonna, Folengo, Ruzante e Cornaro. Ricerche, testi e documenti*, ed. Andrea Canova (Padua: Antenore, 2001).

——, "Alvise Cornaro: un veneziano del Cinquecento nella terraferma padovana," in *Colonna*, pp. 425–66.

——, "Altre osservazioni intorno al Ruzante e al Cornaro," in *Colonna*, pp. 267–303.

———, "Ricerche intorno alla vita e all'ambiente del Ruzante e di Alvise Cornaro," in *Colonna*, pp. 223–66.

———, "Stato economico-sociale del padovano all'epoca del Ruzante," in *Colonna*, pp. 304–37.

Milani, Marisa, "La tradizione del mariazo nella letteratura pavana," in *Convegno internazionale di studi sul Ruzante*, ed. Giovanni Calendoli and Giuseppe Vellucci (Venice: Corbo e Fiore, 1987), pp. 105–15.

Molà, Luca, *The Silk Industry of Renaissance Venice* (Baltimore and London: The Johns Hopkins University Press, 2000).

Molino, Antonio (Il Burchiella), *Delightful Madrigals for Four Voices . . . , Newly . . . Composed and Brought to Light . . . First Book . . . 1568*, ed. Linda L. Carroll, Anthony M. Cummings, Zachary W. Jones, and Philip Weller (Rome: Istituto Italiano per la Storia della Musica, 2014).

Moncallero, Giuseppe Lorenzo, "La politica di Leone X e di Francesco I nella progettata crociata contro i turchi e nella lotta per la successione imperiale," *Rinascimento* 8 (1957): 61–109.

Moro, Giacomo, "Foscarini, Ludovico," *DBI*, 49 (1997).

Morrissey, Thomas E., "'More Easily and More Securely': Legal Procedure and Due Process at the Council of Constance," in *Popes, Teachers, and Canon Law in the Middle Ages*, ed. James Ross Sweeney and Stanley Chodorow (Ithaca: Cornell University Press, 1989), pp. 234–47.

Mortara, Alessandro de, *Catalogo dei manoscritti italiani che sotto la denominazione di codici canoniciani italici si conservano nella Biblioteca Bodleiana a Oxford* (Oxonii: Typographeo Clarendoniano, 1864).

Mueller, Reinhold C., *The Venetian Money Market. Banks, Panics, and the Public Debt, 1200–1500*, Vol. 2 of *Money and Banking in Medieval and Renaissance Venice* (Baltimore: The Johns Hopkins University Press, 1997).

Muir, Edward, *The Culture Wars of the Late Renaissance* (Cambridge: Harvard University Press, 2007).

Mutini, Cesare, "Brocardo, Antonio," *DBI*, 14 (1972).

Nardi, Bruno "Letteratura e cultura veneziana del Quattrocento," *Saggi sulla cultura veneta del Quattro e Cinquecento*, ed. Paolo Mazzantini (Padua: Antenore, 1971), pp. 3–43.

Olivieri, Achille, "Capitale mercantile e committenza nella Venezia del Sansovino," in *Investimenti e civiltà urbana. Secoli XIII–XVIII*, ed. Annalisa Guarducci (Florence: LeMonnier, 1991), pp. 531–69.

Paccagnella Ivano, et al., *Vocabolario del pavano (XIV–XVII secolo)* (Padua: Esedra, 2012).

Padoan, Giorgio, *Momenti del Rinascimento veneto* (Padua: Antenore, 1978).

———, "Angelo Beolco da Ruzante a Perduoçimo," in *Momenti*, pp. 94–192.

———, "La dimora padovana di Michele Gaismar e la richiesta di 'leze e stratuti nuovi'," in *Momenti*, pp. 239–48.

———, "Introduzione" and "Nota ai testi," in Beolco, *La Pastoral*, ed. and trans. G. Padoan, pp. 1–57.

———, "Sulla fortuna della *Pastoral*, della *Veniexiana* e di altri testi," in *Momenti*, pp. 193–207.

———, "La *Veniexiana*: 'Non fabula non comedia ma vera historia'," in *Momenti*, pp. 284–346.

———, *La commedia rinascimentale veneta* (Vicenza: Neri Pozza, 1982).

Pallucchini, Rodolfo, *I Vivarini (Antonio, Bartolomeo, Alvise)*, Saggi e studi di storia dell'arte 4 (Venice: Neri Pozza, n.d. [1961]).

Parronchi, Alessandro, *Donatello e il potere* (Florence: Il Portolano; Bologna: Cappelli, 1980).

Paschini, Pio, *Domenico Grimani Cardinale di S. Marco (+1523)* (Rome: Edizioni di 'Storia e Letteratura', 1943).

Pattini, Dante, "Manenti, Giovanni," *DBI*, 68 (2007).

Petrucci, F., "Cibo, Innocenzo," *DBI*, 25 (1981).

Pieri, Piero, *Il Rinascimento e la crisi militare italiana*, 2nd ed. (Turin: Einaudi, 1952).

Piovan, Francesco, "Tre schede ruzantiane," *Quaderni Veneti* 27–8 (1998): 93–105.

Polano, Sergio, ed., *L'architettura militare veneta del Cinquecento* (Milan: Electa, 1988).

Pozza, Neri, "L'editoria veneziana da Giovanni da Spira ad Aldo Manuzio. I centri editoriali di terraferma," in Arnaldi and Pastore Stocchi, eds, *Dal primo Quattrocento al Concilio di Trento*, pp. 215–44.

Priuli, Girolamo, *I diarii*, ed. Arturo Segre et al., *Rerum Italicarum Scriptores*, 2nd ed. (Città di Castello and Bologna: S. Lapi, 1912–33).

Prizer, William, *Courtly Pastimes. The Frottole of Marchetto Cara* (Ann Arbor: University Microfilms International, 1974).

Pulci, Antonia, *Florentine Drama for Convent and Festival*, annotated and translated by James Wyatt Cook, edited by James Wyatt Cook and Barbara Collier Cook (Chicago: University of Chicago Press, 1996).

Puppi, Lionello, "Il rinnovamento tipologico del Cinquecento," in *Padova Case e Palazzi*, ed. Lionello Puppi and Fulvio Zuliani (Vicenza: Neri Pozza, 1977), pp. 101–40.

Queller, Donald E., *The Venetian Patriciate. Reality versus Myth* (Urbana: University of Illinois Press, 1986).

Raimondi, Ezio, "Bernardino Daniello e le varianti petrarchesche," *Studi petrarcheschi* 5 (1952): 95–130.

Renier, Rodolfo, "Prefazione," in Antonio Cammelli, Il Pistoia, *I sonetti del Pistoia giusta l'apografo trivulziano*, ed. Rodolfo Renier, Biblioteca di Testo Inediti o Rari 2 (Turin: Loescher, 1888), pp. vii–xlviii.

Reynolds, Anne, "Francesco Berni (1497?–1535), An Introductory Biography," in *Francesco Berni, Renaissance Humanism at the Court of Clement VII. Francesco Berni's Dialogue Against Poets in Context. Studies, with an edition and translation by Anne Reynolds* (New York and London: Garland Publishing, Inc., 1997), pp. 35–57.

Riccò, Laura, *"Su le carte e fra le scene." Teatro in forma di libro nel Cinquecento italiano* (Rome: Bulzoni, 2008).

Richardson, Brian, *Print Culture in Renaissance Italy: The Editor and the Vernacular Text 1470–1600* (Cambridge: Cambridge University Press, 1994).

——, *Manuscript Culture in Renaissance Italy* (Cambridge: Cambridge University Press, 2009).

Rigobello, Bruno, *Lendinara Estense*, Vol. 2 of *Storia antica di Lendinara* (Lendinara: Tipografia lendinarese, 1977).

——, "Modi di intervento del capitale veneziano nel polesine e l'insediamento agricolo dei Loredan, dei Corner, dei Badoer, e dei Grimani," in *Palladio e palladianesimo in Polesine* (Rovigo: Minelliana, 1984), pp. 21–35.

Rocke, Michael J., *Forbidden Friendships. Homosexuality and Male Culture in Renaissance Florence* (New York and Oxford: Oxford University Press, 1996).

Romano, Dennis, *The Likeness of Venice. A Life of Doge Francesco Foscari* (New Haven: Yale University Press, 2007).

Roover, Raymond de, *The Rise and Decline of the Medici Bank 1397–1494* (New York: W.W. Norton and Co, 1966).

Rosand, Ellen, *Opera in Seventeenth-Century Venice. The Creation of a Genre* (Berkeley: University of California Press, 1991).

Ruggiero, Guido, *The Boundaries of Eros. Sex Crimes and Sexuality in Renaissance Venice* (New York: Oxford University Press, 1985).

Sabbatino, Pasquale, *La "Scienza" della scrittura: Dal progetto del Bembo al manuale* (Florence: Olschki, 1988).

Saint-Saëns, Alain, ed., *Young Charles V, 1500–1529* (New Orleans: University Press of the South, 2000).

Sambin, Paolo, *Per le biografie di Angelo Beolco, il Ruzante, e di Alvise Cornaro*, restauri di archivio rivisti e aggiornati da Francesco Piovan (Padua: Esedra, 2002).

——, "Altre testimonianze (1525–1540) di Angelo Beolco," in *Per le biografie*, pp. 59–77.

——, "Briciole biografiche del Ruzante e del suoi compagno d'Arte Marco Aurelio Alvarotti (Menato)," in *Per le biografie*, pp. 87–114.

——, "Lazzaro e Giovanni Francesco Beolco, nonno e padre del Ruzante (Relazioni e aspetti di famiglia, lavoro e cultura)," in *Per le biografie*, pp. 7–57.

Sannazaro, Jacopo, *Opere volgari*, ed. Alfredo Mauro (Bari: Laterza, 1961).

Sanuto, Marino, *I diarii*, ed. Rinaldo Fulin et al., 58 vols (Venice: Visentini, 1879–1902).

——, *Itinerario per la Terraferma veneziana*, edizione critica e commento a cura di Gian Maria Varanini, Cliopoli 1 (Rome: Viella, 2014).

Sartori, Antonio, "Documenti padovani sull'arte della stampa nel secolo XV," in Barzon, *Libri e stampatori*, pp. 111–228.

Savarese, Gennaro, *La cultura a Roma tra Umanesimo ed ermetismo (1480–1540)* (Anzio: De Rubeis, 1993).

Schulz, Anne Markham, *Giammaria Mosca called Padovano: A Renaissance Sculptor in Italy and Poland*, 2 vols (University Park, PA: The Pennsylvania State University Press, 1998).

Schulz, Juergen, "The Testamento of Federigo Corner 'Il Grande'," in *From Florence to the Mediterranean and Beyond. Essays in Honour of Anthony Molho*, ed. Diogo Ramada Curto, Eric R. Dursteler, Julius Kirschner, and Francesca Trivellato with the assistance of Niki Koniordos, 2 vols (Florence: Olschki, 2009), 2: 683–94.

Selvatico, Pietro, *Sulla architettura e sulla scultura in Venezia dal medio evo sino ai nostri giorni* (Venice: Carpano, 1847).

Seneca, Federico, *Venezia e Papa Giulio II* (Padua: Liviana, 1962).

Setton, Kenneth M., *The Papacy and the Levant*, 4 vols, Memoirs of the American Philosophical Society, vols 127 *The Fifteenth Century*, 161 *The Sixteenth Century to the Reign of Julius III* (Philadelphia: The American Philosophical Society, 1976–84).

Simionato, Umberto, *Cognomi padovani e antiche famiglie di Padova e del suo territorio. Ricerca storico-linguistica sulle antiche famiglie di Padova e della sua provincia*, 2 vols (Padua: Tip. STEDIV, 1995–99).

Stabel, Peter, "Venice and the Low Countries: Commercial Contacts and Intellectual Inspirations," *Renaissance Venice and the North. Crosscurrents in the Time of Bellini, Dürer, and Titian*, ed. Bernard Aikema and Beverly Louise Brown, for the Ministero per i Beni e le Attività culturali, and Giovanna Nepi Scirè (Milan: Rizzoli, 1999), pp. 30–43.

Steer, John, *Alvise Vivarini: His Art and Influence* (Cambridge: Cambridge University Press, 1982).

Stella, Aldo, "Bonifiche benedettine e precapitalismo veneto tra Cinquecento e Seicento," in *S. Benedetto e otto secoli (XII–XIX) di vita monastica nel Padovano* (Padua: Antenore, 1980), pp. 171–93.

Surtz, Edward, S.J., *The Praise of Pleasure. Philosophy, Education, and Communism in More's* Utopia (Cambridge: Harvard University Press, 1957).

——, *The Praise of Wisdom. A Commentary on the Religious and Moral Problems and Backgrounds of St. Thomas More's* Utopia (Chicago: Loyola University Press, 1957).

Taviani, Carlo, *Superbia discordia: Guerra, rivolta e pacificazione nella Genova del primo Cinquecento*, I libri di Viella 80 (Rome: Viella, 2008).

Tierney, Brian, *Foundations of the Conciliar Theory* (Cambridge: Cambridge University Press, 1955).

Tiziano e Venezia (Vicenza: Neri Pozza, 1980).

Toscan, Jean, *Le carnaval du langage. Le lexique érotique des poètes de l'équivoque de Burchiello a Marino (XVe–XVIIe siècles)*, 4 vols (Lille: Presses Universitaires de Lille, 1981).

Tucci, Ugo, "The Psychology of the Venetian Merchant in the Sixteenth Century," in *Renaissance Venice*, ed. J.R. Hale (London: Faber, 1973), pp. 346–78.

Ulianich, B., "Accolti, Pietro," in *DBI*, 1 (1960).

Vallone, Aldo, "Trifone Gabriele e Bernardino Daniello dinanzi a Dante," *Studi mediolatini e volgari*, 10 (1962): 263–98.

Varanini, Gian Maria, "Proprietà fondiaria e agricoltura," *Storia di Venezia dalle origini alla caduta della Serenissima*, 8 vols (Rome: Istituto dell'Enciclopedia Italiana, 1992–98), vol. 5 *Il Rinascimento. Società ed Economia*, ed. Alberto Tenenti and Ugo Tucci (1996), pp. 807–79.

Ventura, Angelo, "Badoer, Andrea," *DBI*, 5 (1963).

——, "Considerazioni sull'agricoltura veneta e sull'accumulazione originaria del capitale nei secoli XVI e XVII," in *Agricoltura e sviluppo del capitalismo*. Atti del convegno organizzato dall'Istituto Gramsci (Rome 1968) (Rome: Editori Riuniti, 1970), pp. 519–60.

——, "Cappello, Paolo," *DBI*, 18 (1975).

La Veniexiana. Commedia di anonimo veneziano del Cinquecento, Testo critico, tradotto ed annotato da Giorgio Padoan (Padua: Antenore, 1974).

Venturelli, Paola, *Gioelli e gioiellieri milanesi. Storia, arte, moda (1450–1630)* (Cinisello Balsamo [MI]: Amilcare Pizzi, 1996).

Venturi, Lionello, "Le Compagnie della Calza (sec. XV–XVI)," *Nuovo Archivio Veneto* n.s. 16.2 (1909): 3–157.

Verità, Girolamo, *Girolamo Verità. Filosofo e poeta veronese*, ed. Lamberto Carlini (Verona: Franchini, 1905).

Viggiano, Alfredo, *Governanti e governati. Legittimità del potere ed esercizio dell'autorità sovrana nello Stato veneto della prima età moderna* (Treviso: Fondazione Benetton, Canova, 1993).

Virgili, Antonio, *Francesco Berni* (Firenze: Le Monnier, 1881).

Weaver, Elissa, *Convent Theatre in Early Modern Italy. Spiritual Fun and Learning for Women* (Cambridge and New York: Cambridge University Press, 2002).

Weinberg, Bernard, *A History of Literary Criticism in the Italian Renaissance*, 2 vols (Chicago: University of Chicago Press, 1961).

Zamperetti, Sergio. *I piccoli principi. Signorie locali, feudi e comunità soggette nello Stato regionale veneto dall'espansione territoriale ai primi del '600* (Venice: Il Cardo, 1991).

Zapperi, Roberto, "Borromeo, Achille," in *DBI*, 13 (1971).

Zorzi, Ludovico, "Note *La Pastoral*," in Beolco, *Teatro*, pp. 1283–1309.

——, "Note al *Parlamento*," in Beolco, *Teatro*, pp. 1361–78.

Index

Accolti, Bernardo (Unico Aretino) 72, 84
Accolti, Pietro 77–81, 84
Adrian VI 59, 60, 66, 76–81, 91–3, 95, 120
Afaitadi (Affaitadi) family 115, 120
Afaitadi (Affaitadi), Ludovico 59–60, 119
Afaitadi (Affaitadi), Lunardo 60
Africa 1, 9, 10, 22, 115, 116, 124; *see also* Alexandria, Barbary coast
Agnadello 8, 46, 58, 62–3, 75, 94, 155
Agrati, Annalisa 101, 101n180
Alberti, Duccio degli 36
Alberti, Leon Battista: *Deifira* 101
Alexander V 47
Alexander VI 4
Alexandria 9, 67–8, 112–5, 118, 121, 135, 145
Alfonso d'Este duke of Ferrara 103, 114, 137, 153
Alvaroto (Alvarotto) family 49, 61, 131, 134
Alvaroto (Alvarotto), Giacomo 53, 114, 131, 146, 153
Alvaroto (Alvarotto), Marc'Aurelio (Menato) 48, 52, 61, 87–8, 115, 116, 125–35, 140, 142–3, 146, 149
Amadi (Amai) family 75
Amanio, Nicolò 98–9
Anzelieri (Angelieri), Alvise 46, 109, 132, 139
Arcangeli, Letizia 5n8, 11n25, 45n89, 56, 56n165, 120n45
Ardelia 100, 106, 146
Arimondo, Andrea 113, 118
Arimondo, Nicolò 107, 113, 114, 118
Ariosto, Ludovico 66, 83, 85

Armellini, Francesco 77–81
Arnaldi, Girolamo 4n5

Badoer, Agnesina 128
Badoer, Andrea 117, 125–35, 139
Badoer, Albertin 107, 113, 114
Badoer, Giacomo 120
Badoer, Marietta 89–97
Badoer, Piero 125–35
Badoer, Zuan 115, 139
Badoer, Zuan Alvise 113, 114
Badoer, Zuan Francesco 122, 129–30, 145
Bagarotto, Bertucci 49
Ballarin, Alessandro 104n190
Bambarara, Hironimo 59, 119–24, 152
Baratto, Mario 14n34, 46n93, 101n183
Barbarigo family 17, 132, 140, 141
Barbarigo, Cristoforo 114
Barbarigo, Daniele 88
Barbarigo, Hironimo 93, 125–36, 140, 147
Barbarigo, Isabetta 85–97
Barbarossa 47
Barbary coast 9, 10, 22, 38, 40, 57, 112, 114–16, 121, 123, 132, 133
Barbo, Zuan (Giovanni) 107, 140
Barzon, Antonio 2n2,
Basaiti, Marco 19, 38
Bellini, Giovanni 40; *Feast of the Gods* 103; *Frari Triptych: Madonna and Child with Saints Peter, Nicholas, Benedict and Mark* 19, 34
Beltrame, Zuan (Giovanni) 42
Bembo, Bartolomeo 109
Bembo, Lorenzo 107, 116, 125–36
Bembo, Marin 116

Bembo, Pietro 12, 33n4, 34n9, 34n10, 37n29, 38n43, 39n45, 39n47, 44n83, 44n86, 44n86, 49n114, 66, 72–3, 73n36, 76, 81, 84–5, 98, 105, 138n137, 140n152, 141n162
Bembo, Zaccaria 130, 140
Benzon, Soncin 137–38
Beolco family 11, 12, 32, 45, 47–8, 52–6, 58, 61, 88, 107, 111, 112, 113, 127, 130, 132, 134, 136, 138, 139, 141, 154
Beolco, Angelo (Il Ruzante) 5, 8, 11, 13, 14, 32, 46–7, 49, 51–5, 58–9, 61, 63, 71, 82–3, 86, 87–8, 105–6, 107, 109, 115, 116, 120, 125–35, 136, 140, 141, 142, 146, 149–53, 154; *Anconitana* 57, 58, 83n90, 138; *Betia* 42, 46, 47, 50, 52, 55, 56, 57, 61, 74, 135–44, 154–5; *Fiorina* 57, 143; *Lettera giocosa* 83, 100, 129, 132; *Moscheta* 63; *Pastoral* 9, 48, 70–73, 83, 99, 100–1, 105, 106, 136; *Piovana* 54; *Prima oratione* 49, 56, 57, 58, 109, 128, 154; *Reduce* 52, 63; *Seconda oratione* 56; *Vaccaria* 48, 54
Beolco, Francesco 63, 120
Beolco, Lazaro (de) 5, 45, 47, 48, 52, 55
Beolco, Ludovico 55
Beolco, Melchiorre 11n26
Beolco, Zuan (Giovanni) (de) 4, 5, 45, 56, 59, 83, 120, 134, 153
Beolco, Zuan Francesco (Giovanni Francesco) 5, 11, 11n26, 45, 48, 55, 56, 57, 63, 120, 154
Beolco, Zuan Jacopo (Giovanni Giacomo) 5, 11n26, 45, 48, 52, 52n137, 120, 133, 141
Bernardo family 4, 12, 17, 35–6, 36n19, 43, 46, 53, 61, 111, 140
Bernardo, Alvise 54
Bernardo, Hironimo 62, 107, 130
Bernardo, Mafio 43, 60, 117–18, 121, 130–2
Bernardo, Nicolò 35, 49
Bernardo, Nicolò qu. Pietro 45, 49, 53, 54, 61–2, 122, 125–35, 138, 139, 144, 145, 147
Bernardo, Piero (Pietro) 19, 43, 44, 45, 55, 61, 140
Bernardo, Sebastiano (Sebastian) 44, 45, 61, 139, 140

Berni, Francesco 83
Bertelli, Sergio 149n6
Bertoldi, Beneto 74n40, 133n102
Besalù-Beltrame family 60, 75, 86–7, 97, 122–4
Besalù (Bexalù), Francesco 19, 42
Besalù (Bexalù), Gaspare 13, 60, 119–20
Besalù (Bexalù), Raphael 42
Biadego, Giuseppe 71n30
Bibbiena, Bernardo da 8, 83, 83n91, 90; *Calandria* 8, 83
Bibbiena, Marietta 85–97
Bibbiena, Pietro 86–90, 96
Bisignano, Prince of *see* Sanseverino, Pier Antonio
Bloemendal, Jan 3n3
Boccaccio, Giovanni 71
Bonardi, Antonio 50n119, 139n147
Bonora, Elena 79n66
Borromeo, Achille 75–6
Borromeo, Alessandro 75–6
Borromeo, Benvegnuda 75–6
Borromeo, Francesco 76
Borromeo, Margherita 75–6
Branca, Vittore 42n67
Bregno, Lorenzo: Funeral monument of Benedetto Pesaro 19
Brescia 39, 41, 47, 50
Brocardo, Antonio 66, 72–3, 83–4, 98
Brognoligo, Gioacchino 70n22
Brown, Rawdon 35n12, 44n85, 44n86, 50n125
Bulesca 100, 106
Buranello, Roberto 84n92

Cabotto, Giovanni (John Cabot), 43
Caga-in-Calle, Angela 42, 135–6
Calore, Andrea 46n95
Cambrai, League of 2, 10, 14, 37, 41, 42, 43, 44, 47, 50, 62, 67, 68, 75, 92, 95, 108, 112, 118, 127–35, 138, 139, 151, 154
Cammello, Antonio (Il Pistoia) 84
Campeggio, Lorenzo 77–81, 148
Campeggio, Tommaso 151
Canisio, Egidio 77–81
Cantù, Cesare 11n24
Caodevaca, Antonio 49
Capello (Cappello) family 4, 42, 88–9, 97, 136, 140, 152

Capello, Antonio 86–7, 108, 111
Capello, Bernardo 108, 111
Capello, Cristoforo 128
Capello, Filippo 89, 95
Capello, Lorenzo 89, 112
Capello, Marietta 86–97
Capello, Marin 108, 111, 113, 125–35
Capello, Michiel 113
Capello, Pangrati 112
Capello, Polo 95, 111, 122, 129, 137, 144
Capello, Silvano 41
Capello, Vicenzo 88, 95
Caravello, Maria 85–97, 150
Caravello, Moro 95
Carvajal, Bernardino de 77–81
Casini, Matteo 14n36, 71n30, 143, 143n168
Castegnola family 134
Castegnola, Zuan Batista 48
Castoldi, Massimo 65n1, 97n167, 98n168, 98n170, 99n172
Caterina Corner Queen of Cyprus 38, 95
Cesarini, Alessandro 77–81
Cesi, Paolo 77–81
Charles V 10, 11, 12, 14, 16, 32, 44, 51, 58, 60, 62–3, 73, 79, 84, 91, 94, 95, 104–6, 111, 115–24, 127, 147–53
Charles VIII 4, 44
Cherea (Francesco dei Nobili) 59, 82, 142–3, 149–53
Chojnacki, Stanley 7n14, 67n11
Cibo, Innocenzo 77–81
Cicogna, Emmanuele Antonio 65n4
Clement VII 77–81, 91, 105, 121–4, 129–30, 147–53
Cocco, Antonio 90
Cocco, Laura 86–97
Coco (Cocco), Lunardo 104
Cognac, League of 10, 12, 44, 52, 152–3
Colonna, Pompeo 77–81
Coltro, Dino 139n149
compagnie della calza 8, 13, 14, 17, 87, 107, 118, 131, 143, 154
Concina, Ennio 51n128, 93n143
Contarini family 43, 88, 93, 114, 140
Contarini, Agostino 95
Contarini, Alexandro 123, 141
Contarini, Alvise 109, 112
Contarini, Antonio 113

Contarini, Ferigo 109
Contarini, Francesco 115–16
Contarini, Gaspare qu. Alvise 14, 51, 109–10, 113, 117, 121, 141
Contarini, Gaspare qu. Francesco Alvise 133
Contarini, Hironimo 82
Contarini, Marc'Antonio 122, 145
Contarini, Tommaso 111, 113, 141
Contarini, Vincenzo 51, 109, 111–13, 125–35, 141
Contarini, Zaccaria 41
Contarini, Zuan 116
Contarini, Zuan Antonio 121
Contarini, Zustignan (Giustiniano) 79, 81
Conte, Artusio 51
Conte (Conti) di Collalto family 53, 93, 109, 141
Corfino, Lodovico 71
Cornaro, Alvise 12, 14, 14n35, 46–7, 52, 57, 61, 86, 109, 112, 116, 131–3, 135, 138, 139–41, 143, 154
Corner family 19, 33, 37, 38, 38n38, 38n40, 39, 43, 46, 56, 57, 62, 91–2
Corner, Alvise qu. Donà 95
Corner, Andrea 81, 94
Corner, Fantin 46, 56, 86–7
Corner, Ferigo 38
Corner, Francesco 44, 56
Corner, Giacomo 56
Corner, Marco 8, 47, 56, 58, 60, 76–82, 90, 91, 93, 94, 95, 128, 135, 141
Corner, Zorzi (Giorgio) 56–7, 95
Corner, Zuan (Giovanni) di Fantin 46–7, 52, 56
Corner, Zuan (Giovanni) di Zorzi (Giorgio) 82
Corte, Zuan Antonio da 33n4, 33n5, 75, 75n48, 83, 83n90, 88n98, 94n146, 105n196, 105n198
Cosaza, Zuan 127
Covini, Maria Nadia 5n8
Cozzi, Gaetano 6, 6n10, 40n55, 93n134, 93n137, 132, 132n93
Crema 2, 47, 68, 138
Cremona 37, 51, 149
Crescenzi, Victor 12n30, 69n17, 88n107, 88n109, 89n118
Crollalanza, G.B. di 11n25, 74n40

Cruciani, Fabrizio 94n150
Cummings, Anthony M. 126n58
Cupi, Giovanni Francesco 77–81

Dal Legname, Jacopo 82, 101–10
Dall'Oro, Piero 60, 119, 143
D'Ancona, Alessandro 15n37
Dandolo family 93, 109
Dandolo, Andrea 88
Dandolo, Cecilia 85–97
Daniello, Bernardino (Bernardino da
    Lucca) 66, 72, 80–5, 94, 97–9
Da Rif, Bianca Maria 65n3, 70n23, 101, 101n
Del Bo, Beatrice 5n8, 45n89, 56, 56n164,
    56n165
Del Torre, Giuseppe 57n168
Diedo, Alvise 92
Diedo, Andrea 86–8, 92, 97
Diedo, Isabetta 85–97
Dionisotti, Carlo 65, 72, 72n32, 73n34,
    81n73
Dolfin, Dolfin 71, 71n29, 71n30
Dolfin, Lorenzo 71, 71n29
Dolfin, Nicolò 71, 71n29
Dolfin, Pietro 71, 71n29
Dolfin, Zuan 125–35
Donà, Francesco 83, 129, 132
Donà, Pietro 40
Donà, Polo 125–35, 139, 147
Dondi Dall'Orologio, Francesco Scipione
    33n5, 36n23, 40n55, 74n41, 82n80
Dorighello, Francesco 45n90, 57n178

Emo, Marina 86–97
Emo, Zuan 90, 96, 152
England 12, 22, 32, 35, 43, 44, 49, 116–18,
    122, 133, 147
Este 49, 50, 57
Este family 48, 111, 127
Este, Isabella d' 15, 73, 83n91
Eugenio IV 42
Eversmann, Peter G.F. 3n3

Farnese, Alessandro 77–81
Fassini, Antonio 93n135
Favaretto, Lorena 111n10, 131n84,
    139n147
Federico II Gonzaga 8, 14, 15, 63, 73, 108,
    114

Ferrara 47, 54–5, 56, 111, 127, 137, 149,
    151, 153
Ferrero, Bonifacio 77–81, 87, 91–2
Fieschi, Nicolò 77–81
Filelfo, Mario 39
Finlay, Robert 10n23, 36n26, 54, 54n151,
    129, 129n78
Finocchi Ghersi, Lorenzo 40n52, 93n137,
    103n188
Flanders 22, 43, 49, 50, 53, 82, 112,
    114–18, 121, 124, 129, 132, 154
Florence 36, 38, 42, 43, 59, 77, 90, 119,
    149
Flourent, Adrian *see* Adrian VI
Fogolari, Gino 33n7
Forman, Valerie 3n3
Forzaté family 92
Foscari family 35, 36, 36n22, 36n24,
    36n25, 38, 40, 53, 58, 62, 91–2, 112
Foscari, Agostino (Agustin) 4, 5, 46, 90
Foscari, Alvise 47
Foscari, Francesco 4, 5, 46, 88, 89
Foscari, Francesco doge 19, 36, 37, 42, 53,
    62, 130
Foscari, Francesco qu. Alvise 46, 93
Foscari, Francesco qu. Nicolò 47, 53
Foscari, Lauretta 86–97
Foscari, Marco 89, 91, 93, 95
Foscari, Nicolò 46
Foscari, Pietro 46–7
Foscari, Zuan (Giovanni) 46–7, 89, 93
Foscarini family 41, 46, 57–8, 136, 140
Foscarini, Alvise 19, 38, 43, 58
Foscarini, Antonio 57–8, 136
Foscarini, Cecilia 88
France 4, 12, 16, 31, 35, 38, 44, 45, 50,
    59–60, 63, 81, 82, 84, 90, 91, 94–7, 104,
    108, 115–21, 128, 129, 133, 134, 137,
    140, 144–6, 148, 155
Francesco Maria della Rovere duke of
    Urbino 51, 73
Francesco Maria Sforza duke of Milan 120
Francesco Sforza duke of Milan 37, 43, 56
Francis I 10, 12, 14, 16, 51, 52, 56, 73,
    92, 104–5, 108, 111, 118, 120–4, 127,
    144–6, 147–53
Frangipani, Cristoforo 69
Frari *see* Santa Maria Gloriosa dei,
    Basilica

Frati, Ludovico 101n182
Frescobaldi family 5, 53, 59
Fugger family 5, 132

Gabriele, Trifon 73
Gaeta, Franco 149, 149n6
Gallo, Rodolfo 96n164
Garisendi, Gian Andrea 98, 101, 104
Garzoni family 4, 35, 42, 53, 111, 112, 113, 140, 151
Garzoni, Andrea 48n, 140
Garzoni, Marin 111, 113
Garzoni, Paula 111, 113
Garzoni, Vetor 113, 116
Garzoni, Vicenzo 117
Gentilini, Graziella 6n12
Gian Francesco Gonzaga marquis of Mantua 73
Giannetto, Nella 38n41
Gilbert, Felix 8n17, 42n66
Gilliodts-van Severin, Louis 34n8, 38n41
Gios, Pier Antonio 33n5
Giotto 38, 46, 56, 62
Giovio, Paolo 85
Girgensohn, Dieter 36, 36n
Giustinian, Andrea 125–35, 147
Giustinian, Antonio 83
Giustinian, Chiara 102
Giustinian, Hironimo 82, 125–36, 147
Giustinian, Isabetta 68–9
Giustinian, Lorenzo 82
Giustinian, Lucietta 71, 71n29
Giustinian, Lunardo 102
Giustinian, Pangrati 82
Gleason, Elisabeth G. 109n9, 111n11
Gloria, Andrea 33n4, 33n5, 36n23, 37n32, 37n33, 38n43, 40n50, 56n151
Goffen, Rona 33n7, 34n9, 35n12, 36n20, 37n34, 38n38, 40n52, 40n57, 41, 41n58, 42n67, 62, 62n204, 93n140
Gonzaga, Eleonora 73
Gonzaga, Sigismondo 77–81
Gouwens, Kenneth 85n93
Gradenigo family 16–17, 139, 140, 141
Gradenigo, Marco 113
Gradenigo, Justo 109, 113, 125–35
Gradenigo, Piero 119, 140
Gradenigo, Zuan Polo 109, 137–38, 140
Grafton, Anthony 58n181

Grassis, Achille de 77–81
Grimani family 17, 88–9, 91–2, 140
Grimani, Antonio doge 87, 90, 92, 93, 96, 103n189, 120, 128, 131, 150
Grimani, Antonio di Vicenzo di Antonio 150
Grimani, Bianca 86–97
Grimani, Chiaretta 111
Grimani, Domenico 76–81, 90, 93
Grimani, Francesco 43
Grimani, Hironimo 65n2, 107, 111–2, 114, 121, 125–36
Grimani, Marco 58, 59–60, 87–97, 116, 119–20, 125–35, 147, 150–1
Grimani, Marin 111, 143
Grimani, Marino qu. Hironimo 58
Grimani, Piero 89
Grimani, Vetor 129, 151
Grimani, Vicenzo di Antonio 89, 150
Gritti, Andrea, doge 9, 120, 125, 139, 144–5, 150–1
Grubb, James S. 40n55, 69n21
Guicciardini, Francesco 150-
Guidoti (Guidotti, Guioti) family 54–5, 57, 61, 138, 152
Gullino, Giuseppe 2n2, 4n6, 16–17, 36, 36n21, 38n40, 39n45, 45n89, 47n98, 47n99, 48n107, 83n86, 89n115, 95n156, 95n157, 120n46, 124n56, 150n14
Gussoni family 4, 96, 109, 140
Gussoni, Andrea 125–35
Gussoni, Giacomo 112
Gwyn, Peter 32n2, 44n81, 91n128, 117n36

Hale, J.R. 108n3, 109n4
Hallman, Barbara McClung 76n55, 90n122
Hallmark, Anne 74n41
Henry VIII 10, 44, 91, 94, 116, 121, 123–4, 132, 147
Holy Roman Empire 1, 19, 31, 32, 45, 46, 50, 51, 53, 56, 59, 63, 69, 76, 81, 82, 87, 91–2, 96–7, 108, 116, 129, 144–6, 148, 155

Immortali 8, 14, 46–7, 50, 52, 55, 57, 61, 73, 88, 89, 96, 108, 109, 111, 118, 127, 130, 131, 132, 133, 142, 154
Innocenti, Piero 149n6

Isabella d'Este Gonzaga 15
Isella family 48

Jacobacci, Domenico 77–81
Jardine, Lisa 58n181
Jordan, Peter 13n31
Justinian *see* Giustinian

King, Margaret 3n4, 39n46, 40n55,
    58n181
Knapton, Michael 40n55, 93n134, 93n137,
    132, 132n93
Kolb, Carolyn 88n107, 94n148, 128n66

Lane, Frederic C. 4n6, 10n22, 32n1,
    93n137, 117n36, 118, 118n38, 131n85,
    132n93, 145, 145n172
Laura, Bellisario 85, 97
Lazara, Giovanni 2n2, 33n5, 34n11,
    39n44, 40n53, 49n12, 54n149, 57n172,
    82n84
Lazzarini, Vittorio 33n4
Lenci, Angiolo 140n151
Leo X 9, 12, 59, 72, 73, 76–80, 86, 90,
    104, 123, 124
Leze, Maria da 86–97
Leze, Zuan da 89, 96, 133
Ling, Lesley A. 2n2, 37n32, 139n144
Lion, Maria 86–97
Lipomano (Lippomano) family 4, 42, 52
Lomellino family 5, 120
London 4, 32, 34, 35, 43, 91, 93, 94, 116, 134
Loredan, Leonardo doge 68, 112, 127
Loredan, Lorenzo di Leonardo 125–35
Loredan, Lorenzo di Marco 127
Loredan, Marc'Antonio 130
Loredan, Marco di Antonio 127
Loredan, Zuan Francesco 130
Lorenzo de' Medici duke of Urbino 78,
    126n58
Lovarini, Emilio 5n8, 5n9, 11, 11n24,
    45n90, 47n105, 50n122, 51, 52, 55n159,
    58, 58n180, 70n23, 100, 100n177,
    100n178, 115n31, 135, 135n124, 136,
Lowe, K. J. P. 78n58
Lowry, Martin 4n5, 149n13
Ludovico Sforza duke of Milan 54, 120,
    134, 149
Lyon 59

Machiavelli, Niccolò 3, 148–53;
    Mandragola 6, 9, 59, 148–50
Magno, Andrea 5, 9, 41, 48, 65–70, 74, 75,
    81–3, 90, 93, 94, 98, 101, 102, 104, 105
Magno, Stefano 67, 69
Magno, Stefano di Andrea, 5, 9, 15, 48,
    65, 66, 67–71, 81–2, 84, 97–9, 100–2,
    105–6, 113, 131, 134, 136, 146; *Annali
    veneti* 4n6, 32n3, 70, 70n26, 149;
    Cronaca Magno 67n10, 68n13, 69n19,
    70, 70n26, 82–3; *Origine delle case
    patrizie* 70, 70n26
Magno, Stefano qu. Pietro 90
Magno, Vicenzo 69, 113
Mainoni, Patrizia 5n8, 45n89
Malipiero, Donado 60, 119
Malipiero, Michiel 125–35
Malipiero, Nicolò 112
Malipiero, Polo 125–35
Malipiero, Tomà 107, 112
Malipiero, Zuan Antonio 141
Mallett, M.E. 108n3, 109n4
Manenti, Zuan (Giovanni) 3, 9, 59–60,
    116, 119–24, 125–35, 142–3, 147–53
Mantua 39, 78, 82, 108, 121, 151
Manzoni, Alessandro 10
Marcello family 4, 32, 32n3, 33n4, 46, 47,
    55, 136, 140, 148
Marcello, Alvise 48
Marcello, Andrea qu. Antonio 48
Marcello, Andrea di Bernardo 48–9, 107,
    121, 141
Marcello, Bernardino 33
Marcello, Bernardo 105, 141
Marcello, Donà 120
Marcello, Ferigo 47, 55
Marcello, Hironimo 47, 50
Marcello, Jacopo 19, 32, 50, 104–5
Marcello, Nicolò 47
Marcello, Piero (Pietro) 33, 48
Marcello, Piero qu. Giacomo 47
Marechal, Joseph 34n8
Maredini, Francesco 79
Marso, Giovanni Antonio 7, 44
Massimiliano Sforza duke of Milan 120
Martelli family 42, 59
Martinengo family 52, 52n137, 93
Martinengo, Antonio 50, 53, 95, 140
Martinengo, Bernardino 41

Martini, Alvise di Piero 13
Maximilian I 60, 67, 108–9, 115, 117, 133
Medici bank 42, 43, 53
Medici family 95
Medici, Cosimo de' 42, 59
Medici, Giovanni de' 'dalle Bande Nere'
    151
Medici, Giulio *see* Clement VII
Medici, Lorenzo de' (Lorenzo il
    Magnifico) 53
Menegazzo, Emilio 11, 11n25, 45n90,
    46n95, 49n116, 51, 52, 52n134, 53,
    109–10n10, 132n89, 133n103, 138n138,
    139, 140n151
Mezzo, Tommaso 6, 7
Milan 5, 10, 11, 15, 23, 32, 37, 38, 39, 42,
    43, 45, 48, 53, 56, 57, 59, 63, 82, 91,
    119–24, 129, 130, 136, 145, 148, 151,
    154
Milani, Marisa 15n38
Mocenigo, Alvise 113, 117, 122, 130,
    135–6, 139, 140, 141, 145, 148
Mocenigo, Antonio 107, 113, 125–36
Mocenigo, Francesco 105, 111, 136
Mocenigo, Lazaro 125–35, 140, 148
Mocenigo, Lucia 53, 141
Mocenigo, Lunardo 122, 145
Mocenigo, Tommaso 40, 144
Molà, Luca 2n2, 132n94, 141n162
Molin, Hironimo da 118
Molin, Marco da 75, 125–35, 144
Molin, Pietro da 118
Molino, Antonio (Il Burchiella) 15, 15n37
Molza, Francesco Maria 66, 98
Moncallero, Giuseppe Lorenzo 96n165
Monselice 33, 48
Montagnana, Jacopo da 34
Monte, Antonio Ciocchi dal 77–81
Montelupo, Baccio da: Funeral monument
    of Benedetto Pesaro 19
Monterosso, Antonio 17, 33n4, 33n5,
    34n10, 35n18, 37n27, 37n29, 37n33,
    38n43, 39n47, 40n49, 40n50, 40n54,
    40n55, 48n109, 51n128, 54n149,
    54n150, 55n156, 55n160, 56n167,
    57n178, 67n9, 74n44, 130n81, 132n95,
    136n133, 149n11
Morosini family 147, 149–50

Morosini, Almorò 107
Morosini, Marc'Antonio 40, 149
Morosini, Nicolò 107, 113
Morrissey, Thomas E. 74n41
Mortara, Alessandro de 65n1, 66, 66n,
    98n168, 98n171
Mosca, Giammaria (Padovano): Funeral
    monument of Alvise Pasqualigo 19, 43
Mueller, Reinhold 4n6, 34n10, 35n14, 38n42,
    42n67, 42n68, 42n69, 43n72, 48n107,
    53n139, 56n164, 59n187, 92n131, 94n145,
    130n81, 131n87, 145, 145n174
Muir, Edward 13n31

Naples 51, 58, 130, 145
Nardi, Bruno 44n83, 57n178, 136n134
Navagero, Andrea 66, 83, 85, 97
Nerli family 53, 59, 148–51
Nerli, Ferigo de' 60, 119, 122–4
Nogarola, Ginevra 58
Nogarola, Isotta 39, 58
Numai, Cristoforo 77–81

Olivieri, Achille 2n2
Onofrio Veronese 66, 85, 97, 99
Orazio, Ludovico di 60, 119–24, 147–8
Orio, Marco 41
Orsini, Franciotto 77–81
Orsini, Generosa 38
Orsini, Niccolò 39, 74
Orsini, Lorenzo (Renzo) da Cere 55, 75
Ortolani 50, 55, 56, 57, 59, 60, 71, 87, 92,
    94, 95, 108, 111, 116, 122, 127, 128,
    131, 140, 154
Osnaghi family 56
Ottoman empire *see* Turkish Porte

Pace, Richard 124
Padoan, Giorgio 8, 9n19, 53n138, 58n180,
    65n3, 67n9, 70–1, 70n23, 71n28, 82n81,
    82n82, 100–1, 100n179, 101n180,
    101n184, 135n124
Padovano, Jacopo 38
Padua 2, 5, 10, 14, 15, 16, 17, 33, 34, 35,
    36, 37, 38–9, 40, 41, 43, 44, 45, 46, 48,
    49, 50, 51, 53, 54, 55, 56, 57, 58, 61,
    62, 66–7, 68, 70, 72, 73, 74, 75, 76, 81,
    82, 83, 87–8, 90, 92, 93, 94, 95, 96, 98,
    99–100, 104, 105, 109, 112, 124, 127–9,

131, 132, 136, 137, 138, 139, 140, 143, 149, 154
Paduan countryside 16, 37, 39, 40, 41, 46, 47, 49, 57, 61, 68, 112, 129, 131, 133, 134, 137, 154–5
Pallavicini, Giovanni Battista 77–81
Pallucchini, Rodolfo 38n37, 38n39
Panigarola family 56
papacy 3, 4, 8, 9, 16, 19, 23, 31, 42, 82, 87, 90, 92, 93, 95–7, 137
Parronchi, Alessandro 42n67, 59, 59n185
Paschini, Pio 78n59
Pasqualigo family 7, 12, 61
Pasqualigo, Alvise 19, 43–44, 61
Pasqualigo, Lorenzo 43–4
Pasqualigo, Pietro 14, 43–4, 61
Passerini, Silvio 77–81
Pastore Stocchi, Manlio 4n5
Pavia 11, 51, 53, 91, 122, 127, 130, 147, 148, 152
Pernumia family 113
Pernumia, Antonio da 83, 141
Pernumia, Paola da 83
Pesaro family 4, 33, 34n10, 40–1, 46, 49–51, 57, 58, 62, 89, 93
Pesaro, Alvise 49
Pesaro, Andriana 85–97
Pesaro, Antonio 41, 58–9
Pesaro, Antonio 49
Pesaro, Benedetto (Beneto) 19, 34, 36, 93
Pesaro, Bianca 41
Pesaro, Fantin 34, 41, 50
Pesaro, Francesco 15, 38, 51, 93
Pesaro, Francesco di Fantin 41
Pesaro, Francesco qu. Marco 93
Pesaro, Hironimo (Girolamo) 34, 50, 51
Pesaro, Jacopo (Giacomo) 19, 36, 40, 58, 93, 151–2
Pesaro, Nicolò 49
Pesaro, Piero (Pietro) 34n10, 49–53, 88, 93–4, 140, 147
Pesaro, Zuan (Giovanni) 41
Petrarch (Francesco Petrarca) 85
Petrucci, Raffaele 77–81
Piccolomini, Giovanni 77–81
Pieri, Piero 140n151
Piovan, Francesco 46n91
Piove di Sacco 33, 43, 54–5, 57, 61, 109–10, 132, 136, 139, 141
Pisani family 4, 58, 97, 116, 136, 138, 144–6

Pisani, Almorò 112
Pisani, Alvise 60, 86, 112, 117, 118, 128, 147, 150
Pisani, Donada 112, 132, 135
Pisani, Francesco 48–9
Pisani, Francesco di Alvise 76–81, 96
Pisani, Francesco di Zuan 94
Pisani, Zuan (Giovanni) 88
Polesine 47, 48, 55, 57, 58, 127, 133, 136, 138
Polano, Sergio 57n169
Poncetti, Ferdinando 77–81
Portugal 1, 4, 11, 22, 23, 32, 35, 44, 64, 112, 116
Potenza, Gerolamo da 39n45
Pozza, Neri 39n44
Priuli family 92–4, 97, 112, 132, 140, 151
Priuli, Alvise 87–97, 144
Priuli, Andrea 125–35
Priuli, Antonio 118, 152
Priuli, Federico 43
Priuli, Girolamo 8, 94n145; *I diarii* 34n10
Priuli, Zaccaria 127–8
Prizer, William 66, 66n7, 99n173
Pucci, Lorenzo 77–81
Pulci, Antonia 6n11
Puppi, Lionello 76n53

Queller, Donald 67n12
Querini, Paola 88
Querini, Stefano 88

Raimondi, Ezio 81n73
Ram (Rames), Piero 60, 119–20, 122
Rangone 77–81
Renier, Andrea 107
Renier, Rodolfo 66, 66n8
Reynolds, Anne 83n91
Riccò, Laura 44n84
Richardson, Brian 65, 65n5, 70n25, 71n29, 81n76
Ridolfi, Niccolò 77–81
Rigobello, Bruno 39n44, 108n3, 128n64, 133n108
Rizzo, Antonio: Funeral monument of Doge Nicolò Tron 19
Rocke, Michael J. 79n68
Romano, Dennis 36, 36n21
Roover, Raymond de 4n6, 42n67, 42n68, 43n70, 43n72, 59n187
Rosand, Ellen 12n29

Ruggiero, Guido 7, 7n13
Ruzante *see* Beolco, Angelo

Sabbatino, Pasquale 12n28
Sadoleto, Jacopo 83
Salamon, Zuan Francesco 107
Salvago family 5
Salviati, Giovanni 77–81
Sambin, Paolo 5n9, 11n24, 14n35, 45n90, 47n102, 48n107, 49n116, 52n136, 52n137, 115n31, 116n34, 140n151
Sannazaro, Jacopo 72–3, 85, 99
Sanseverino, Pier Antonio 87, 92, 94, 95
Sanseverino, Roberto da 54, 149
Santa Maria Gloriosa dei Frari 2, 4, 12, 19, 35, 39, 42, 45, 49, 50, 60, 62, 119, 122, 136, 149, 154
Santa Maura, battle of 41
Sanudo, Andrea 107
Sanudo, Francesco 109
Sanudo, Laura 89–97, 140
Sanudo, Marin (Sanuto, Marino) 8, 16, 35, 51, 58, 59, 61, 67, 68, 69, 85, 86–7, 107, 125–35, 142–3, 149, 150, 151, 152; *Itinerario* 34n10, 37n28, 38n43, 93n134, 133n108, 149n10
Sartori, Antonio 3n5, 39n44
Savarese, Gennaro 78n65
Schinner, Matteo 77–81
Schulz, Anne Markham 37n30, 43n75
Schulz, Juergen 38n38
Scuola dei Fiorentini 19, 42, 59
Scuola dei Milanesi 19, 37, 56
Selvatico, Pietro 35n13
Seneca, Federico 149n9
Setton, Kenneth M. 1n1, 8n16, 16, 16n, 34n9, 41n59, 91n127, 105n195, 123n54, 130, 130n80, 148n4
Sforza family 5, 45, 63
Simionato, Umberto 138n141
Soderini, Francesco 77–81
Soranzo, Alvise 89
Soranzo, Camillo 70
Soranzo, Isabetta 89, 95
Soranzo, Jacomo 125–35
Soranzo, Lucietta 89, 95
Spain 4, 10, 22, 31, 32, 38, 41, 42, 44, 58, 60, 91, 93, 115, 117, 119, 121, 124, 144–6, 148
Spannocchi family 59

Speroni, Sperone 83–84
Stabel, Peter 32n3, 53n139
Steer, John 38n37
Stella, Aldo 2n2
stradioti 15, 34, 52–3, 139–40
Strietman, Elsa 3n3
Surtz, Edward 94n150
Syria 2, 11, 67, 141

Taviani, Carlo 78n59
Tebaldeo, Antonio 80–3
Tiepolo family 17
Tierney, Brian 74n41
Titian (Tiziano Vecellio): *Assunta* 19, 36, 62; *Madonna di Ca' Pesaro* 19, 40, 58–9, 62
Toscan, Jean 99n174
Trevisan family 37, 55, 140, 148
Trevisan, Andrea 122, 145
Trevisan, Anzelo 55
Trevisan, Beneto 55
Trevisan, Domenico (Domenego) 40, 55–7, 122, 147
Trevisan, Marin 55, 56, 58
Trevisan, Melchiorre 37, 40, 43, 55, 149–50
Trevisan, Nicolò 125–35
Trevisan, Piero 4
Treviso and territory 41, 51, 68, 88, 102, 129, 131
Trissino, Gian Giorgio 98, 101, 104–6
Trissino, Lunardo 104
Triumphanti 3, 11, 12, 14, 16, 48, 53, 55, 56, 60, 62, 88, 105, 107–47, 150, 154
Trivulzio (Triulzi), Agostino 77–81
Trivulzio, Scaramuccia 77–81
Tron family 139
Tron, Antonio 56
Tron, Filippo di Nicolò 54
Tron, Filippo qu. Priamo 54–5
Tron, Franceschina 36
Tron, Luca 37, 54, 114, 117, 121–2, 125–35, 145, 147
Tron, Nicolò 56
Tron, Nicolò doge 19, 36, 54, 129
Tron, Santo 54, 140
Tron, Vicenzo 54
Tucci, Ugo 6, 6n10
Turkish Porte 1, 2, 4, 9, 11, 16, 19, 22–3, 32, 34, 35, 37, 40, 44, 50, 58, 64, 91, 93, 107, 113, 115, 118–19, 121, 123, 128, 152, 154

Valaresso, Fantin 125–35
Valaresso, Ferigo 107, 133
Valaresso, Polo 54, 134
Valier family 41, 155
Valier, Carlo 41, 82–3
Valier, Zuan Francesco 8, 59, 82–4, 90
Valle, Andrea della 77–81
Vallone, Aldo 81n73
Varanini, Gian Maria 2n2
Vedoa, Hironimo di la 115
Vendramin, Andrea 82
Vendramin, Antonio 41
Vendramin, Luca 41
Vendramin, Nicolò 82, 102
Venice, Venetian Republic: *avogadori di
    comun* (state's attorneys) 54; Collegio
    (Colegio) 113, 122–4, 147–52; Council
    of Ten (Consiglio di Dieci) 42, 43, 46,
    48, 53, 61, 67, 68, 76, 87, 114, 117, 119,
    120, 125–35, 147–52; *governadori di
    l'entrade* 41, 134; Maggior Consiglio 47,
    67, 68, 114, 131; *provedadori a l'Arsenal*
    115; *provedador sopra lo armar* 50;
    provedadori sora il cotimo di Alexandria
    118; *provedadori sora la mercadantie*
    114; Provveditori di Comun 59–60, 68;
    savi ai ordeni 114, 116, 117; *savi dil
    consejo* 16, 90, 122, 125–35, 138, 144–6,
    147; *savi di terraferma* 122, 125–35;
    Senate 3, 5, 10, 11, 16, 48, 49, 54, 61, 74,
    83, 94, 113, 114, 115, 117, 119, 121–3,
    125–35, 137, 140, 144–6, 147–52;
    Ufficio ale Raxon Vecchie 69
Venier, Antonio doge 86
Venier, Domenico 122
Venier, Hieronima 86–97
Venier, Isabetta 86–97
Venier, Lucrezia 85–97
Venier, Lunardo 89
Venier, Marc'Antonio 86–97
Venier, Marin 62, 130
Venier, Nicolò 41, 90
Venier, Paola 85–97
Venier, Piero 88
Veniexiana, La 8, 82–3, 100, 106
Ventura, Angelo 2n2
Venturelli, Paola 5n8

Venturi, Lionello 107, 107n1
Verità, Girolamo 65n3, 69, 70, 97–8, 100,
    104
Verona 9, 39, 48, 51, 58, 67, 69–71, 73,
    93, 101, 104, 108–9, 144, 151
Vicenza 15, 41, 48, 77, 104
Vich, Raimond 77–81
Vicoaro, Jacomo da 52–3, 139–40
Viggiano, Alfredo 40n54
Vio, Tommaso de 77–81
Virgil 70, 98
Virgili, Antonio 83n91
Vivarini, Alvise: *St. Ambrose and Saints*
    19, 38
Vivarini, Bartolomeo: *Bernardo Triptych*
    19, 35, 38; *Triptych of St. Mark with Sts.
    John the Baptist, Jerome, Nicholas and
    Paul* 19
Volpe, Taddeo di la 47

Weaver, Elissa 6n11
Weinberg, Bernard 81n73
women 72–6, 84–97, 140, 143–4, 151

Zabarella, Francesco 74
Zabarella, Giacomo 74
Zabarella, Paolo 74
Zamberti, Bartolomeo 7
Zamperetti, Sergio 37n32
Zane, Antonio 94
Zane, Bernardo 42, 94
Zane, Elena 86–97
Zen family 40, 40n57, 57
Zen, Andrea 42
Zen, Antonio 40
Zen, Helena 86–97
Zen, Jacopo 40, 90
Zen, Giovanni Battista 40, 41
Zen, Luca 19, 39, 40, 57
Zen, Piero 90
Zen, Tomà 40
Ziliol, Andrea 138n137
Zorzi, Fantin 107, 114–18
Zorzi, Lucrezia 88
Zorzi, Ludovico 114n29
Zorzi, Marin 10, 82, 94, 114, 144–6
Zuan Polo 51, 103n189, 125–35, 142–3

For Product Safety Concerns and Information please contact our
EU representative GPSR@taylorandfrancis.com Taylor & Francis
Verlag GmbH, Kaufingerstraße 24, 80331 München, Germany